WOMEN IN URBAN RURAL GOVERNMENT

WOMEN IN URBAN RURAL GOVERNMENT

B.R. Trivedi

CYBER TECH PUBLICATIONS
4264/3, Ansari Road, Daryaganj, New Delhi-110002 (India)
Ph.: 011-23244078, 011-43559448 Fax: 011-23280028
E-Mail: cyberpublicationsdelhi@yahoo.com
Website: www.cybertechpublications.com

WOMEN IN URBAN RURAL GOVERNMENT

B.R. Trivedi

First Edition 2010

Published by : Asian Offset Printers

G.S. Rawat for **Cyber Tech Publications**
4264/3, Ansari Road, Daryaganj, New Delhi-110002 (India)
Ph.: 011-23244078, 011-43559448 Fax: 011-23280028
E-Mail: cyberpublicationsdelhi@yahoo.com
Website: www.cybertechpublications.com

Preface

The modern municipal government in urban units is essentially a creation and legacy of British rule. It was imported in India by Britishers from their own land. However, it is said that the origin of local self-government had very deep roots in ancient India. On the basis of historical records, excavations and archaeological investigations, it is believed that some form of local selfgovernment did exist in the remote past. Madras was the first city to have a local government established under a charter, dated December 30, 1687, issued by the Company. The Municipality came into existence on September 29,1688. The United Provinces Municipalities Act of 1916 (which replaced the Act of 1900) is a landmark in the development of city government in U.P. After independence the U.P. Government took a decision to set-up Municipal Corporation in five big cities of Kanpur, Agra, Varanasi, Allahabad and Lucknow, popularly known as KAVAL Towns. As a result, the state of U.P. adopted a new Act for Municipal Corporation in 1959.

Uttar Pradesh is spread over an area of 2,43,286 square kilometers with a population of 166,197,921, the state constitutes 16.17 percent of the total population of the country, the literacy rate of the state is 56.26 percent. Being agrarian in character, villages (97,134) far outnumber urban units (627) in the state. As per Census 2001, every fifth person in the state is residing in Urban Areas. Presently constituting 20.78 percent of population in urban areas in the state. Concurrent with the growth in urban population, number of urban settlements in the state has increased from 293 in 1971 to 659 in 1981 and further to 702 in 1991. In 2001 total urban centers in the state were recorded as 708 (including 66 census towns & 13 cantonment boards). In addition to being the most populous state in the country Uttar Pradesh enjoys the status of having the second largest number of urban local bodies in the country.

— *Author*

CONTENTS

1

INTRODUCTION

The term women's rights refers to the freedoms inherently possessed by women and girls of all ages, which may be institutionalized, ignored or suppressed by law, custom, and behavior in a particular society.

These liberties are grouped together and differentiated from broader notions of human rights because they often differ from the freedoms inherently possessed by or recognized for men and boys, and because activism surrounding this issue claims an inherent historical and traditional bias against the exercise of rights by women.

Some of the issues commonly associated with these notions include rights to:

- bodily integrity and autonomy;
- vote (universal suffrage);
- hold public office;
- work;
- fair wages or equal pay;
- own property and to enter into legal contracts;
- education;
- serve in the military; and
- to have marital, parental and religious rights.

Activists have campaigned, and in some places continue to campaign, for the same rights as modern men.

HISTORICAL BACKGROUND

Till the mid nineteenth century, writers assumed that a patriarchal order was a natural order that had existed as JS Mill wrote, since "the very earliest twilight of human society". This was not seriously challenged till the eighteenth century when Jesuit missionaries found matrilineality in native North American peoples.

In the 16th century, the Reformation allowed more women to add their voices, including the English writers Jane Anger, Aemilia Lanyer, and the prophetess Anna Trapnell. However, it has been claimed that the Dissolution and resulting closure of convents had deprived many such women of one path to education. Giving voice in the secular context became more difficult when deprived of the rationale and protection of divine inspiration. Queen Elizabeth I demonstrated leadership amongst women, even if she was unsupportive of their causes, and subsequently became a role model for the education of women.

The Enlightenment and a Vindication of the Rights of Woman

The Age of Enlightenment was characterized by secular intellectual reasoning, and a flowering of philosophical writing. The most important feminist writer of the time was Mary Wollstonecraft, often described as the first feminist philosopher. A Vindication of the Rights of Woman (1792). Wollstonecraft argued that it was the education and upbringing of women that created limited expectations. Despite some inconsistencies (Brody refers to the "Two Wollestoncrafts") reflective of problems that had no easy answers, this book remains a foundation stone of feminist thought.

In other parts of Europe, Hedvig Charlotta Nordenflycht was writing in Sweden, and what is thought to be the first scientific society for women was founded in Middelburg, in the south of Holland in 1785. This was the Natuurkundig Genootschap der Dames (Women's Society for Natural Knowledge). which met regularly until 1881, finally dissolving in 1887. However Deborah Crocker and Sethanne Howard point out that women have been scientists for 4,000 years. Journals for women which focused on science became popular during this period as well.

Suffrage, the Right to Vote

The ideas that were planted in the late 1700s took root during the 1800s. Women began to agitate for the right to vote and participate in government and law making. The ideals of Women's suffrage developed alongside that of universal suffrage, and women's movements took lessons from those in other countries.

United States

American women advocated women's right to vote from the 1820s onward. This was first achieved in the relatively sparsely-populated territories of Wyoming (1869) and briefly in Utah (1870), although Utah women were disenfranchised by the U.S. Congress in 1887.

The push to grant Utah women's suffrage was at least partially fueled by outsiders' belief that, given the right to vote, Utah women would dispose of polygamy. After Utah women exercised their suffrage rights in favor of polygamy the U.S. Congress disenfranchised Utah women. Other territories and states granted women the right to vote in the late 19th and early 20th century, but national women's suffrage did not come until the Nineteenth Amendment to the United States Constitution was ratified in 1920.

US Timeline

- 1848 - The first Women's Rights Convention (Seneca Falls Convention) is held in Seneca Falls, NY
- 1849 - Women doctors are now permitted to legally practice medicine
  - Elizabeth Blackwell (doctor) becomes the first female to receive a medical degree in the United States
- 1852 - Susan B. Anthony and Elizabeth Cady Stanton form the Women's New York Temperance Society
- 1860-1865 - American Civil War

- 1868 - The Fourteenth Amendment to the United States Constitution is ratified
- 1869 - Lucy Stone , Henry Blackwell , and Julia Ward Howe are instrumental in forming the American Woman Suffrage Association
- 1872 - Susan B. Anthony is arrested for attempting to vote
- 1890 - Wyoming becomes the first state to allow women to vote
- 1920 - The Nineteenth Amendment to the United States Constitution is ratified

United Kingdom

Throughout the 19th century British women reformers developed their own dialogue through many various reforming groups until, by 1903, they had formed into two distinct organisations; the democratic National Union of Women's Suffrage Societies, and the militant Women's Social and Political Union. Leaders in the struggle were the peaceful Millicent Fawcett and radical Emmeline Pankhurst with her daughter Christabel. Their fight also proved slow and frustrating. In 1918 the British Parliament finally passed a bill allowing women over the age of 30 to vote. In 1928 the age limit was lowered to 21.

Other Countries

In some nations women were granted full voting rights earlier than in the United States and Britain. Women first won the right to vote in New Zealand in 1893, Australia in 1902, and Finland in 1906. But many other nations proved much slower to change. For example, women in France were not given voting rights until 1944. However, in some of these countries only women in the ruling population were able to vote at first. For example, Aboriginal women in Australia were not allowed to vote until they became citizens in 1967.

Today women in some conservative Arab countries still do not have the right to vote, or barely any rights at all.

THE MODERN MOVEMENT

In the subsequent decades women's rights again became an important issue in the English speaking worlds. By the 1960s the movement was called "feminism" or "women's liberation." Reformers wanted the same pay as men, equal rights in law, and the freedom to plan their families or not have children at all. Their efforts were met with mixed results.

In the UK a public groundswell of opinion in favour of legal equality had gained pace, partly through the extensive employment of women in men's traditional roles during both world wars. By the 1960s the legislative process was being readied, tracing through MP Willie Hamilton's select committee report, his Equal Pay For Equal Work Bill, the creation of a Sex Discrimination Board, Lady Sear's draft sex anti-discrimination bill, a government Green Paper of 1973, until 1975 when the first British Sex Discrimination Act, an Equal Pay Act, and an Equal Opportunities Commission came into force. With encouragement from the UK government, the other countries of the EEC soon followed suit with an agreement to ensure that discrimination laws would be phased out across the European Community.

In the USA, the US National Organization of Women (NOW) was created in 1966 with the purpose of bringing about equality for all women. NOW was one important group that fought for the Equal Rights Amendment (ERA). This amendment stated that "equality of rights under the law shall not be denied or abridged by the United States or any state on account of sex." But there was disagreement on how the proposed amendment would be understood. Supporters believed it would guarantee women equal treatment. But critics feared it might deny women the right be financially supported by their husbands. The amendment died in 1982 because not enough states had ratified it. ERAs have been included in subsequent Congresssses, but have still failed to be ratified.

In the last three decades of the 20th century, Western women knew a new freedom through birth control, which enabled women to plan their adult lives, often making way for both career and family. The movement had been started in the 1910s by US pioneering social reformer Margaret Sanger and in the UK and internationally by Marie Stopes.

Over the course of the 20th century women took on a greater role in society. For example, many women served in government. In the U.S. government some served as U.S. Senators and others as members of the U.S. Cabinet. Many women took advantage of opportunities to become educated. In the United States at the beginning of the 20th century less than 20 percent of all college degrees were earned by women. By the end of the century this figure had risen to about 50 percent.

Opportunities also expanded in the workplace. Fields such as medicine, law, and science opened to include more women. At the beginning of the 20th century about 5 percent of the doctors in the United States were women.

As of 1998, 23 percent of all doctors were women, and today, women make up more than 50 percent of the medical student population. While the numbers of women in these fields increased, many women still continued to hold clerical, factory. retail, or service jobs. For example, they worked as office assistants, on assembly lines, or as cooks.

US Timeline

- 1931-1945 - World War II
- 1960 - Margaret Sanger opens the first U.S. birth-control clinic in Brooklyn, NY (The clinic was shut down ten days later and Sanger was arrested)
- 1960 - The FDA approves birth-control pills
- 1963 - Congress passes the Equal Pay Act
- 1966 - The National Organization for Women is founded
- 1970 - 50,000 people march in New York City for the first women's Strike for Equality
- 1971 - United States Supreme Court rule ends sex discrimination in hiring
- 1981 - Sandra Day O'Connor becomes the first female justice

- 1997 - Madeleine Albright becomes the first female United States Secretary of State
- 2005 - Condoleezza Rice becomes the first female African American Secretary of State

The United Nations and Women's Rights

In 1946 the United Nations established a Commission on the Status of Women. Originally as the Section on the Status of Women, Human Rights Division, Department of Social Affairs, and now part of the Economic and Social Council (ECOSOC). In 1948 the UN issued its Universal Declaration of Human Rights which protects "the equal rights of men and women", and addressed both the equality and equity issues.

Since 1975 the UN has held a series of world conferences on women's issues, starting with the World Conference of the International Women's Year in Mexico City. These conferences created an international forum for women's rights, but also illustrated divisions between women of different cultures and the difficulties of attempting to apply principles universally Emerging from the 1985 Nairobi conference was a realization that feminism is not monolithic but "constitutes the political expression of the concerns and interests of women from different regions, classes, nationalities, and ethnic backgrounds. There is and must be a diversity of feminisms, responsive to the different needs and concerns of women, and defined by them for themselves. This diversity builds on a common opposition to gender oppression and hierarchy which, however, is only the first step in articulating and acting upon a political agenda." At the Fourth World Conference on Women in Beijing, The Platform for Action was signed. This included a commitment to achieve "gender equality and the empowerment of women".

Reproductive Rights

Reproductive rights are rights relating to sexual reproduction and reproductive health. The idea of these rights were first discussed as a subset of human rights at the United Nation's 1968 International Conference on Human Rights. The sixteenth article of the Proclamation of Teheran states, "Parents have a basic human right to determine freely and responsibly the number and the spacing of their children." Since then, reproductive rights have been established as human rights in international human rights documents, particularly with the ratification of the Convention to End Discrimination Against Women (CEDAW), and the adoption of the the Cairo Programme and the Beijing Platform. Reproductive rights are often held to include the right to control one's reproductive functions, the right to access quality reproductive healthcare, the right to education and access in order to make reproductive choices free from coercion, discrimination, and violence.

FEMINISM

Feminism comprises a number of social, cultural and political movements, theories and moral philosophies concerned with gender inequalities and equal rights for women.

According to some, the history of feminism consists of three waves. The first wave was in the nineteenth and early twentieth centuries, the second was in the 1960s and 1970s and the third extends from the 1990s to the present. Feminist Theory developed from the feminist movement. It takes a number of forms in a variety of disciplines such as feminist geography, feminist history and feminist literary criticism.

Feminism has altered aspects of Western society, ranging from culture to law. Feminist political activists have been concerned with issues such as a woman's right of contract and property, a woman's right to bodily integrity and autonomy (especially on matters such as reproductive rights, including the right to abortion, access to contraception and quality prenatal care); for protection from domestic violence; against sexual harassment and rape; for workplace rights, including maternity leave and equal pay; and against other forms of discrimination.

Throughout much of its history, most of the leaders of feminist social and political movements, as well as many feminist theorists, have been predominantly middle-class white women from western Europe and North America. However, at least since Sojourner Truth's 1851 speech to US Feminists, women of other races have proposed alternative feminisms.

This trend accelerated in the 1960s with the Civil Rights movement in the United States and the collapse of European colonialism in Africa, the Caribbean, parts of Latin America and Southeast Asia. Since that time, women in former European colonies and the Third World have proposed alternative "post-colonial" and "Third World" feminisms as well. Some Postcolonial feminists, such as Chandra Talpade Mohanty, are critical of Western feminism for being ethnocentric. Black feminists, such as Angela Davis and Alice Walker, share this view.

Since the 1980s, standpoint feminists have argued that the feminist movement should address global issues (such as rape, incest, and prostitution) and culturally specific issues (such as female genital mutilation in some parts of Africa and the Middle East and glass ceiling practices that impede women's advancement in developed economies) in order to understand how gender inequality interacts with racism, homophobia, lesbophobia, colonialism, and classism in a "matrix of domination." Other feminists have argued that gendered and sexed identities, such as "man" and "woman", are social constructs meaning that some gender roles are socially conditioned rather than innate.

Feminists have divided the movement's history into three "waves". The first wave refers to that of the nineteenth through early twentieth centuries, which dealt mainly with the Suffrage movement. The second wave (1960s-1980s) attempted to right legal and cultural inequalities. The third wave (1990s-present) is seen as both a continuation and a response to the perceived failures of the second wave.

First-wave Feminism

First-wave feminism refers to a period of feminist activity during the nineteenth century and early twentieth century in the United Kingdom and the United States. Originally it focused on the promotion of equal contract and property rights for women and the opposition to chattel marriage and ownership of married women (and their children) by their husbands. However, by the end of the nineteenth century, activism focused primarily on gaining political power, particularly the right of women's suffrage. Yet, feminists such as Voltairine de Cleyre and Margaret Sanger were still active in campaigning for women's sexual, reproductive, and economic rights at this time.

In Britain the Suffragettes campaigned for the women's vote. In 1918 the Representation of the People Act 1918 was passed granting the vote to women over the age of 30 who owned houses. In 1928 this was extended to all women over eighteen. In the United States leaders of this movement included Elizabeth Cady Stanton and Susan B. Anthony, who each campaigned for the abolition of slavery prior to championing women's right to vote.

Other important leaders include Lucy Stone, Olympia Brown, and Helen Pitts. American first-wave feminism involved a wide range of women some belonging to conservative Christian groups (such as Frances Willard and the Woman's Christian Temperance Union), others resembling the diversity and radicalism of much of second-wave feminism (such as Matilda Joslyn Gage and the National Woman Suffrage Association). In the United States first-wave feminism is considered to have ended with the passage of the Nineteenth Amendment to the United States Constitution (1919), granting women the right to vote.The term first wave, was coined retrospectively after the term second-wave feminism began to be used to describe a newer feminist movement that focused as much on fighting social and cultural inequalities as political inequalities.

Second-wave Feminism

Second-wave feminism refers to a period of feminist activity beginning in the early 1960s and lasting through the late 1980s and, as Imelda Whelehan suggests, it was a continuation of the earlier phase of feminism involving the suffragettes in the UK and USA. Second-wave feminism has existed continuously since that time and coexists with what is termed third-wave feminism. Second-wave feminists saw cultural and political inequalities as inextricably linked and encouraged women to understand aspects of their personal lives as deeply politicized as well as reflective of a sexist structure of power. With her essay "The Personal is Political", Carol Hanisch coined a slogan that became synonymous with the second wave. If first-wave feminism focused on rights such as suffrage, second-wave feminism was largely concerned with other issues of equality, such as the end to discrimination.

Women's Liberation in the USA

The phrase "Women's Liberation" was first used in the United States in 1964 and first appeared in print in 1966. By 1968, although the term Women's Liberation Front appeared in the magazine Ramparts, it was starting to refer to the whole women's movement. Bra-burning also became associated with the movement.

One of the most vocal critics of the women's liberation movement has been bell hooks, who argues that the movement's glossing over of race and class was part of its failure to address "the issues that divided women". She has highlighted the lack of minority voices in the women's movement.

The Feminine Mystique

Betty Friedan's The Feminine Mystique (1963) criticized the idea that women could only find fulfillment through childrearing and homemaking. According to Friedan's obituary in the The New York Times, The Feminine Mystique "ignited the contemporary women's movement in 1963 and as a result permanently transformed the social fabric of the United States and countries around the world" and "is widely regarded as one of the most influential nonfiction books of the 20th century." In the book Friedan hypothesizes that women are victims of a false belief system that requires them to find identity and meaning in their lives through their husbands and children. Such a system causes women to completely lose their identity in that of their family.

Friedan specifically locates this system among post-World War II middle-class suburban communities. At the same time, America's post-war economic boom had led to the development of new technologies that were supposed to make household work less difficult, but that often had the result of making women's work less meaningful and valuable.

Third-wave Feminism

Third-wave feminism began in the early 1990s, arising as a response to perceived failures of the second wave and also as a response to the backlash against initiatives and movements created by the second wave. Third-wave feminism seeks to challenge or avoid what it deems the second wave's essentialist definitions of femininity, which (according to them) over-emphasize the experiences of upper middle-class white women. A post-structuralist interpretation of gender and sexuality is central to much of the third wave's ideology. Third-wave feminists often focus on "micro-politics" and challenge the second wave's paradigm as to what is, or is not, good for females. The third wave has its origins in the mid-1980s. Feminist leaders rooted in the second wave like Gloria Anzaldua, bell hooks, Chela Sandoval, Cherrie Moraga, Audre Lorde, Maxine Hong Kingston, and many other black feminists, called for a new subjectivity in feminism. They sought to negotiate prominent space within feminist thought for consideration of race-related subjectivities.

In 1991, Anita Hill accused Clarence Thomas, a man nominated to the United States Supreme Court, of sexual harassment. Thomas denied the accusations and, after extensive debate, the United States Senate voted 52-48 in favor of Thomas. In response to this case, Rebecca Walker published an article entitled "Becoming the Third Wave" in which she stated, "I am not a post-feminism feminist. I am the third-wave."

Third-wave feminism also consists of debates between difference feminists, such as Carol Gilligan, who believe that there are imnortant differences between the sexes (which may or may not be inherent, but which cannot be ignored), and those who believe that there are no essential differences between the sexes (social roles are due to conditioning). Gilligan's book In a Different Voice: Psychological Theory and Women's Development (1982) criticized Lawrence Kohlberg's research on the moral development of children, which at that time showed that girls on average reached a lower level of moral development than did boys. She pointed out that the participants in Kohlberg's basic study were mostly male, and that Kohlberg's scoring method tended to favor a principled way of reasoning, which is more common to boys, over a relational ethics, which is more common to girls. Kohlberg revised his scoring methods as a result of Gilligan's critique, after which boys and girls scored unevenly. In the opening chapter of her book, she demonstrates that female psychology has been considered inferior because it does not correspond with male psychology.

Post-feminism

Post-feminism describes a range of viewpoints reacting to feminism. The term was first used in the 1980s to signify a backlash against second-wave feminism. It now denotes a wide range of theories, some of which argue that postmodernism has destabilized the notion of a universal femininity, and take critical approach to previous feminist discourses, including challenges to the second wave's ideas. Other post-feminists contend that feminism is no longer relevant to today's society. Amelia Jones has written that the post-feminist texts which emerged in the 1980s and 1990s portrayed second-wave feminism as a monolithic entity and criticized it using generalizations.

One of the earliest uses of the term was in Susan Bolotin's 1982 article "Voices of the Post-Feminist Generation," published in New York Times Magazine. This article was based on a number of interviews with women who largely agreed with the goals of feminism, but did not identify as feminists.

Some contemporary feminists, such as Katha Pollitt or Nadine Strossen, consider feminism to hold simply that "women are people". Views that separate the sexes rather than unite them are considered by these writers to be sexist rather than feminist.

Christina Hoff Sommers, in her 1994 book Who Stole Feminism? How Women Have Betrayed Women, considers much of modern academic feminist theory and the feminist movement, which she says is aimed at the abolition of gender roles, to be gynocentric and misandrist. She labels this "Gender feminism" and proposes "Equity feminism"-an ideology that aims for full civil and legal equality. She argues that while the feminists she designates as gender feminists advocate preferential treatment and portray women as victims, equity feminism provides a viable alternative form of feminism. These descriptions and her other work have caused Hoff Sommers to be described as an antifeminist by other feminists.

Susan Faludi in her book Backlash: The Undeclared War Against American Women, argues that a backlash against second wave feminism in the 1980s has successfully re-defined feminism through its terms. She argues that it constructed the women's liberation movement as the source of many of the problems alleged to be plaguing women in the late 1980s. She also argues that many of these problems are illusory, constructed by the media without reliable evidence. According to Faludi, the backlash is also a historical trend, recurring when it appears that women have made substantial gains in their efforts to obtain equal rights.

French Feminism

French feminism usually refers to a branch of feminist thinking from a group of feminists in France from the 1970s to the 1990s. French feminism, compared to Anglophone feminism, is distinguished by an approach which is at once more philosophical and more literary. Its writings tend to be effusive and metaphorical, rather than pragmatic. It is less concerned with immediate political doctrine, or "materialism", and generally focuses on theories of "the body".

People of Interest

- Simone de Beauvoir
- Helene Cixous
- Bracha Ettinger
- Luce Irigaray
- Julia Kristeva

Simone de Beauvoir

The French author and philosopher Simone de Beauvoir wrote novels; monographs on philosophy, politics, and social issues; essays, biographies, and an autobiography. She is now best known for her metaphysical novels, including She Came to Stay and The Mandarins, and for her 1949 treatise The Second Sex, a detailed analysis of women's oppression and a foundational tract of contemporary feminism. It sets out a feminist existentialism which prescribes a moral revolution. As an existentialist, de Beauvoir accepts Jean-Paul Sartre's precept that existence precedes essence; hence "one is not born a woman, but becomes one". Her analysis focuses on the concept of The Other; that is, is the social construction of Woman as the quintessential Other that Beauvoir identifies as fundamental to women's oppression. She argues that women have historically been considered deviant and abnormal. She submits that even Mary Wollstonecraft considered men to be the ideal toward which women should aspire. Beauvoir says that this attitude has limited women's success by maintaining the perception that they are a deviation from the normal-outsiders attempting to emulate "normality". For feminism to move forward, this assumption must be set aside.

1970s-present

French feminists approach feminism with a the concept of écriture féminine (which translates as female, or feminine, writing). Helene Cixous argues that writing and philosophy are phallocentric and along with other French feminists such as Luce Irigaray emphasize "writing from the body" as a subversive exercise. Julia Kristeva's work on the semiotic and abjection influenced feminist literary criticism in particular. However, as Elizabeth Wright points out, "none of these French feminists align themselves with the feminist movement as it appeared in the Anglophone world". Bracha L. Ettinger contends that the specificity of the female body allows it to articulate a "matrixial trans-subjectivity" which has specific aesthetic and ethical implications.

FEMINIST THEORY

Feminist theory is the extension of feminism into theoretical or philosophical fields. It encompasses work in a variety of disciplines, including anthropology, sociology, economics, women's studies, literary criticism, art history, psychoanalysis and philosophy. Feminist theory aims to understand gender inequality and focuses on gender politics, power relations, and sexuality. While providing a critique of these social and political relations, much of feminist theory also focuses on the promotion of women's rights and interests. Themes explored in feminist theory include discrimination, stereotyping, objectification (especially sexual objectification), oppression, and patriarchy.

Elaine Showalter describes the phased development of feminist theory. The first she calls "feminist critique", in which the feminist reader examines the ideologies behind literary phenomena. The second Showalter calls "gynocritics", in which the "woman is producer of textual meaning" including "the psychodynamics of female creativity; linguistics and the problem of a female language; the trajectory of the individual or collective female literary career [and] literary history". The last phase she calls "gender theory", in which the "ideological inscription and the literary effects of the sex/gender system" are explored". This model has been criticized by Toril Moi who sees it as an essentialist and deterministic model for female subjectivity and for failing to account for the situation of women outside the West.

Feminism's Many Forms

Several subtypes of feminist ideology have developed over the years; some of the major subtypes are listed below.

Liberal Feminism

Liberal feminism asserts the equality of men and women through political and legal reform. It is an individualistic form of feminism, which focuses on women's ability to show and maintain their equality through their own actions and choices.

Liberal feminism uses the personal interactions between men and women as the place from which to transform society. According to liberal feminists, all women are capable of asserting their ability to achieve equality, therefore it is possible for change to happen without altering the structure of society. Issues important to liberal feminists include reproductive and abortion rights, sexual harassment, voting, education, "equal pay for equal work", affordable childcare, affordable health care, and bringing to light the frequency of sexual and domestic violence against women.

People of Interest

- Shirley Chisholm
- Betty Friedan
- Pauli Murray
- Eleanor Smeal
- Gloria Steinem
- Rebecca Walker
- Naomi Wolf

Organizations of Interest

- National Organization for Women (U.S.)
- Feminist Majority Foundation (U.S.)

Closely Aligned With

- Black feminism
- Civil Rights Organizations
- Ecofeminism

RADICAL FEMINISM

Radical feminism sees the capitalist sexist hierarchy as the defining feature of women's oppression. Radical feminists believe that women can free themselves only when have done away with what they consider an inherently oppressive and dominating system. Radical feminists feel that there is a male-based authority and power structure and that it is responsible for oppression and inequality, and that as long as the system and its values are in place, society will not be able to be reformed in any significant way. Radical feminists see capitalism as one of the most important barriers to ending oppression. Most radical feminists see no alternatives other than the total uprooting and reconstruction of society in order to achieve their goals. Separatist feminism is one form of radical feminism. It does not support heterosexual relationships because its proponents argue that the sexual disparities between men and women are unresolvable. Separatist feminists generally do not feel that men can make positive contributions to the feminist movement and that even well-intentioned men replicate patriarchal dynamics. Author Marilyn Frye describes separatist feminism as "separation of various sorts or modes from men and from institutions, relationships, roles and activities that are male-defined, male-dominated, and operating for the benefit of males and the maintenance of male privilege - this separation being initiated or maintained, at will, by women".

People of Interest

- Charlotte Bunch
- Susan Brownmiller
- Mary Daly
- Andrea Dworkin
- Melissa Farley
- Shulamith Firestone
- Catharine Mackinnon
- Adrienne Rich

SEX-POSITIVE FEMINISM

Both the sex-positive and sex-negative forms of present-day feminism can trace their roots to early radical feminism. Some feminists joined the sex-positive feminist movement in response to anti-pornography feminists, such as Catharine MacKinnon, Andrea Dworkin, Robin Morgan and Dorchen Leidholdt, who argued that heterosexual pornography was a central cause of women's oppression. Sex-positive feminism, sometimes known as pro-sex feminism, sex-radical feminism, or sexually liberal feminism, is a movement that was formed in order to address issues of women's sexual pleasure, sex work, and inclusive gender identities. The initial period of intense debate and acrimony between sex-positive and anti-pornography feminists during the early 1980s is often referred to as the Feminist Sex Wars. Other, less academic, sex-positive feminists became involved not in opposition to other feminists, but in direct response to what they saw as patriarchal control of sexuality, such as the organization Feminists for Free Expression.

Ellen Willis's 1981 essay, "Lust Horizons: Is the Women's Movement Pro-Sex?" is the origin of the term, pro-sex feminism. In it, she argues against feminists making alliances with the political right in opposition to pornography and prostitution, as occurred, for example, during the Meese Commission hearings in the United States. Willis argues for a feminism that embraces sexual freedom, including men's sexual freedom, rather than one that condemns pornography, consensual BDSM, and in some cases sexual intercourse and fellatio.

People of Interest

- Kathy Acker
- Susie Bright
- Avedon Carol
- Patrick Califia
- Nina Hartley
- Inga Muscio
- Carol Queen
- Candida Royalle
- Annie Sprinkle
- Gayle Rubin

Anarcha-feminism

Another offshoot of radical feminism is anarcha-feminism (also called anarchist feminism or anarcho-feminism), an ideology which combines feminist and anarchist beliefs. Anarcha-feminists view patriarchy as a manifestation of hierarchy, believing that the fight against patriarchy is an essential part of the class struggle and the anarchist struggle against the state. Anarcha-feminists such as Susan Brown see the anarchist struggle as a necessary component of the feminist struggle.

In Brown's words, "anarchism is a political philosophy that opposes all relationships of power, it is inherently feminist". Recently, Wendy McElroy has defined a position (she describes it as "ifeminism" or "individualist feminism") that combines feminism with anarcho-capitalism or libertarianism, arguing that a pro-capitalist, anti-state position is compatible with an emphasis on equal rights and empowerment for women. Individualist anarchist-feminism has grown from the US-based individualist anarchism movement.

BLACK FEMINISM

Black feminism argues that sexism, class oppression, and racism are inextricably bound together. Forms of feminism that strive to overcome sexism and class oppression but ignore race can discriminate against many people, including women, through racial bias.

Black feminists argue that the liberation of black women entails freedom for all people, since it would require the end of racism, sexism, and class oppression.

One of the theories that evolved out of this movement was Alice Walker's Womanism. It emerged after the early feminist movements that were led specifically by white women who advocated social changes such as woman's suffrage. These movements were largely white middle-class movements and ignored oppression based on racism and classism. Alice Walker and other Womanists pointed out that black women experienced a different and more intense kind of oppression from that of white women.

Angela Davis was one of the first people who articulated an argument centered around the intersection of race, gender, and class in her book, Women, Race, and Class. Kimberle Crenshaw, a prominent feminist law theorist, gave the idea a name while discussing identity politics in her essay, "Mapping the Margins: Intersectionality, Identity Politics and Violence Against Women of Color".

People of Interest

- Angela Davis
- Hattie Gossett
- Patricia Hill Collins
- Barbara Smith
- Alice Walker
- bell hooks

SOCIALIST AND MARXIST FEMINISMS

Socialist feminism connects the oppression of women to Marxist ideas about exploitation, oppression and labor. Socialist feminists see women as being held down as a result of their unequal standing in both the workplace and the domestic sphere. Prostitution, domestic work, childcare, and marriage are all seen as ways in which women are exploited by a patriarchal system which devalues women and the substantial work that they do. Socialist feminists focus their energies on broad change that affects society as a whole, and not just on an individual basis. They see the need to work alongside not just men, but all other groups, as they see the oppression of women as a part of a larger pattern that affects everyone involved in the capitalist system.

Marx felt that when class oppression was overcome, gender oppression would vanish as well. According to socialist feminists, this view of gender oppression as a sub-class of class oppression is naive and much of the work of socialist feminists has gone towards separating gender phenomena from class phenomena. Some contributors to socialist feminism have criticized these traditional Marxist ideas for being largely silent on gender oppression except to subsume it underneath broader class oppression.

Other socialist feminists, notably two long-lived American organizations Radical Women and the Freedom Socialist Party, point to the classic Marxist writings of Frederick Engels and August Bebel as a powerful explanation of the link between gender oppression and class exploitation.

In the late nineteenth century and early twentieth century both Clara Zetkin and Eleanor Marx were against the demonization of men and supported a proletarian revolution that would overcome as many male-female inequalities as possible.

People of Interest

- Michelè Barrett
- Friedrich Engels
- Clara Fraser
- Emma Goldman
- Sheila Rowbotham
- Clara Zetkin
- Eleanor Marx

POST-STRUCTURAL AND POSTMODERN FEMINISM

Post-structural feminism, also referred to as French feminism, uses the insights of various epistemological movements, including psychoanalysis, linguistics, political theory (Marxist and post-Marxist theory), race theory, literary theory, and other intellectual currents for feminist concerns. Many post-structural feminists maintain that difference is one of the most powerful tools that females possess in their struggle with patriarchal domination, and that to equate the feminist movement only with equality is to deny women a plethora of options because equality is still defined from the masculine or patriarchal perspective.

Postmodern feminism is an approach to feminist theory that incorporates postmodern and post-structuralist theory. The largest departure from other branches of feminism, is the argument that gender is constructed through language. The most notable proponent of this argument is Judith Butler. In her 1990 book, Gender Trouble, she draws on and criticizes the work of Simone de Beauvoir, Michel Foucault and Jacques Lacan. Butler criticizes the distinction drawn by previous feminisms between biological sex and socially constructed gender. She says that this does not allow for a sufficient criticism of essentialism. For Butler "woman" is a debatable category, complicated by class, ethnicity, sexuality, and other facets of identity. She suggests that gender is performative. This argument leads to the conclusion that there is no single cause for women's subordination and no single approach towards dealing with the issue.

In A Cyborg Manifesto Donna Haraway criticizes traditional notions of feminism, particularly its emphasis on identity, rather than affinity. She uses the metaphor of a cyborg in order to construct a postmodern feminism that moves beyond dualisms and the limitations of traditional gender, feminism, and politics. Haraway's cyborg is an attempt to break away from Oedipal narratives and Christian origin-myths like Genesis. She writes: "The cyborg does not dream of community on the model of the organic family, this time without the oedipal project. The cyborg would not recognize the Garden of Eden; it is not made of mud and cannot dream of returning to dust."

A major branch in postmodern feminist thought has emerged from the contemporary psychoanalytic French feminism. Other postmodern feminist works highlight stereotypical gender roles, only to portray them as parodies of the original beliefs. The history of feminism is not important in these writings-only what is going to be done about it. The history is dismissed and used to depict how ridiculous past beliefs were. Modern feminist theory has been extensively criticized as being predominantly, though not exclusively, associated with Western middle class academia. Mainstream feminism has been criticized as being too narrowly focused and inattentive to related issues of race and class.

People of Interest

- Judith Butler
- Helene Cixous
- Bracha Ettinger
- Mary Joe Frug
- Donna Haraway

- Luce Irigaray
- Julia Kristeva
- Monique Wittig

POSTCOLONIAL FEMINISM AND THIRD-WORLD FEMINISM

Postcolonial feminists argue that oppression relating to the colonial experience, particularly racial, class, and ethnic oppression, has marginalized women in postcolonial societies. They challenge the assumption that gender oppression is the primary force of patriarchy. Postcolonial feminists object to portrayals of women of non-Western societies as passive and voiceless victims and the portrayal of Western women as modern, educated and empowered.

Postcolonial feminism emerged from the gendered history of colonialism: colonial powers often imposed Western norms on colonized regions. In the 1940s and 1950s, after the formation of the United Nations, former colonies were monitored by the West for what was considered "social progress". The status of women in the developing world has been monitored by organizations such as the United Nations and as a result traditional practices and roles taken up by women-sometimes seen as distasteful by Western standards-could be considered a form of rebellion against colonial oppression. Postcolonial feminists today struggle to fight gender oppression within their own cultural models of society rather than through those imposed by the Western colonizers.

Postcolonial feminism is critical of Western forms of feminism, notably radical feminism and liberal feminism and their universalization of female experience. Postcolonial feminists argue that cultures impacted by colonialism are often vastly different and should be treated as such. Colonial oppression may result in the glorification of pre-colonial culture, which, in cultures with traditions of power stratification along gender lines, could mean the acceptance of, or refusal to deal with, inherent issues of gender inequality.[88] Postcolonial feminists can be described as feminists who have reacted against both universalizing tendencies in Western feminist thought and a lack of attention to gender issues in mainstream postcolonial thought.

Third-world feminism has been described as a group of feminist theories developed by feminists who acquired their views and took part in feminist politics in so-called third-world countries. Although women from the third world have been engaged in the feminist movement, Chandra Talpade Mohanty criticizes Western feminism on thc grounds that it is ethnocentric and does not take into account the unique experiences of women from third-world countries or the existence of feminisms indigenous to third-world countries. According to her, women in the third world feel that Western feminism bases its understanding of women on "internal racism, classism and homophobia". This discourse is strongly related to African feminism and postcolonial feminism. Its development is also associated with concepts such as black feminism, womanism, "Africana womanism", "motherism", "Stiwanism", "negofeminism", chicana feminism, and "femalism".

People of Interest

- Trinh T. Minh-ha
- Uma Narayan
- Taslima Nasrin
- Amrita Pritam
- Gayatri Spivak
- Sarojini Sahoo
- Chandra Talpade Mohanty

ECOFEMINISM

Ecofeminism links ecology with feminism. Ecofeminists see the domination of women as stemming from the same ideologies that bring about the domination of the environment. Patriarchal systems, where men own and control the land, are seen as responsible for the oppression of women and destruction of the natural environment. Since the men in power control the land, they are able to exploit it for their own profit and success. In this same situation, women are exploited by men in power for their own profit, success, and pleasure. Women and the environment are both exploited as passive pawns in the race to domination. Those people in power are able to take advantage of them distinctly because they are seen as passive and rather helpless. Ecofeminism connects the exploitation and domination of women with that of the environment. As a way of repairing social and ecological injustices, ecofeminists feel that women must work towards creating a healthy environment and ending the destruction of the lands that most women rely on to provide for their families.

Ecofeminism argues that there is a connection between women and nature that comes from their shared history of oppression by a patriarchal Western society. Vandana Shiva explains how women's special connection to the environment through their daily interactions with it have been ignored. She says that "women in subsistence economies, producing and reproducing wealth in partnership with nature, have been experts in their own right of holistic and ecological knowledge of nature's processes. But these alternative modes of knowing, which are oriented to the social benefits and sustenance needs are not recognized by the [capitalist] reductionist paradigm, because it fails to perceive the interconnectedness of nature, or the connection of women's lives, work and knowledge with the creation of wealth." Ecofeminists also criticize Western lifestyle choices, such as consuming food that has traveled thousands of miles and playing sports (such as golf and bobsledding) which inherently require ecological destruction.

However, feminist and social ecologist Janet Biehl has criticized ecofeminism for focusing too much on a mystical connection between women and nature and not enough on the actual conditions of women.

People of Interest

- Mary Daly
- Gerda Lerner
- Wangari Maathai

- Val Plumwood
- Rosemary Radford Ruether
- Vandana Shiva
- Charlene Spretnak
- Karen J. Warren

INDIVIDUALIST FEMINISM

Individualist feminism is defined in opposition to, what writers such as Wendy McElroy and Christina Hoff Sommers term, political or gender feminism. Some individualist feminists trace the movement's roots to the classical liberal tradition. It is closely linked to the libertarian ideas of individuality and personal responsibility for both women and men. Some other feminists believe that it reinforces patriarchal systems because it does not view the rights or political interests of men and women as being in conflict nor does it rest upon class or gender analysis.

Individualist feminists attempt to change legal systems in order to eliminate class privileges and gender privileges and to ensure that individuals have equal rights, including an equal claim under the law to their own persons and property. Individualist feminism encourages women to take full responsibility for their own lives. It also opposes any government interference into the choices adults make with their own bodies, because it contends such interference creates a coercive hierarchy (such as patriarchy).

People of Interest

- Dora Marsden
- Wendy McElroy
- Carol Moorc
- Ezra Heywood
- Cathy Young
- Sharon Presley
- Heidi Wyss

FEMINISM AND SOCIETY

The feminist movement has effected change in Western society, including women's suffrage; the right to initiate divorce proceedings and "no fault" divorce; and the right of women to make individual decisions regarding pregnancy (including access to contraceptives and abortion); and the right to own property.

Civil Rights

Feminism has effected many changes in Western society, including women's suffrage, broad employment for women at more equitable wages, the right to initiate divorce proceedings and the introduction of "no fault" divorce, the right to obtain contraception and safe abortions, and access to university education. According to studies by the United Nations, when both paid employment and unpaid household tasks are accounted for, on average women work more than men. In rural areas of selected developing countries women performed an average of 20% more work than men, or an additional 102 minutes per day.

In the OECD countries surveyed, on average women performed 5% more work than men, or 20 minutes per day. At the UN's Pan Pacific Southeast Asia Women's Association 21st International Conference in 2001 it was stated that "in the world as a whole, women comprise 51 percent of the population, do 66 percent of the work, receive 10 percent of the income and own less than one percent of the property".

Language

Gender-neutral language is a description of language usages which are aimed at minimizing assumptions regarding the biological sex of human referents. The advocacy of gender-neutral language reflects, at least, two different agendas: one aims to clarify the inclusion of both sexes or genders (gender-inclusive language); the other proposes that gender, as a category, is rarely worth marking in language (gender-neutral language). Gender-neutral language is sometimes described as non-sexist language by advocates and politically-correct language by opponents.

Heterosexual Relationships

The increased entry of women into the workplace beginning in the twentieth century has affected gender roles and the division of labor within households.

Sociologist Arlie Russell Hochschild in The Second Shift and The Time Bind presents evidence that in two-career couples, men and women, on average, spend about equal amounts of time working, but women still spend more time on housework. Feminist criticisms of men's contributions to child care and domestic labor in the Western middle class are typically centered around the idea that it is unfair for women to be expected to perform more than half of a household's domestic work and child care when both members of the relationship also work outside the home. Several studies provide statistical evidence that the financial income of married men does not affect their rate of attending to household duties.

In Dubious Conceptions, Kristin Luker discusses the effect of feminism on teenage women's choices to bear children, both in and out of wedlock. She says that as childbearing out of wedlock has become more socially acceptable, young women, especially poor young women, while not bearing children at a higher rate than in the 1950s, now see less of a reason to get married before having a child.

Her explanation for this is that the economic prospects for poor men are slim, hence poor women have a low chance of finding a husband who will be able to provide reliable financial support. Although research suggests that to an extent, both women and men perceive feminism to be in conflict with romance, studies of undergraduates and older adults have shown that feminism has positive impacts on relationship health for women and sexual satisfaction for men, and found no support for negative stereotypes of feminists.

CULTURE

Women's Writing

Women's writing came to exist as a separate category of scholarly interest relatively recently. In the West, second-wave feminism prompted a general reevaluation of women's historical contributions, and various academic sub-disciplines, such as women's history and women's writing, developed in response to the belief that women's lives and contributions have been underrepresented as areas of scholarly interest. Virginia Balisn et al. characterize the growth in interest since 1970 in women's writing as "powerful". Much of this early period of feminist literary scholarship was given over to the rediscovery and reclamation of texts written by women.

Studies such as Dale Spender's Mothers of the Novel (1986) and Jane Spencer's The Rise of the Woman Novelist (1986) were ground-breaking in their insistence that women have always been writing. Commensurate with this growth in scholarly interest, various presses began the task of reissuing long-out-of-print texts. Virago Press began to publish its large list of nineteenth and early-twentieth-century novels in 1975 and became one of the first commercial presses to join in the project of reclamation. In the 1980s Pandora Press, responsible for publishing Spender's study, issued a companion line of eighteenth-century novels written by women. More recently, Broadview Press has begun to issue eighteenth- and nineteenth-century works, many hitherto out of print and the University of Kentucky has a series of republications of early women's novels. There has been commensurate growth in the area of biographical dictionaries of women writers due to a perception, according to one editor, that "[m]ost of our women are not represented in the 'standard' reference books in the field".

Feminist Science Fiction

In the 1960s the genre of science fiction combined its sensationalism with political and technological critiques of society. With the advent of feminism, questioning women's roles became fair game to this "subversive, mind expanding genre". Two early texts are Ursula K. Le Guin's The Left Hand of Darkness (1969) and Joanna Russ' The Female Man (1970). They serve to highlight the socially constructed nature of gender roles by creating utopias that do away with gender. Both authors were also pioneers in feminist criticism of science fiction in the 1960s and 70s, in essays collected in The Language of the Night

(Le Guin, 1979) and How To Suppress Women's Writing (Russ, 1983). Other major works of feminist science fiction have been The Handmaid's Tale by Margaret Atwood and Kindred by Octavia Butler.

Riot Grrrl Feminism

Riot grrrl (or riot grrl) is an underground feminist punk movement that started in the 1990s and is often associated with third-wave feminism (it is sometimes seen as its starting point). However, riot grrrl's emphasis on universal female identity and separatism often appears more closely allied with second-wave feminism than with the third wave. Riot grrrl bands often address issues such as rape, domestic abuse, sexuality, and female empowerment. Some bands associated with the movement are: Bikini Kill, Bratmobile, Excuse 17, Free Kitten, Heavens To Betsy, Huggy Bear, L7, and Team Dresch. In addition to a music scene, riot grrrl is also a subculture; zines, the DIY ethic, art, political action, and activism are part of the movement. Riot grrrls hold meetings, start chapters, and support and organize women in music.

People of Interest

- Allison Wolfe
- Kathleen Hanna
- Molly Neuman
- Corin Tucker
- Tobi Vail

RELIGION

Feminist theology is a movement that reconsiders the traditions, practices, scriptures, and theologies of religions from a feminist perspective. Some of the goals of feminist theology include increasing the role of women among the clergy and religious authorities, reinterpreting male-dominated imagery and language about God, determining women's place in relation to career and motherhood, and studying images of women in the religion's sacred texts.

Christian Feminism

is a branch of feminist theology which seeks to interpret and understand Christianity in light of the equality of women and men. Because this equality has been historically ignored, Christian feminists believe their contributions are necessary for a complete understanding of Christianity. While there is no standard set of beliefs among Christian feminists, most agree that God does not discriminate on the basis of biologically-determined characteristics such as sex. Their major issues are the ordination of women, male dominance in Christian marriage, and claims of moral deficiency and inferiority of abilities of women compared to men. They also are concerned with the balance of parenting between mothers and fathers and the overall treatment of women in the church.

Islamic Feminism

Islamic feminism is concerned with the role of women in Islam and aims for the full equality of all Muslims, regardless of gender, in public and private life. Islamic feminists advocate women's rights, gender equality, and social justice grounded in an Islamic framework. Although rooted in Islam, the movement's pioneers have also utilized secular and Western feminist discourses and recognize the role of Islamic feminism as part of an integrated global feminist movement. Advocates of the movement seek to highlight the deeply rooted teachings of equality in the Quran and encourage a questioning of the patriarchal interpretation of Islamic teaching through the Quran, hadith (sayings of Muhammed), and sharia (law) towards the creation of a more equal and just society.

People of Interest

- Fadela Amara
- Asma Barlas
- Samira Bellil
- Mukhtaran Bibi
- Zilla Huma Usman
- Amina Wadud

Jewish Feminism

Jewish feminism is a movement that seeks to improve the religious, legal, and social status of women within Judaism and to open up new opportunities for religious experience and leadership for Jewish women. Feminist movements, with varying approaches and successes, have opened up within all major branches of Judaism. In its modern form, the movement can be traced to the early 1970s in the United States. According to Judith Plaskow, who has focused on feminism in Reform Judaism, the main issues for early Jewish feminists in these movements were the exclusion from the all-male prayer group or minyan, the exemption from positive time-bound mitzvot, and women's inability to function as witnesses and to initiate divorce.

People of Interest

- Rachel Adler
- Tova Hartman
- Susan Sontag
- Yona Wallach
- Yona Wallach
- Jeanette Rankin

REGIONAL FEMINIST MOVEMENTS

Iran

Perhaps the most notable figure of the women's movement during the Iranian revolution and in post-revolution Iran was Shirin Ebadi. She won the Nobel Prize for advocating democracy and human rights, especially the rights of women and children. Ebadi in collaboration with figures like Simin Behbahani, Mehrangiz Kar, Elaheh Koulaei, Shahla Sherkat, Jila Bani Yaghoob, Mahboubeh Abbas-Gholizadeh, Azam Taleghani, Shahla Lahiji, and others directed the women's movement in Iran in the late 20th century and at the turn of the new millennium. In 1992, Shahla Sherkat founded Zanan (Women) magazine, which focused on the concerns of Iranian women and tested the political waters with its edgy coverage of reform politics, domestic abuse, and sex. It is the most important Iranian women's journal published after the Iranian revolution, systematically criticizing the Islamic legal code. It argues that gender equality is Islamic and that religious literature has been misread and misappropriated by misogynists. Mehangiz Kar, Shahla Lahiji, and Shahla Sherkat, the editor of Zanan, leads the debate on women's rights and demanded reforms. On August 27, 2006, a new women's rights campaign was launched in Iran. The "One Million Signatures" campaign aims to end legal discrimination against women in Iranian laws by collecting a million signatures. The supporters of this campaign include many Iranian women's rights activists and also international activists as well as many Nobel laureates.

India

With the rise of feminism across the world, a new generation of Indian feminists has emerged. Women have developed themselves according to the situations and has become advanced in various fields. They have become independent in respect of their reproductive right. Contemporary Indian feminists are fighting for: individual autonomy, rights, freedom, independence, tolerance, cooperation, nonviolence and diversity, domestic violence, gender, stereotypes, sexuality, discrimination, sexism, non-objectification, freedom from patriarchy, the right to an abortion, reproductive rights, control of the female body, the right to a divorce, equal pay, maternity leave, breast feeding, prostitution, and education. Medha Patkar, Madhu Kishwar, and Brinda Karat are feminist social workers and politicians who advocate women's rights in post-independent India. Writers such as Amrita Pritam, Sarojini Sahoo and Kusum Ansal advocate feminist ideas in Indian languages. Rajeshwari Sunder Rajan, Leela Kasturi, Sharmila Rege, and Vidyut Bhagat are Indian feminist essayists and critics writing in English.

Japan

Japanese feminism as an organized political movement dates back to the early years of the 20th century, when Kato Shidzue pushed for birth-control availability as part of a broad spectrum of progressive reforms. Shidzue went on to serve in the National Diet following the defeat of Japan in World War II and the promulgation of the Peace Constitution by US forces. Other figures such as Hayashi Fumiko and Ariyoshi Sawako illustrate the broad socialist ideologies of Japanese feminism, that seeks to accomplish broad goals rather than celebrate the individual achievements of powerful women.

Norway

Feminism in Norway has its political origins in the movement for women's suffrage. Women's issues were first articulated in the public sphere by Camilla Collett (1813-1895), widely considered the first Norwegian feminist. Originating from a literary family, she wrote a novel and several articles on the difficulties facing women of her time, and in particular forced marriages. Amalie Skram (1846-1905) also gave voice to a woman's point of view with her naturalist writing.

The Norwegian Association for Women's Rights was founded in 1884 by Gina Krog and Hagbart Berner. The organization raised issues related to women's rights to education and economic self-determination, and above all, universal suffrage. Women's right to vote was passed by law, June 11, 1913 by the Norwegian Parliament. Norway was the second country in Europe after Finland to have full suffrage for women.

Poland

The development of feminism in Poland and Polish territories[133] has traditionally been divided into seven successive "waves". The 1920s saw the emergence of radical feminism in Poland. Its representatives, Irena Krzywicka and Maria Morozowicz-Szczepkowska, advocated women's independence from men.

Krzywicka and Tadeusz Zelenski both promoted planned parenthood, sexual education, rights to divorce and abortion, and equality of sexes. Krzywicka published a series of articles in Wiadomosci Literackie in which she protested against interference by the Roman Catholic Church in the intimate lives of Poles.

After the Second World War, the Polish Communist state (established in 1948) forcefully promoted women's emancipation at home and at work. However, during Communist rule (until 1989), feminism in general, and second-wave feminism in particular, were practically absent.

Although feminist texts were produced in the 1950s and afterwards, they were usually controlled and generated by the Communist state. After the fall of Communism, the Polish government, dominated by 'pro-Catholic' political parties, introduced a de facto legal ban on abortions. Since then some feminists have adopted argumentative strategies borrowed from the American 'Pro-Choice' movement of the 1980s.

FEMINISM AND POLITICAL MOVEMENTS

Feminism and Socialism

Some strands of early twentieth century feminism allied with socialism. In 1907 there was an International Conference of Socialist Women in Stuttgart where suffrage was described as a tool of class struggle. Clara Zetkin of the Social Democratic Party of Germany called for women's suffrage to build a "socialist order, the only one that allows for a radical solution to the women's question".

In Britain, the women's movement was allied with the Labour party. In America, Betty Friedan emerged from a radical background to take command of the organized movement. Radical Women, founded in 1967 in Seattle is the oldest (and still active) socialist feminist organization in the U.S. During the Spanish Civil War, Dolores Ibárruri (La Pasionaria) led the Communist Party of Spain. Although she supported equal rights for women, she opposed women fighting on the front and clashed with the anarcho-feminist Mujeres Libres.

Revolutions in Latin America brought changes in women's status in countries such as Nicaragua where Feminist ideology during the Sandinista Revolution was largely responsible for improvements in the quality of life for women but fell short of achieving a social and ideological change.

Feminism and Fascism

In Nazi Germany and the other fascist states of the 1930s and 1940s, the political agenda illustrated the disastrous consequences for women of an antifeminist state ideology.

In Germany there was a rapid dissolution of the gains made during the prewar period. In Francisco Franco's Spain, the right-wing Catholic conservatives undid the gains of the Republic. Fascist society emphasized virility, were very hierarchical, and subordinated women to men.

Feminism and Science

Feminists has been critical of scientific discourse, arguing that the field has historically been biased towards a masculine perspective. Evelyn Fox Keller argues that the rhetoric of science reflects a masculine perspective, and she questions the idea of scientific objectivity. Primatologist Sarah Blaffer Hrdy notes the prevalence of masculine-coined stereotypes and theories, such as the non-sexual female, despite "the accumulation of abundant openly available evidence contradicting it". Some natural and social scientists have examined feminist ideas using scientific methods.

Feminism and the Biology of Gender

Modern feminist science is based on the view that many differences between the sexes are based on socially constructed gender identities rather than on biological sex differences. For example, Anne Fausto-Sterling's book Myths of Gender explores the assumptions embodied in scientific research that purports to support a biologically essentialist view of gender. However, in The Female Brain, Louann Brizendine argues that brain differences between the sexes are a biological reality with significant implications for sex-specific functional differences. Steven Rhoads' book Taking Sex Differences Seriously illustrates sex-dependent differences across a wide scope.

Carol Tavris, in The Mismeasure of Woman, uses psychology and sociology to critique theories that use biological reductionism to explain differences between men and women. She argues rather than using evidence of innate gender difference there is an over-changing hypothesis to justify inequality and perpetuate stereotypes.

Feminism and Evolutionary Biology

Sarah Kember-drawing from numerous areas such as evolutionary biology, sociobiology, artificial intelligence, and cybernetics in development with a new evolutionism-discusses the biologization of technology. She notes how feminists and sociologists have become suspect of evolutionary psychology, particularly inasmuch as sociobiology is subjected to complexity in order to strengthen sexual difference as immutable through pre-existing cultural value judgments about human nature and natural selection. Where feminist theory is criticized for its "false beliefs about human nature," Kember then argues in conclusion that "feminism is in the interesting position of needing to do more biology and evolutionary theory in order not to simply oppose their renewed hegemony, but in order to understand the conditions that make this possible, and to have a say in the construction of new ideas and artefacts."

Men and Feminism

The ɪelationship between men and feminism has been complex. Men have taken part in significant responses to feminism in each 'wave' of the movement. There have been positive and negative reactions and responses, depending on the individual man and the social context of the time. These responses have varied from pro-feminism to masculism to anti-feminism. In the twenty-first century new reactions to feminist ideologies have emerged including a generation of male scholars involved in gender studies, and also men's rights activists who promote of male equality (rights to equal treatment in family, divorce and anti-discrimination law).

Historically a number of men have engaged with feminism. Philosopher Jeremy Bentham demanded equal rights for women in the eighteenth century. In 1866, philosopher John Stuart Mill (author of "The Subjection of Women") presented a women's petition to the British parliament; and supported an amendment to the 1867 Reform Bill. Others have lobbied and campaigned against feminism. Today, academics like Michael Flood, Michael

Messner and Michael Kimmel are involved with men's studies and pro-feminist.

Other men have campaigned against feminism. During the suffragettes' campaign anti-suffragists numbered 160 in 1902 in Britain. In New York, the New York State Association Opposed to Woman Suffrage was founded in 1897, and by 1908 it had over 90 members.

A number of feminist writers maintain that identifying as a feminist is the strongest stand men can take in the struggle against sexism. They have argued that men should be allowed, or even be encouraged, to participate in the feminist movement. Other female feminists argue that men cannot be feminists simply because they are not women. They maintain that men are granted inherent privileges that prevent them from identifying with feminist struggles, thus making it impossible for them to identify with feminists. Fidelma Ashe has approached the issue of male feminism by arguing that traditional feminist views of male experience and of "men doing feminism" have been monolithic. She explores the multiple political discourses and practices of pro-feminist politics, and evaluates each strand through an interrogation based upon its effect on feminist politics.

OTHER CONCEPTS

Pro-feminism

Pro-feminism is the support of feminism without implying that the supporter is a member of the feminist movement. The term is most often used in reference to men who are actively supportive of feminism and of efforts to bring about gender equality. The activities of pro-feminist men's groups include anti-violence work with boys and young men in schools, offering sexual harassment workshops in workplaces, running community education campaigns, and counseling male perpetrators of violence. Pro-feminist men also are involved in men's health, activism against pornography including anti-pornography legislation, men's studies, and the development of gender equity curricula in schools. This work is sometimes in collaboration with feminists and women's services, such as domestic violence and rape crisis centers. Some activists of both genders will not refer to men as "feminists" at all, and will refer to all pro-feminist men as "pro-feminists".

Anti-feminism

Antifeminism is opposition to feminism in some or all of its forms. Feminists such as Camille Paglia, Christina Hoff Sommers, Jean Bethke Elshtain and Elizabeth Fox-Genovese have been labeled "anti-feminists" by other feminists. Patai and Koertge argue that in this way the term "anti-feminist" is used to silence academic debate about feminism. Paul Nathanson and Katherine K. Young's books Spreading Misandry and Legalizing Misandry explore what they argue is feminist-inspired misandry. Christina Hoff-Sommers argues feminist misandry leads directly to misogyny by what she calls "establishment feminists" against (the majority of) women who love men in Who Stole Feminism: How Women Have Betrayed Women. "Marriage rights" advocates criticize feminists like Shelia Cronan who take the view that marriage constitutes slavery for women, and that freedom for women cannot be won without the abolition of marriage.

2

HUMAN RIGHTS AND WOMEN

WHAT ARE THE HUMAN RIGHTS OF WOMEN?

Every woman and girl is entitled to the realization of all human rights -- civil, political, economic, social and cultural - on equal terms with men, free from discrimination. Women and girls also enjoy certain human rights specifically linked to their status as women. The world has recognized that the human rights of women and of the girl-child are "an inalienable, integral and indivisible part of universal human rights." (Vienna Declaration and Programme of Action, para. 18.)

Women are guaranteed equal treatment and freedom from discrimination in the most basic human rights treaties, and women's human rights are the subject of a specific treaty, the Convention on the Elimination of All Forms of Discrimination Against Women. Far-reaching Governmental commitments to ensuring the human rights of women have been made at each of the recent world conferences, and women's human rights are central to the unanimously approved Beijing Declaration and Platform for Action. The Beijing Declaration and Platform for Action, organized into Critical Areas of Concern, raises issues involving fundamental human rights of women.

WOMEN, HUMAN RIGHTS & POVERTY

What is the Human Right to Freedom from Poverty?

A life of dignity is every person's human right. This is true no matter where he or she lives or what his or her sex, race, or ethnic origin may be. And every woman, man, youth and child has basic needs that must be met if he or she is to live in dignity. A life of poverty means that basic needs go unfulfilled, and fundamental human rights are violated.

More than 1 billion people live in poverty around the world, and a great majority of them are women. Women's poverty results in widespread violations of their human rights. When a woman faces a lack of access to adequate housing, food, or health care, her human rights are violated. When she lives in an unsafe and unhealthy environment or lacks access to clean water, she is not enjoying her fundamental human rights to a life of dignity and to an adequate standard of living.

Poverty can also be caused by violations of human rights, particularly women's human right to non-discrimination. When women are denied equal access to employment opportunities, are paid less than men for equal work, or are prevented by law or custom from owning or inheriting land, they are made vulnerable to poverty. When women are denied equal access to education, when they do not have the equal right to decide on the number and spacing of children, or when they have an unequal share of the responsibility for raising children, their ability to earn an income and to be protected from poverty is greatly compromised.

THE HUMAN RIGHTS AT ISSUE

Human Rights relating to poverty are set out in basic human rights treaties and include:

- The human right to an adequate standard of living, including access to housing, food, clean water, and basic social services.
- The human right to a healthy and safe environment.
- The human right to primary health care and medical attention in case of illness.
- The human right to freedom from discrimination based on sex, in all aspects of life and work.
- The human right to equal access to education and training.

- The human right to equal access to productive resources, including land and credit.
- The human right to work and receive wages that contribute to an adequate standard of living.
- The human right to equal pay for equal work, and to equality of opportunity in hiring and promotion.
- The human right to proper consideration of women's reproductive rights and sexuality, including job security during and after pregnancy, flexible working conditions, and access to child care.
- The human right to equality within the family and shared responsibilities for children's upbringing.
- The human right to social security in the event of unemployment, disability, old age, or other lack of livelihood.
- The human right to be treated with dignity, and to freedom from violence and exploitation.
- The human right to full and equal participation in shaping decisions of importance to women, their families and communities, including decisions relating to poverty eradication and development.
- The human right to sustainable development.
- The human right to peace.

What is the Human Right to Education?

Every woman, man, youth and child has the human right to education, training and information, and to other fundamental human rights dependent upon realization of the human right to education. Equality of access to all levels of education is crucial to empowering women and girls to participate in economic, social and political life of their societies.

Education unlocks a woman's potential, and is accompanied by improvements in health, nutrition, and well-being of women and their families. Despite widespread agreement that all people have the fundamental human right to education, 100 million children, at least 60% of them girls, do not have access to primary education. 960 million adults in the world are illiterate, and more than two-thirds of them are women. Women and girls continue to face discrimination at all levels of education, a fact which poses tremendous obstacles to their advancement.

Human rights relating to education are set out in basic human rights treaties and include:

- The human right to free and compulsory elementary education and to readily available forms of secondary and higher education.
- The human right to freedom from discrimination based on sex or any other status in all areas and levels of education, including access to scholarships and fellowships, and to equal access to career development, continuing education and vocational training.
- The human right to information about health, nutrition, reproduction and family planning.

The human right to education is inextricably linked to other fundamental human rights -- rights that are universal, indivisible, interconnected and interdependent including:

- The human right to equality between men and women and to equal partnership in the family and society. Realization of this human rights depends on eliminating gender-based stereotypes in education which deny women opportunities for full and equal partnership.
- The human right to work and receive wages that contribute to an adequate standard of living.
- The human right to freedom of thought, conscience, religion and belief.
- The human right to an adequate standard of living.
- The human right to participate in shaping decisions and policies affecting one's community, at the local, national and international levels.

What is the Human Right to Health?

Every woman, man, youth and child has the human right to the highest attainable standard of physical and mental health. Enjoyment of the human right to health is vital to all aspects of a person's life and well-being. Many women and girls face serious obstacles to realization of their human right to health, including inequality of access to health care, food and nutrition, and customary practices detrimental to their health and well-being. All inequalities relating to health and practices harmful to women violate their fundamental human rights. Human rights relating to health are set out in basic human rights treaties and include:

- The human right to the highest attainable standard of physical and mental health, including reproductive and sexual health.
- The human right to equal access to adequate health care and health related services, regardless of sex, race, or other status.
- The human right to equitable distribution of food.
- The human right to access to safe drinking water and sanitation.
- The human right to an adequate standard of living and adequate housing.
- The human right to a safe and healthy environment.
- The human right to a safe and healthy workplace, and to adequate protection for pregnant women in work proven to be harmful to them.
- The human right to freedom from discrimination and discriminatory social practices, including female genital mutilation, prenatal gender selection, and female infanticide.
- The human right to access to information relating to health, including reproductive health and family planning to enable couples and individuals to decide freely and responsibly all matters of reproduction and sexuality.

- The human right to equality in marriage, including the equal right of women and men to decide on the number and spacing of children.
- The human right to access to adequate social services, including access to safe, effective, affordable and acceptable methods of family planning of their choice, as well as other methods of their choice for regulation of fertility, and the right of access to appropriate health-care services that will enable women to go safely through pregnancy and childbirth.
- The human right to privacy.
- The human right to full respect for the inherent dignity of the person.
- The human right to freedom from coercion and violence, sexual exploitation and forced prostitution.
- The human right of the child to an environment appropriatė for physical and mental development.

What is the Human Right to Freedom from Violence?

Violence against women violates fundamental human rights and is an affront to women's inherent human dignity. Physical, psychological, and sexual violence against women and girls, public and private, plagues all societies and classes and poses tremendous obstacles to the achievement of equality, development and peace. Governments have the obligation not to engage in any form of violence against women and to prevent violence against women wherever it occurs.

Human rights relating to violence against women are set out in basic human rights treaties and include:

- The human right to life.
- The human right to full respect for human dignity.
- The human right not to be subjected to torture or other cruel, inhuman or degrading treatment or punishment.
- The human right to the highest attainable standard of physical and mental health.

- The human right to freedom from discrimination and violence, public or private, due to any status, including gender, race, ethnicity or age.
- The human right to full equality between women and men.
- The human right to full equality between women and men in power and decision-making.
- The human right to freedom from sexual abuse, physical abuse, and psychological violence.
- The human right to a workplace free from violence and abuse.
- The human right to freedom from dowry-related violence.
- The human right to freedom from marital rape.
- The human right to freedom from female genital mutilation and other traditional practices harmful to women.
- The human right to freedom from all harmful customary practices.
- The human right to freedom from trafficking and forced prostitution.
- The human right to freedom from violence associated with armed conflict, including murder, systematic rape, sexual slavery, and forced pregnancy.
- The human right to freedom from forced sterilization and forced abortion.
- The human right to freedom from coercive use of contraceptives.
- The human right to freedom from female infanticide.
- The human right to freedom from prenatal sex selection.
- The human right to equal access to justice, equal protection of the law, and effective remedies for victims of violence.
- The human right to access to services, including physical and mental health services.

WOMEN, HUMAN RIGHTS & PEACE

What is the Human Right to Peace?

The human right of every woman, man, youth and child to peace and the absence of conflict lies at the heart of the realization of all human rights. War and violence result in the systemic and sweeping denial of civil and political rights, along with economic, social, and cultural rights as scarce resources are expended on weapons and preparation for war. In turn, enduring peace will be attained only when people's fundamental human rights are fulfilled. Human Rights relating to poverty are set out in basic human rights treaties and include: The human right to peace is inextricably linked to all other human rights -- rights that are universal, indivisible, interconnected and interdependent. Human rights relating to peace are set out in basic human rights treaties and include:

- The human right to life.
- The human right to freedom from violence, torture and cruel, inhuman treatment or punishment.
- The human right to freedom from arbitrary executions, detention, and disappearance.
- The human right to freedom from genocide, ethnic cleansing and rape as a strategy of war.
- The human right to freedom from religious intolerance.
- The human right to freedom from foreign occupation or domination.
- The human right to self-determination of peoples.
- The human right to the highest attainable standard of physical and mental health.
- The human right to protection and assistance to displaced and refugee women.
- The human right to live by the rule of law.
- The human right to an adequate standard of living, including adequate food, medical care and necessary social services.

- The human right to sustainable development.
- The human right of the child to an environment appropriate for his or her physical, mental, spiritual and moral well-being and development.
- The human right of all people to full and equal participation in decision-making and efforts aimed at the prevention and resolution of conflicts.

What is the Human Right to Full and Equal Participation in Power and Decision-Making?

Issues of women's empowerment and their full and equal participation in public life are human rights issues. Human rights norms and standards guarantee women the human rights to non-discrimination in all aspects of political, economic, and social life, and to full and equal participation in decision-making and access to power at all levels. At the same time, realization of the full spectrum of human rights for women depends on women's full and equal participation in decision-making.

The human right to full and equal participation in power and decision-making includes:

- The human right to participate on equal terms with men in shaping and implementing decisions and policies affecting themselves, their families, communities, and societies, at the local, national and international levels.
- The human right to equal access to public service.
- The human right to equal access to education and information.
- The human right to freedom of expression and opinion.
- The human right to equality between men and women and to full and equal partnership in the family and society.

What is the Human Right to a Healthy and Safe Environment?

Every woman, man, youth and child has the human right to a safe and healthy environment, and to other fundamental human rights linked to and dependent upon a healthy environment. Human rights relating to the environment are set out in basic human rights treaties and include:

- The human right to a safe and healthy environment.
- The human right to the highest attainable standard of health.
- The human right to ecologically sustainable development.
- The human right to an adequate standard of living, including access to safe food and water.
- The human right to freedom from any type of discrimination.
- The human right to safe working conditions, including adequate safeguards for pregnant and lactating women.
- The human right to education and information, including information relating to links between health and the environment.
- The human right to full and equal participation in environmental decision-making and development planning, and in shaping decisions and policies affecting one's community, at the local, national and international levels.
- The human right to share in the benefits of scientific progress.
- The human right of the child to live in an environment appropriate for physical and mental development.

What are the Human Rights of the Girl-Child?

Human Rights are universal, and civil, political, economic, social and cultural rights belong to all human beings, including children and young people. Children and youth also enjoy certain human rights specifically linked to their status as minors and to their need for special care and protection. Girl-children are particularly vulnerable to certain human rights violations, and therefore require additional protections. The human rights of children and the girl-child are explicitly set out in the Convention on the Rights of the Child, the most widely ratified human rights treaty in history. They are also contained in other human rights documents including the Universal Declaration, the Covenants, CEDAW, and other widely adhered to international human rights treaties and Declarations. The human rights of children and the girl-child include the following indivisible, interdependent and interrelated human rights:

- The human right to freedom from discrimination based on gender, age, race, colour, language, religion, ethnicity, or any other status, or on the status of the child's parents.
- The human right to a standard of living adequate for a child's intellectual, physical, moral, and spiritual development.
- The human right to a healthy and safe environment.
- The human right to the highest possible standard of health and to equal access to health care.
- The human right to equal access to food and nutrition.
- The human right to life and to freedom from prenatal sex selection.
- The human right to freedom from cultural practices, customs and traditions harmful to the child, including female genital mutilation.
- The human right to education -- to free and compulsory elementary education, to equal access to readily available forms of secondary and higher education, and to freedom from all types of discrimination at all levels of education.
- The human right to information about health, sexuality and reproduction.
- The human right to protection from all physical or mental abuse.
- The human right to protection from economic and sexual exploitation, prostitution, and trafficking.
- The human right to freedom from forced or early marriage.

- The human right to equal rights to inheritance.
- The human right to express an opinion about plans or decisions affecting the child's life.

HUMAN RIGHTS IMPACT ASSESSMENTS FOR FOREIGN INVESTMENT PROJECTS

Rights & Democracy (International Centre for Human Rights and Democratic Development) is an independent Canadian institution created by an Act of Parliament. It has an international mandate to promote, advocate for and defend the democratic and human rights set out in the International Bill of Human Rights. In cooperation with civil society and governments in Canada and abroad, Rights & Democracy initiates and supports programmes to strengthen laws and democratic institutions, principally in developing countries.

PLACE GREATER EMPHASIS ON ACCOMPANIMENT

Communities and local research teams require reliable moral and professional support throughout the course of the human rights impact assessment process and its follow-up. This is important for capacity building, but also for the personal security of the community members and researchers themselves.

PROVIDE A MORE REALISTIC BUDGET AND TIME ALLOCATION

Methodologies for human rights impact assessments should include a time and budget guide as part of the initial assessment process. Such a guide would flag potential costs that might not otherwise be considered and would provide the accompanying organization and research team members with a better estimate of the amount of time they require for each stage of the assessment process.

REVISE THE METHODOLOGY AND RESEARCH GUIDE

The ten-step methodology should be broken down into smaller, better-defined tasks that provide explicit guidance on implementation. Some elements of the methodology were not sufficiently developed, such as how to structure the final reports.

There is a tension between producing a user-friendly research guide and a comprehensive research guide. There should be a simpler way of selecting questions appropriate to each case study, perhaps by developing a digital tool.

The Case Study Reports

In three cases (Argentina, Peru, Philippines) the research teams were able to link human rights impacts directly to the investment project. In the two others (Democratic Republic of Congo and Tibet) enough information was produced to merit additional study and action.

Philippines

In 2005, the Canadian company TVI Pacific Inc. officially opened the Canatuan mine on the island of Mindanao in the Philippines. The mining operations displaced many families; divided the local indigenous people, known as the Subanon; deprived thousands of small-scale miners of their livelihood; and negatively affected rice farmers and fishers living downstream because of increased levels of sediment and metals in local rivers and creeks.

One of the most controversial aspects of the mine is that it is located on the peak of Mount Canatuan, which the Subanon living in the area consider as sacred. The research team focused heavily on the rights of Indigenous People as described in the UN Declaration on Indigenous Peoples. The central finding of this report is that the investment has had a negative impact on the ability of the Subanon to enjoy the human right to self-determination, to human security, to an adequate standard of living, to adequate housing, to work and to education.

Tibet

In March 2005, the Canadian company Nortel announced it had entered into an agreement with China's Ministry of Railways to provide a digital wireless communications network for a new railway being built in Tibet. The technology, called the Global System for Mobile Communications for Railways, is a key component in the railway's communication system. Railway communications systems are themselves part of China's

Golden Shield Project, an all-encompassing surveillance network that monitors and controls the flow of information and people. The case study is ex-ante; it looks at the potential future impacts of the communications technology on the Tibetan people's rights to privacy, to security of the person, to freedom of expression and to self-determination.

The case study raises the issue of corporate complicity within public-private partnerships, particularly in non-democratic states where human rights violations are systemic. It also looks at the human rights obligations of the company's home state with regard to the export of dual-use technology.

Democratic Republic of Congo (DRC)

In 2001, SOMIKA, a processor of heterogenite (copper and cobalt), set up operations in the Katanga region of the DRC. The company processes ore from various neighboring sites where extraction is contracted out to artisanal miners. SOMIKA's installations are located on a major water table that supplies drinking water to 70% of the population of Lubumbashi. There is a risk that the water could potentially be contaminated by SOMIKA's operations. In addition, there are persistent concerns about discriminatory hiring procedures and working conditions including health and safety risks that have not been adequately addressed. This case study remains incomplete. A number of difficulties were experienced during the research process and therefore it is not possible to present definitive conclusions of the impact assessment here. Nevertheless, preliminary results indicate that there is reason for concern that violations of labour rights and the rights to water and health may have occurred as a result of the investment.

Argentina

In 1993, the government of Argentina created what was then the largest privatized water concession in the world when it awarded a contract to Aguas Argentinas S.A., a consortium of European and Argentine companies, to operate the water and sewage systems in Buenos Aires and surrounding municipalities. The research team studied the performance of both Aguas Argentinas and the Republic of Argentina over the life of the contract, which was terminated by the Argentine government in early 2006. This case study is the only one in the project that focuses on one specific human right - the human right to water. The conceptual framework of the report draws heavily upon General Comment 15, an interpretive statement issued by the United Nations about the human right to water.

The central finding of this research is that the public-private partnership had a negative impact on the ability of the people of Buenos Aires to enjoy access to sufficient, safe, acceptable, accessible and affordable water.

Peru

In 1997, Doe Run Peru S.R.L. purchased a state-owned smelter complex in La Oroya, a Peruvian town in the Andes Mountains. The complex, in operation since 1922, produces copper, lead, zinc, silver, gold, and other products, and emits a toxic cocktail of pollutants. In 2006, La Oroya was named one of the 10 most polluted areas in the world. The case study looks in particular at the impact of the smelter complex on the human rights of women, including the human right to health, housing and water, as well as the human right to work, to information, and to freedom of expression.

The key finding of this case study is that the operations of Doe Run Peru, and the failure of the state to take appropriate steps, have had a negative impact on the ability of the people of La Oroya, especially women, to enjoy their human rights.

INTRODUCTION

When we launched a three-year project in 2004 to develop and test a human rights impact assessment methodology for investment, we knew that the task ahead would not be simple. We had been examining the links between human rights and economic globalization for many years and concerns related to foreign investment were impossible to avoid. We were receiving an ever-increasing number of appeals from communities around the world who often held dramatically different opinions about the benefits of foreign investment than did their governments or the corporations involved. While we acknowledge that investment itself is neither inherently good nor bad for human rights, these stories illustrated that if foreign direct investment projects are to contribute towards sustainable and equitable development, their human rights impacts will have to be both acknowledged and addressed. This requires a process through which the impacts of specific investment projects can be understood in human rights terms.

At its first meeting in November 2004, the project's international advisory committee grappled with the challenges presented by such an ambitious idea. They understood that governments, businesses and the affected communities each have distinct roles and responsibilities with regard to the protection of human rights, albeit with very different levels of influence. They agreed also that basic human rights principles emphasize attention to the most vulnerable and that a process aimed at community empowerment would therefore be the most appropriate.

As a result of these deliberations, Rights & Democracy and the project's international advisory committee, decided to develop a draft methodology and research guide aimed at empowering communities to conduct human rights impact assessments of foreign investment projects. The model they developed was subsequently tested in five case studies, the results of which are presented here in two parts: our reflection on the experience (part one); the case study reports (part two).

The case study reports are the result of a year-long process that involved members of the affected communities, local researchers and our international advisory committee. It is unfortunate that the richness of that experience cannot be fully represented in these few pages. However, the information provided is faithful to the experience and to the data generated by using the draft methodology, although some editing of the final reports has been done by Rights & Democracy for the purposes of consistency.

You will find additional background information about this initiative on the Rights & Democracy website at www.dd-rd.ca, including the original versions of the draft methodology and the research guide. A revised methodology and research guide, based on lessons learned from this process, will be provided in a forthcoming publication.

THE CHALLENGE: ADDRESSING THE INVESTMENT AND HUMAN RIGHTS NEXUS

In recent years, corporate involvement in human rights violations has become a high-profile issue. In some cases, corporations have been held directly responsible for specific violations of human rights, such as abusive labour practices or forced evictions. In other cases, corporations have been viewed as complicit in human rights violations perpetrated by the state, for example by using government security forces to suppress opposition. What is common in most cases is that the people whose lives may be fundamentally transformed by the corporate activity are ill-equipped to negotiate with the companies, to participate in government decision-making or even to understand the international processes that facilitate project bidding and financing.

To address this challenge, we determined that a community-led human rights impact assessment would be an important tool. What was needed was an assessment model that would allow those most affected by the investment to identify its specific human rights impacts and to seek appropriate remedies.

DUTY-BEARERS IN THE BOARDROOM?

One of the primary challenges of applying a human rights framework to investment is that the very nature of corporate obligations remains undefined. It is certainly true that states bear the primary responsibility for protecting and promoting human rights. Nevertheless, the integration of economies and the free flow of capital across borders has made it much more difficult for them to do so. The pressing need for foreign exchange and technology transfer often leads to the reluctance of states to enact or enforce regulations they believe might deter foreign investment. Even in a company's home state, the government commonly acts in the interests of its private sector and gives insufficient attention to the human rights impacts or potential impacts of corporate activities overseas. Human rights advocates acknowledge that the state, the market and civil society are complex, interacting entities. In today's world, focusing on the state as the only human rights duty-bearer does not reflect the increased influence of the market and its primary actors, corporations. However, the human rights responsibilities of companies are not the same as the obligations of states. Our view is that businesses must comply with national and international law, including human rights law, and that this is best understood as a requirement to respect human rights, not to benefit from violations of human rights, and not to be complicit in human rights abuses. In fact, the Universal Declaration of Human Rights states in its opening preamble that "every organ of society" must respect human rights and secure their observance.

In recent years, there have been a number of initiatives designed to more clearly articulate the responsibilities of the private sector in relation to human rights. For example, the UN Global Compact, the Kimberly Process, the Voluntary Principles on Security and Human Rights and the OECD Guidelines for Multinational Enterprises have all attempted to regulate and influence corporate activity to some degree. In 2003, the UN Sub-commission on the Protection and Promotion of Human Rights adopted the UN Norms on the Responsibilities for Business and Other Transnational Corporations with Regard to Human Rights (the Norms), although there was no corresponding consensus among states to adopt them at the Commission on Human Rights itself (now the Human Rights Council). Instead, in 2005 UN Secretary-General Kofi Annan appointed John Ruggie as his Special Representative on Business and Human Rights. Part of his mandate is described as the development of "materials and methodologies for undertaking human rights impact assessments of the activities of transnational corporations and other business enterprises".

There are other initiatives led by civil society organizations. The Danish Institute for Human Rights has developed a human rights compliance assessment model for use by business. The International Business Leaders Forum, in partnership with the International Finance Corporation, has developed its own methodology.

These projects are designed to assist businesses to better understand human rights and to better respond to the range of human rights challenges encountered when operating overseas.

In Canada, the federal government has overseen a process that brought representatives of civil society, government and the private sector together to address corporate responsibility in the extractive sector. The process evolved from a June 2005 report issued by the House of Commons Standing Committee on Foreign Affairs and International Trade.

It concluded that public support for corporations, including project financing and embassy services, should be conditional on the respect of human rights. In its response to the report, the Government of Canada announced that it would convene a series of roundtables across the country focused specifically on the extractive sector. Each roundtable included consultations with the public as well as closed-door sessions with experts on a number of related themes. A multi-stakeholder advisory group with representatives from industry, civil society and academia worked with a government steering committee to oversee implementation of the roundtable process. Following completion of the roundtables, the advisory group prepared a report with a series of recommendations for the Government of Canada.

SHIFTING THE POWER DYNAMIC

All these initiatives have succeeded in reminding states of their human rights responsibilities in relation to foreign investment. They have also made valuable contributions to the debate about the precise nature of corporate obligations with respect to human rights.

Yet there has been scant attention paid to the active involvement of the rights holders themselves in these processes. The individuals and communities who are directly affected by specific investment projects have been largely excluded from international debates about corporate accountability.

There are many reasons for this. Communities often have little leverage over the states that govern them and even less over foreign investors and their home governments. They are also disadvantaged by a lack of information and insufficient access to financial resources. There may be additional security concerns and threats to their personal safety. Yet this entire debate purports to be about the impact of foreign investment as experienced by these very communities.

It has been argued that environmental and social impact assessments provide an adequate response to this challenge. In fact, such assessments are now widely used for large-scale investment projects, including those supported by the World Bank. Environmental and social impact assessments, however, do not adequately confront the challenge of unequal power among stakeholders. The value of reconceiving impact assessments within a human rights framework lies in clarifying the roles of duty-bearer (the state) and rights-holder (those living under the state's jurisdiction).

This idea is illustrated by looking at the standards upon which assessments are based. In a social impact assessment, for example, the baseline data is the current situation and all else is measured from that starting point. Repeated assessments throughout the project cycle identify impacts. A human rights impact assessment, on the other hand, emphasizes standards established by international law and reflected in domestic legislation and policies. While it is also important to measure progressive improvement from a human rights perspective, the main objective of a human rights impact assessment is to measure the gap between the legal norm and the experience. To assist us in understanding exactly how this approach is applied, it is useful to look at some of the primary principles that govern human rights.

Participation: A human rights framework requires the meaningful participation of the rights holders, be they individuals or communities. This reflects the right to take part in public affairs directly or through chosen representatives.6 A human rights impact assessment therefore requires the active involvement of people living in affected communities. This in turn requires enjoyment of the human rights to information, freedom of expression and opinion, security of the person, and the right to privacy.

Accountability: A human rights framework emphasizes the accountability of duty-bearers, including government and corporate actors. This reflects the right of individuals and communities to an effective remedy when the state has failed to respect and ensure their rights. A human rights impact assessment therefore requires attention to judicial processes or legislative and administrative procedures that will offer recourse to the victims of human rights violations.

Transparency: A human rights framework assumes transparency in both process and content. This reflects the human right to seek and receive information. A human rights impact assessment therefore requires full disclosure of information unless restrictions are provided by law, including for the protection of national security.

Non-discrimination: A human rights framework gives special attention to policies and practices that result in discriminatory outcomes. This reflects the right to equality before the law and to equal protection before the law. A human rights impact assessment therefore demands identification of the most vulnerable groups in a given situation and the incorporation of specific steps aimed at their protection and empowerment. Such steps might include designing an impact assessment tool specifically for use by affected communities.

Indivisibility: A human rights framework adopts the view that all human rights - social, economic, cultural, civil and political - are interrelated and interdependent. This principle is derived from the preambles of both the International Covenant on Civil and Political Rights and the International Covenant on Economic, Social and Cultural Rights. A human rights impact assessment therefore looks not only at living standard indicators, for example, but gives equal attention to the ability of affected groups to safely participate in the project process or to express dissent related to the project. The relevance of human rights principles is sometimes unclear to the communities, the states and the companies involved in the project assessment. A fisher who can no longer eat the fish he catches because the water has been polluted might immediately understand the environmental impact but may not know that access to safe and nutritious food is actually a human right to which he is entitled. Similarly, a mining company might think that building a health clinic for the community is an act it can cite as an example of goodwill, but may not realize that the attainment of the highest standard of health is a human right required by and protected in international law. In order to encourage better understanding of human rights it is necessary to integrate education and capacity building as central components of the human rights impact assessment process.

THE RESPONSE: FITTING THE APPROACH TO THE CHALLENGE

It is generally understood that a human rights impact assessment could be applied to policies, processes or projects. We have chosen to focus on the impact of investment at the level of the project. This choice reflects our predisposition to work with affected communities where human rights violations are experienced first-hand. Clearly however, an assessment conducted at the project level focuses largely on the symptom rather than the cause, and some examination of the other levels (such as trade and investment policies or national development plans aimed at fulfillment of social objectives) would be valuable.

In making the choice to focus on a community-led process at the project level, we understood that our emphasis would be on established projects (ex-post) rather than projects still in the planning stage (ex-ante). Although the International Association for Impact Assessment defines assessment as a "process of identifying the future consequences of a current or proposed action", our decision from the outset was to emphasize actual impacts of current investment projects as experienced by affected communities. Furthermore, conducting an ex-ante study at the community level is particularly difficult because communities rarely have adequate information about projects that are in the planning or bidding phases.

A unique dimension of ex-post impact assessments is that in addition to identifying both negative and positive impacts, they may also reveal specific violations that have occurred as a direct result of the investment. However, adequate documentation of violations would require additional steps and expertise within the research process as well as a commitment on the part of the accompanying organization to support community efforts for remedial action, including perhaps court actions, civil suits or even UN complaint procedures.

One might argue that it is in the corporate interest to ensure the free, prior and informed consent of communities in the planning stages of any investment project in order to avoid responsibility for violations down the road. At the moment, however, this is not the case.

Having made these strategic decisions for the project, Rights & Democracy and its international advisory committee launched three concurrent processes with the idea that each pillar would inform the other. The three processes were:

- o Design a methodology specifically for community-led human rights impact assessments;
- o Create a research guide for use during community training and investigation (also referred to as the indicators);
- o Select five case studies to test and revise the methodology and the guide.

THE METHODOLOGY

Much has been written about the value of participatory evaluation processes. Essentially, a participatory process emphasizes the active involvement of the affected person or group in the evaluation or assessment being conducted.

Active involvement means not only provision of information to researchers, but actual ownership of the research process itself. In this sense, the accompanying organization serves only to facilitate communication between various stakeholders and to provide technical assistance to researchers, depending on the situation and the need. Such an approach empowers affected communities to actively engage the assessment process, to take hold of situations affecting their well-being, and to actively assert their human rights when they determine that violations have taken place. They are no longer forced into a position of waiting for someone else to bestow their human rights upon them.

Participatory processes involve a number of departures from more conventional methods of project assessment. The level of objectivity, for example, might be quite different and there will be less emphasis on quantitative indicators. The process will also require fitting the method to the situation and not the other way around.

For the affected community, however, the outcomes of a process like this are often more relevant to their actual situation. Other stakeholders benefit from the richness of data collected from an investigative process that draws upon an element of trust between the researcher and the person or group being interviewed.

In putting forward a methodology that would assist the case study researchers through a participatory impact assessment process, we attempted to address all the various challenges summarized in the previous pages, while incorporating the basic human rights principles as described. We also sought to ensure that procedures were accessible and easily implemented by communities with a minimum of financial and other resources. The resulting roadmap, the Ten-Step Methodology, can be summarized in four general categories: preparation of the case study; application of the research guide; report preparation; and follow-up.

TEN-STEP METHODOLOGY

Steps 1-3: Preparation of the Case Study

Step 1: Scoping

Preliminary scoping includes an overview of the human rights situation at the national level including international human rights instruments ratified by the state; reports published by non-governmental organizations (NGOs), UN agencies, and experts; national policies and legislation; and other related data. Initial scoping should also identify key stakeholders such as specific groups within affected communities; NGOs; the company or its representatives; governments; and other experts.

Step 2: Specific Research on the Investment Project

This step includes the collection of available data about the company and the investment. It includes information such as contracts; records of company interaction with the both home and host states; existing environmental and social impact assessments related to the project; and company policy on social responsibility.

It might also include corporate filings and information about financing from export credit agencies, banks or other multilateral agencies.

Step 3: Adapt the Tool to the Project

Based on the information gathered in steps 1 and 2, the research team adapts the research guide to the case study. Relevant questions and/or indicators are selected and in some cases, when projects focus primarily on one particular human right, a more detailed list of questions and indicators is developed. Depending on the political climate in which the case study is undertaken, some of the questions may need to be reworded.

Steps 4-6: Application of the Research Guide

Step 4: Seek Expert Opinion on Key Human Rights Issues

Identify academics, independent experts, or representatives of non-governmental organizations that have expertise in specific issues identified in the initial scoping. This step allows the research team to incorporate existing data and legal and technical expertise not available within the community.

Information gathered contributes to the "general portrait" of the state's compliance with the specific human rights being addressed by the case study.

Step 5: Interview Representatives of the Community, Workers, Company and Government

The ways in which interviews take place naturally differ from case to case. They range from community meetings to private conversations. The process is iterative and therefore a second round of interviews is recommended in order to obtain supplemental information. As much as possible, interviews are conducted in local languages, and care is taken to protect confidential sources and informants.

Step 6: Verify Information, Identify Factual Disputes

The research team corroborates all information through a careful comparison of collected data, team peer review, and community verification whenever possible. When information is disputed by one party, efforts to resolve that dispute through dialogue are engaged. Background and contextual information provided as part of the research is supported by appropriate documentation.

Step 7: Develop a Draft Report

Once the previous steps have been completed, a draft report will be written to summarize the results of the research, including background documentation, an explanation of how the guide was adapted, and the actual findings of the research. The draft report will be circulated for comment among all parties.

The nature of unresolved disputes should be clearly articulated and included in the final report, but the research team maintains responsibility for the final content.

Step 8: Develop Conclusions and Recommendations for Corrective Action

The research team draws conclusions from its experience and proposes appropriate corrective measures. Although recommendations are directed first and foremost at the state, which bears primary responsibility for the defense and promotion of human rights, special attention is also given to the responsibilities of the company and next steps for civil society.

Step 9: Final Report

The final report is a product of the community and its representatives, as well as the accompanying organization. The final report compiles all relevant information, including a map, acknowledgements and a bibliography. It may include dissenting views if parties have agreed to do so. The report is translated into the language of the affected community and is distributed free of charge.

Step 10: Follow-up Action

Step 10: Monitoring and Ongoing Evaluation

Human rights impact assessment reports are not the end of the process, but rather the beginning of ongoing monitoring and evaluation. Additional actions might include in-country distribution of the report, conflict resolution or mediation procedures, advocacy for legislative or policy reform, or the establishment of a dialogue between the community, government and company.

THE RESEARCH GUIDE (INDICATORS)

The research guide is a 75-page compilation of questions derived from international human rights law. It is based primarily on the Universal Declaration of Human Rights, which was adopted by the United Nations in 1948 and has since been expanded upon in a number of treaties widely ratified by states. Much of the Universal Declaration is now considered to be part of international customary law; its associated treaties are part of international law and comprise binding obligations on the states that have ratified them. The questionnaire was structured according to the UN Norms on the Responsibilities for Business and Other Transnational Corporations with Regard to Human Rights.

This decision was made in part so as not to revisit the debates that had informed drafting of the Norms and that had already resulted in some degree of agreement between states and civil society. The Norms provided us with additional advantages because they:

o Codify human rights for the private sector;

- o Organize information into clusters of rights;
- o Draw upon a broad selection of human rights instruments;
- o Are authoritative and comprehensive.

Open-ended questions were developed for each article contained within the Norms. When necessary, a short definition of the right was provided. For certain articles, there was an additional explanation about the nature of state obligations for that particular right. This was followed by a paragraph detailing company responsibilities.

Formulation of the questions was informed in large measure by the "general comments" (interpretive statements) produced by UN treaty monitoring bodies, as well as by the various treaties themselves, primarily the International Covenant on Civil and Political Rights, the International Covenant on Economic, Social and Cultural Rights, and the core conventions of the International Labour Organization.

The questions provided in the resulting research guide were not intended to be used as a script by the research team. They were meant to be adapted according to the local situation and for use in interviews, workshops, or other forms of data collection. The objective was to create a comprehensive document that would enable communities to generate two types of data: first, a general portrait of how a specific right is protected in the national context; and second, information specific to the actual impact of the investment on the enjoyment of human rights.

For example, in the case of the human right to adequate housing, the general portrait seeks information about national legislation and programs designed to fulfill the right.

- o Is there a national housing plan?
- o Do women enjoy equal property rights?
- o What are the rules for expropriation of land?

Questions related to the actual impact of the investment on the human right to adequate housing situate the experience in relation to the context.

- o Were evictions carried out in the construction of the project?
- o Has the project affected the average cost of housing in the area?

The research team traveled by road along the route of the In the example of freedom from discrimination at work and in the community, the questions are designed to produce a general portrait focused largely on the perspective of migrant workers and women.

- o Has the government ratified international treaties concerning forced labour?
- o Is national law consistent with international standards at the International Labour Organization?
- o Are there legal provisions to support the right of women to equality?

Questions related to the actual impact of the investment on freedom from discrimination in the workplace seek to understand the ways in which the company has contributed to improvement or retrogression of the right.

- o Do employees have an employment contract?
- o Has the investor demonstrated a distinction, exclusion or preference for any group of workers through the recruitment, hiring, training or pay processes?
- o Is there subcontracting to vulnerable groups (those who are excluded from the workplace?)

Excerpt From the Research Guide

This excerpt provides a snapshot of how the research guide is organized, based on Section C, the Human Right to Security of the Person.

It does not include all the questions included within the sampled sub-sections and not all sub-sections are represented. Much of this part of the research guide is derived from the Rome Statue of the International Criminal Court (ICC).

Right to Security of Person

Transnational corporations and other business enterprises shall not engage in nor benefit from war crimes; crimes against humanity; genocide; aggression; torture; forced disappearance; forced or compulsory labour; hostage-taking; extrajudicial, summary or arbitrary executions; other violations of humanitarian law; and other international crimes against the human person as defined by international law, in particular human rights and humanitarian law.

State Obligations

The violations covered by Article 3 of the UN Norms are among the most serious human rights violations, with most having a status of jus cogens from which no derogations are permitted.

These principles are widely accepted by the international community of states and there is also a legal obligation for states to take action to prevent their occurrence. This special status has been recognized in new legal enforcement mechanisms at the international level. The statutes of the ad hoc tribunals for the former Yugoslavia and Rwanda, and the Statute for the International Criminal Court contain specific provisions for the prosecution of genocide, war crimes and crimes against humanity.

Company Responsibilities

While it is possible that companies and their human principals will commit the offences named above, it is more likely that they will be accused of being complicit with armed forces (state-sponsored or not). The notion of corporate complicity with crimes against security of the person is evolving and no clear legal definitions exist.

The obligation in the Norms is to "not engage in or benefit from" the international wrong. This should require an examination of whether the company was directly complicit (positively assisting), indirectly complicit (benefiting from human rights violations), or silently complicit (silence or inaction in the face of human rights violations).

General Portrait

Summarize existing documentation and the country's record with regard to violation of these human rights. Is there credible and well-documented evidence of the existence of war crimes, crimes against humanity, and torture during the past five years in this country? Has there been any prosecution for these crimes? Have the UN or regional bodies invoked any special procedures to deal with these crimes and has the state taken specific action to eradicate them? Is the state a party to the International Criminal Court? Has the state enacted legislation to implement the ICC Statute into domestic law? In cases where there is no conflict and no violence, it is probable that this entire section can be omitted from the human rights impact assessment.

C.2. Actual Impact

Is it an international conflict between two or more nations? (If so, go to sub-section C.2.1 on international conflict.)

Is it a conflict not between two countries? (If so, go to sub-section C.2.2 on civil war.)

Is there a widespread or systematic attack against a civilian population? (If so, go to sub-section C.2.3 on crimes against humanity.)

Is there a systematic attack committed with intent to destroy, in whole or in part, a national, ethnic, racial or religious group? (If so, go to sub-section C.2.4 on genocide.)

Are there acts by which severe pain or suffering (mental or physical) is intentionally inflicted on a person in custody or under the control of a public official or a person acting in an official capacity? (If so, go to sub-section C.2.5 on torture.)

Are there extrajudicial, summary or arbitrary executions committed in the country? (If so, go to sub-section C.2.6 on extrajudicial, summary or arbitrary executions.)

C.2.1. If it is an international conflict, has the company, anyone associated with the company, or any government at the request of, or with the support of, or to support the company, committed any of the following acts?

- o Directed attacks (on purpose) against the population at large or individual civilians who are not taking direct part in the armed conflict?
- o Directed attacks (on purpose) against people, places or things involved in humanitarian assistance or peacekeeping missions?
- o Directed attacks (on purpose) against houses, churches, mosques, synagogues or other places clearly dedicated to humanitarian purposes such as houses of worship, schools, hospitals, museums, art galleries or the like?
- o Transported parts of a foreign civilian population into the territory while it was occupied by a foreign country, or transported all or parts of the local population of that territory within or outside this territory during this occupation?

C.2.2. If there was a conflict, but not between two countries, has the company, anyone associated with the company, or any government at the request of, or with the support of, or to support the company, committed any of the following acts against civilians or against soldiers who were prisoners or wounded?

- o Committed outrages against personal dignity, in particular humiliating and degrading treatment?
- o Directed (on purpose) attacks against the civilian population or against individual civilians not taking direct part in the hostilities?
- o Looted or taken valuables from a town or place?
- o Committeed rape, sexual slavery, enforced prostitution, forced pregnancy, enforced sterilization, or any other form of sexual violence?

Selection of the Five Case Studies

To select case studies, an open call for proposals was issued in the fall of 2004. Forty-six proposals were received, the majority related to investment in the extractive sector. To select the five cases for the project, the international advisory committee established criteria that included attention to community capacity as well as to the nature of the investment itself.

We sought assurances that the community was interested in addressing the particular investment project being proposed and that the research team would be willing to engage in dialogue with those holding opposing views. We also tried to ensure regional and sectoral diversity, a mix of rural and urban stories, and a variety of human rights focus issues, including at least one on indigenous issues and one with a gender focus.

We intended to work in countries with various levels of development as well as in states with varying levels of compliance with human rights. Finally we sought at least one example of a project that was not yet operational.

The five cases selected were from the Philippines, Tibet, the DRC, Argentina, and Peru. Their stories are included in part two of this publication.

The Five Case Studies

Mining Operations in Mindanao, Philippines

This study looks at the operations of TVI Pacific Inc. (Canada) and specifically at its impact on the human rights of indigenous people. This case had already been the subject of two parliamentary hearings in Canada which resulted in the National Roundtables on the Extractive Sector.

Communications Technology Introduced along the Gormo-Lhasa Railroad, Tibet

This study looks at the potential future impact of modern information communications technology provided by Nortel (Canada) in collaboration with China's Public Security Bureau and Ministry of Railways. It is the only ex-ante assessment in the project.

Mineral Refining in the Katanga Region of the DRC

The DRC's wealth of natural resources has turned it into the site of ongoing conflict between armed groups seeking to control its riches. This study assesses the human rights impact of the operations of Somika, a private company that is owned in part by Canadian investors.

Privatization of Water and Sanitation Networks in Buenos Aires, Argentina

Through this investment, a number of foreign companies including Suez (France) became part of a public-private consortium called Aguas Argentinas, created to manage the water and sanitation systems in Buenos Aires. This case is headed for a precedentsetting arbitration at the International Centre for the Settlement of Investment Disputes (World Bank).

Mineral Refining in La Oroya, Peru

This case addresses the cumulative effects of refinery operations conducted by Doe Run Resources Corp. (US) in La Oroya, Peru. It focuses on the human rights to health and water, emphasizing the impact on women of the refinery operations.

The Experience: How it Worked in Practice

All of the research teams reported that the experience enriched their understanding of human rights and built confidence in their ability to demonstrate the human rights impacts of foreign investment projects in the affected communities.

They found that the methodology and research guide became tools of community empowerment. For Rights & Democracy, the experience of applying a draft methodology in five practical examples helped us to gauge the breadth and limitations of such an ambitious endeavour.

As a general reflection, our experience found that the ten-step methodology was too general and required additional explanation. Each step would have benefited from being broken down into smaller, better defined tasks. For example, step one (scoping) involved not only an overview of the national context but also the identification of stakeholders and the composition of the research team. Breaking the steps down would have allowed the research teams to better plan each task and to be more precise with regard to financial requirements.

REFLECTIONS ON THE METHODOLOGY

Steps 1-3: Preparation of the Case Study

The scoping step of the methodology involved collecting all of the relevant contextual information, such as data on the legal framework in the country, related policies adopted by the national government and information about the investment itself. In all cases, access to information was a problem and data collection on the investment itself was particularly difficult. This was particularly true in the Tibet case, where the company did not participate in the assessment. To the extent that companies did cooperate, the role of international researchers and/or Rights & Democracy staff was often a decisive factor. This reinforces our conclusion that the accompanying organization plays a critical role in facilitating communication between parties. This may be particularly true if the accompanying organization is based in the home state of the company.

Much of the information obtained during the scoping phase of the impact assessment comprised complex legal documents that research teams had difficulty analyzing. No funds were set aside at the outset of the process to cover the costs of legal counsel or other forms of expert assistance. For example, the Tibet study required technical assistance to understand the nature of the communications technology in question and its relation to surveillance practices in China.

In Argentina, particular expertise was needed to better understand the implications of the contract between the company and the government. In the Philippines, an expert in bilateral investment treaties might have contributed a better understanding of the implications of the Canada-Philippines Investment Protection Agreement. In both the DRC and the Philippines, independent verification of water quality and ground pollution was not possible because proper water sampling was not foreseen in the project work plan or budget. This type of omission was particularly significant later in step six of the methodology, dealing with fact-checking and verification. Consultation with downstream communities in the Philippines,

The use of technical experts should therefore be integrated into the research work plan and budget at the outset of the assessment process. One option could be to include an explicit step within the preparatory phase of the methodology to identify the type of expert opinion needed and the resources that will be required in order to obtain their services. There are certainly a number of experts from various disciplines who would be willing to work pro bono and we were able to benefit from such services, specifically in the Philippines and Tibet case studies. Nevertheless, a systematic approach should be integrated into the revised methodology.

Research on the investment would have benefited from a standard format that communities could use for mapping relevant company information. This mapping would indicate the type of information that is useful.

For example, is the company public, private or stateowned?

What are the duties of its directors? What aspects of home state laws and regulations might be relevant for the assessment? The mapping might also include information about the relationship between the state, the private sector and civil society where the investment is taking place. For example, in Tibet the Chinese state is very strong, and western governments actively seek investment opportunities there, but civil society is weak. In the DRC, it is the state that is weak and the private sector often operates outside the scope of any national legislation, striking its own deals with civil society groups.

We found that this part of the methodology did not give adequate attention to investigation of the role played by the company's home state in promoting the investment through trade and investment facilitation services, publication of market research reports, trade missions, and negotiation of bilateral and other investment treaties. All these relationships should influence the eventual formulation of conclusions and recommendations resulting from the human rights impact assessment.

As research teams prepared to adapt the research guide questions to their situation, we understood the importance of including human rights education as an explicit step in the methodology. For example, the Congolese team found human rights education to be one of most important outcomes of their research experience.

At the beginning of the process, our team organized a training (session) to allow the researchers to have a better understanding of the object of the study and to be more familiar with the tool. During the training, orientation carried out by experts allowed participants to immerse themselves with the UN Norms and the other international instruments. We organized talks on civil, political, economic, social and cultural rights, and on the conventions of the International Labour Organization. A presentation of the tool, as well as training on research techniques, was also provided. There were a number interesting approaches used in each case study to adapt the questions provided in the research guide to the local situation.

Steps 4-6: Application of the Research Guide

One of the most rewarding experiences of the research process was the creativity of communities in the actual application of the research guide. Each of the case studies had a unique approach that enriched our understanding of how a human rights impact assessment can be successfully applied at the community level. The community reflections, however, also point to the need for substantially more guidance specific to interviews with the companies and with government.

As in scoping, the methodology would therefore have benefited from being broken down into its components; how best to conduct interviews in communities, with governments or with companies.

At the community level, most of the case study teams found that group discussions were effective. In the DRC, large consultative meetings were organized and participants were asked to fill out questionnaires. The Philippine team used map-making, story-telling and time-lining techniques.

We asked them to build, with paper and other material that we have brought, a representation of their land prior to the arrival of the mining project. They showed us where they used to pray and where they used to get their medicinal plants. After that, the research team asked them to draw, or construct a representation of their land after the arrival of the company.

In the Tibet study, the process was more complicated due to the political situation and security concerns.

In fact, it was not possible for the researchers to conduct group consultations, or even to explain the project.

Direct questions about human rights could not be asked. Instead, researchers decided to engage in conversation with individuals they would meet on the street, in restaurants, or at tourist sites. Conversations in Internet cafés, for example, often resulted in interesting discussions.

One businessperson we met told us that he regularly visited China's official Tibet website. One day, he mistakenly entered an incorrect suffix and was surprised to find himself on the website of the Tibetan government in exile. He spent an hour surfing the site, most amazed by the Dalai Lama's travel itinerary posted there. A few days later, officers of the Public Security Bureau visited his office demanding to know who had viewed the forbidden website.

In Peru, the researchers organized workshops with community members and they used techniques, such as drawing, to elicit information about subjects, such as pregnancy or housework. Without asking specific questions, the process allowed documentation of the women's experience. For example, understanding that a particular group of women spend most of their day inside the home, one can deduce that they are at greater risk of contamination because exposure is greater indoors.

Steps 7-9: Report Preparation

The outcome of the initial scoping and interviews produced a large amount of data in many different formats. The data included statements of fact, interpretive narratives, expert opinion and grievances. With its predominantly qualitative orientation, all this information proved to be extremely onerous to compile and analyze, particularly because of the recurring issue of limited time and resources. This in turn, made it difficult to identify conflicting or unclear data for verification. In many cases, a second or third site visit would have been useful. Much can be done electronically, but the use of email disadvantages those with the least resources, usually the affected communities themselves and those who do not speak English, French or Spanish, the working languages of this project.

Synthesizing the collected data in the form of a report presented a challenge in every case study experience. Although an outline for the reports was provided as a way of maintaining some consistency and comparability among them, each research team emphasized certain areas and disregarded others. This of course reflected the different specificities of each case, but also the varying degree of emphasis between contextual information and data collected directly from the community specific to the actual impact of the investment. For example, in the Philippines and Peru, great emphasis was placed on community interviews. In Tibet and the DRC, there was more emphasis on the general context. In Argentina, the report relies heavily on statistics and the legal analysis of experts.

Circulating draft reports for comment took much more time than anticipated. There were additional expenses and time delays incurred in translating texts back and forth between English and the drafting language. In the case of Philippines, it was not possible to translate any version of the report into the local indigenous language, so the researchers had to explain the conclusions of the study orally to the participants.

To do this, they organized different consultations with each group to ensure the draft text adequately represented their views.

The report drafting phase of a human rights impact assessment requires some systemization, including limiting of expectations with regards to participation. Clearly there are boundaries, and at some point the research team must assume responsibility for the content as it appears.

We found that developing recommendations for companies was considerably more difficult because of the great distance that often exists between the community and the company positions.

Furthermore, while companies may claim specific contractual obligations and fiduciary obligations to shareholders, communities are claiming their human rights which are protected in the UN Charter and should prevail. Suddenly, international debates about global governance are real at the community level as issues of corporate accountability and poor enforcement of human rights standards find a human face.

Step 10: Follow-up Action

The very process of carrying out a human rights impact assessment in communities was itself an instrument of mobilization. In some instances, those who carried out the research became increasingly engaged, not only in seeking resolution for the community, but also in the broader cause of protecting human rights. For example, the research in Argentina contributed to the drafting of an amicus curiae brief that was later accepted for consideration by the International Centre for the Settlement of Investment Disputes. During the international advisory committee meeting with case study researchers in Johannesburg, the Argentine research group met and shared its experience with South African communities facing similar water privatization schemes.

The development of recommendations generated expectations about continued monitoring of the individual projects and involvement of the accompanying organization during that monitoring phase. The limitations of accompaniment should be clearly articulated at the initial phase of the assessment process.

It is also necessary to understand, however, that entering a community and involving its members in an often sensitive process does imply some degree of responsibility, particularly once the final report is written and published. This is the time when community members may be most at risk. If continued accompaniment is not possible, a procedure should be identified in the methodology to ensure that communities find suitable alternate support.

REFLECTIONS ON THE RESEARCH GUIDE

Although the research guide was often described as cumbersome and unwieldy, it certainly did provide an excellent resource for communities to develop situationspecific questions for the research process. In undertaking this task, the research teams were driven by different imperatives. For example, the Peruvians found the guide too direct and perhaps confrontational in tone.

At the beginning, we considered that the questions were very straightforward and seemed intended to find the state and the company at fault. The questions would create a defensive attitude from the interviewees, so we paraphrased them to be more objective. We also adapted the questions to the Peruvian style of dialogue and we added more questions on local issues affecting women: "Do you know what a miscarriage is?" or "Are there cases of women who have experienced more than one miscarriage?" or "Where are cases of miscarriages being registered?"

The Philippine group found the questions to be too technical and unreflective of their underlying meaning.

An orientation workshop was undertaken to translate the methodology into the vernacular in order to bring out the understanding of human rights and to encourage discussion about the idea behind the human right and to identify questions that better relate to the cultural and historical context.

We encouraged casual conversations that focused on the Subanon's right to self-determination, such as cultural integrity, non-discrimination, development and self-government. Instead of strict adherence to the questions provided, a more open type of questioning was adopted. Sample questions included: "Tell us what Siocon or Canatuan was like before the company came here?" or "How many kilos of fish do you usually harvest." and finally, "What are the changes you have noticed since the company came?"

Among the main criticisms was that the guide was much too long and there was no advice for selecting key questions from the document based on the parameters of the case study.

Further, there was no differentiation between questions for the community members themselves and those designed for government or the company. The Peruvians dealt with this challenge by adapting the wording of individual questions according to who they were interviewing. For the community, some questions were subdivided to obtain more precise answers and others were transformed into images. For example, with regard to the right to health, the team created images taken from the local culture to draw attention to the issues facing pregnant women as a result of the investment.

The guide focused heavily on generating information about the actual impact of an investment project, rather than about the general human rights context in the project area. Questions related to the actual impact were not as relevant for the Tibet case study which was assessing the potential future impacts of an investment project that was not yet fully operational.

A revised research guide should devote more attention to the different approaches required when conducting ex-ante case studies. Security was a significant challenge at different stages of each of the case studies. This sometimes affected the way in which research teams could apply the methodology or ask questions. For example, the Tibet team had to reformulate questions in a way that would make them less threatening and more a part of everyday conversation.

When we tried to ask questions about security of the person, the research guide was too explicit. For example, asking the question: "Is there a systematic attack committed with intent to destroy, in whole or in part, a national, ethnic, racial or religious group?" made people feel uncomfortable. So instead we asked: "How is everything these days in Tibet?"

Some sections of the questionnaire required additional material. The section on labour rights focused heavily on discrimination in the workplace and failed to adequately address other labour rights issues such as rates of unionization. The section on discrimination focused heavily on the rights of indigenous peoples, without sufficient attention to other forms of discrimination. In fact, all case study teams agreed that discrimination might have been better formulated as a crosscutting principle relevant for each of the rights being addressed. The guide provided inadequate assistance on the issue of freedom of expression, which was a key focus for the Tibet research team.

In Argentina, where the entire case study was devoted to the human right to water, community researchers were preparing an amicus curiae brief, and therefore required detailed questions specific to human right to water. They found that the research guide placed too much emphasis on qualitative indicators, and that at least some attention to quantitative indicators would have been helpful. The research team devoted significant time to developing a list of supplemental questions derived from General Comment 15 on the human right to water. In the case of the Philippines, the research documents the experience of the community in the context of conflict and it relates specifically to the human rights of indigenous people. To emphasize the question of self-government, the researchers drafted additional questions to supplement those found in the research guide on sovereignty and the rights of indigenous people. They also decided to use the structure of the UN Declaration on the Rights of Indigenous Peoples - self-government, cultural integrity, land and natural resources - as a way of organizing their report.

It is important to note that language can be a considerable challenge when working in communities. Even in the scoping phase, many background documents are not available in the local language, requiring efforts to inform and brief communities about the information they contain. While our research guide was prepared in English, French and Spanish, interviews in both the Philippines and Tibet required other languages.

LESSONS LEARNED

This report reviews the initial phase of the human rights impact assessment project - conceptualization and testing. It has not been a theoretical exercise but rather a practical learning process. Throughout, we have confronted numerous unforeseen challenges, but have been consistently inspired by the richness of the experience and the unfailing enthusiasm of our case study partners. Those partners came together with the project's international advisory committee for three days in Johannesburg in September 2006. Together we evaluated the preliminary findings of the case studies and determined four primary recommendations for improving the human rights impact assessment process:

- o Integrate more capacity building;
- o Place greater emphasis on accompaniment;
- o Provide a more realistic budget and time allocation;
- o Revise the methodology and research guide.

Attention to Capacity Building

Our experience has shown that the need to reinforce local capacity continues throughout the course of the human rights impact assessment and it should be viewed as an integral part of the research process. This will require that sufficient time and resources be integrated into the assessment work plan in order to conduct workshops and training sessions with the local partners and their communities.

It is necessary to plan training and capacity building for both the research team and the community. A good understanding of the nature of human rights and their governing principles is essential in order to obtain a credible report at the end of the assessment and also to encourage a sustained interest in human rights within the community. Further, communities may need additional training in basic sociological techniques of inquiry, familiarity with interview techniques and both quantitative and qualitative analysis.

One means of integrating capacity building into the assessment process is to construct research teams that combine international and local researchers. A balance between local and international team members encourages a two-way learning process that is equally valuable to all.

The internationals often bring technical expertise lacking in the community and they receive critically important experience in the practical application of their expertise.

Importance of Accompaniment

It is important to ensure that communities and their research teams enjoy reliable moral and professional support throughout the course of the human rights impact assessment project. Accompaniment is important also for the personal security of the community members themselves and of the research teams. In fact, it cannot be over-emphasized how important it was, in our experience, to provide sustained accompaniment throughout the course of each case study. Workshops held in La Oroya, Peru 2006.

Accompaniment begins with conceptualization of the assessment scope and the composition of the research team. It continues through all phases of the research and report writing and may extend to continued monitoring or follow-up activities. In this research project, Rights & Democracy initially assumed the responsibility for accompaniment but did not fully understand what that would mean in practice.

In the DRC case study for example, much more attention was required. The support provided to this case study was interrupted in mid-process and another field trip to the project site was not possible because of constraints to human and financial resources. This resulted in considerable stress for the local research team and a failure to complete the ten steps of the methodology. In Peru, a similar interruption in accompaniment occurred, but a second site visit was eventually undertaken and the report was completed to everyone's satisfaction.

Another contribution of accompaniment relates to the perceived objectivity of the process. Communities and their research teams are often viewed as biased and as having little or no interest in conducting a fair assessment of the investment. In the case of the Philippines, when the assessment process was launched, there was already a high degree of tension in the community and some members of the research team were clearly identified as anti-mining. Nevertheless, the company agreed to be interviewed by the research team on two occasions and to an ongoing dialogue with Rights & Democracy about the project. This might have been due, in part, to the fact that

Rights & Democracy is located in the company's home state, Canada.

Given these experiences, we do not believe a human rights impact assessment tool for communities can simply be provided on a website with the idea that the communities will download it and go through the exercise on their own. In most cases, some degree of professional accompaniment in the process from outside the community will be critical. One suggestion is to create a consortium of organizations willing to contribute their time for this purpose. If such a consortium existed, then it might be possible to assign an organization from the company's home state with the task of providing accompaniment.

This in turn would encourage more attention to the role and responsibilities of the home state, as well as facilitate interaction with the company's head office.

Provision of an Adequate Budget and Time

In thinking about the challenges of capacity, access and security, it becomes clear that community-led processes require the allocation of considerable time and this in turn implies more financial resources. Traditional consultation and validation processes follow their own pace and are often at odds with the rigid deadlines that characterize research in western countries. Ongoing capacity-building and repeated validation exercises at each phase of the project are time-consuming and even more so if translation is required whenever documents and drafts are circulated. These considerations, and their financial implications, should be better integrated into the initial planning phase of the process.

A comprehensive and credible human rights impact assessment requires considerable financial resources, particularly if the research team and experts are to be compensated as they would be in company or government-led processes. In our case studies, there was heavy reliance on the volunteer participation of community members and the pro bono services of numerous experts and advisors. Such reliance can sometimes result in uneven quality of the work, inconsistencies between various aspects of the research, or in unforeseen delays. We recommend that a time and budget guide be developed as part of the assessment tool. Such a guide would flag potential costs that might not otherwise be considered and would provide the accompanying organization and research team members with a better estimate of the amount of time they should plan for each stage of the assessment process. The following is a general idea of how such a guide might be conceived, using selected steps from the methodology. It is provided here only as a sample and not as a definitive response.

TIME AND BUDGET GUIDE EXAMPLE

Methodology Related Expense Additional

Consideration

In-kind or pro bono service available Estimated time and money needed to complete all phases of the task

Steps 1-3

Preparation of the case study Workshops and training sessions for community groups Planning meetings for researchers Internet connection Travel Will you need to rent meeting space and provide meals?

Will you need to hire facilitators and interpreters?

Are travel expenses incurred?

Will you need to translate and print basic human rights documents?

Are phone lines costly?

Are subscriptions required to obtain access to business publications or information services?

Is meeting space available within the community?

Does the national government have a fund for translation of human rights documentation?

Has the company already translated some of its documentation?

Is any relevant information available from the home and/ or host state?

Include net costs here, as well as time expectations.

Steps 4-6

Application of the methodology

Do you need to hire experts, such as corporate lawyers or technical experts

Where should you host meetings:

- In the affected area
- In the national capital
- In the home state of the company
- With the local company representatives

How often in the process will you need to consult the same expert?

Is translation or interpretation required?

Are travel and related expenses involved?

How many individuals will be included in this process?

Will the purchase of a laptop be required?

Are relevant experts already included on the research team?

If the information gaps are not significant, can verification be done electronically or by telephone?

What is the availability of the expert?

What is the availability of the research team members?

When can appropriate government representatives meet with your research team?

How long will it take to synthesize the amount of information collected?

Methodology Related Expense Additional Consideration

In-kind or pro bono service available Estimated time and money needed to complete all phases of the task

Steps 7-9

Report preparation

Assign the drafting task to one team member.

Organize a community meeting to study the draft report and develop recommendations. Employ required graphic and printing services. Hire legal counsel What are the professional fees charged by the drafter? Will the draft text need to be translated for circulation to various stakeholders?

Will you distribute the report in paper version or only electronically?

Are pro bono legal services available?

Does the accompanying organization have a widely read website?

Is a negotiation and mediation process required at this phase?

Step 10

Follow-up action

Select indicators for ongoing monitoring of impacts

Create a dialogue process

Take legal action

Are professional fees required?

Will travel and meeting space be required?

Will legal fees apply?

Will the community take on this task?

Is the company or the government willing to contribute?

What is the estimated duration of the project?

Will monitoring be required for the duration of the project?

Revision of the Ten-step Methodology and Research Guide

The case study experience taught us that the ten-step methodology should be broken down into smaller, better-defined tasks. While the general categories were sufficient, communities needed more explicit guidance on how to implement each component. For example, a mapping format would have assisted research on the investment and a budget guide might have helped with establishing limits on the research. Some elements of the methodology were not sufficiently developed, such as how to structure the final reports. The revised methodology should give increased attention to practical guidance for researchers as they apply each of the ten steps.

With regard to the research guide, there is a tension between producing a user-friendly model and a comprehensive model. Each of the case study teams told us that questions in the research guide were far too unwieldy to be efficient. Further there was no clear means of selecting questions appropriate to the study. Our primary challenge, then, is to identify a small number of key indicators which would generally apply in every case, for example indicators related to discrimination, and then an additional list from which communities can select in order to capture the context and specificity of their example.

It was suggested by the Tibet research group that this might best be accomplished by producing a digital tool in which certain key words are entered, such as "indigenous", "food" or "freedom of expression", as well as the industrial sector and country.

The tool would then generate a series of appropriate indicators related to those key words. Another approach, recommended by each of the case study partners, would be to create a series of sector-specific guides with the goal of compiling information tailored to mining, surveillance technology or manufacturing, for instance. For example, in the Tibet case study more precise indicators might be developed by adapting the OECD indicators for information and communications technology in China.

During the Johannesburg meeting, a discussion evolved around the importance of comparability between case studies and the balance between quantitative and qualitative indicators. But while everyone agreed that there might be some interest over time in comparing results, especially from a country or sector perspective, the five case studies we had selected for this project had very different characteristics and objectives.

There was a high degree of variance between the national contexts, industrial sectors and communities themselves. We agreed that while quantitative indicators might be more specific and could lend objectivity to our conclusions, the nature of human rights impacts is often less precise and best captured by qualitative responses. The revised research guide will include a combination of quantitative and qualitative indicators and we look with interest at the innovative research currently being undertaken at the Office of the High Commissioner for Human Rights. That project is developing indicators specific to individual rights and these are primarily quantitative in nature. Nevertheless, Rights & Democracy has adopted an approach in which qualitative indicators will remain of central importance.

CONCLUSION

This research experience has shown that it is possible to demonstrate the human rights impacts of foreign investment at the project level. Perhaps more importantly, it has shown that placing the affected communities at the centre of the process enriches the outcomes. All of the case study research teams reported having a better understanding about human rights and they placed significant value on the sense of empowerment experienced with production of the final reports.

In three cases (Argentina, Peru, and the Philippines), the research teams were able to link human rights impacts directly to the investment project. In the other two (DRC and Tibet), enough information was produced to merit additional study and action. What became less clear as the project proceeded is the actual nature of private sector obligations with respect to human rights. Some of our international advisory committee members expressed concern that in trying to identify corporate obligations, we were in fact contributing to the "privatization" of human rights.

It is certainly true that each of the five case study reports emphasized state responsibility in its conclusions, perhaps as an assertion of their view that it is primarily the state, not the company, that must assume responsibility for human rights through national policies, regulations or laws.

Throughout the process, we confronted issues that are mired in conceptual debates at the international level. They will merit more attention as we proceed with research for the Investing in Human Rights series of publications.

The difficult issue of complicity requires further study, particularly from the perspective of public-private partnerships, as in the Argentina and Tibet case studies. The precise nature of extraterritorial obligations when the home state uses public funds to promote foreign investment was a consideration in each of the case studies. The question of "no-go zones" for foreign investment was raised by the difficulties encountered by researchers in Tibet. There is no doubt that working through these complex issues is a challenge for governments, companies, civil society, and the affected communities themselves.

We hope that the experience and lessons learned from this effort to develop and test a practical tool for communities will be a useful contribution to all those working to ensure that foreign investment benefits local people and does not violate their human rights. Traveling by road along the Gormo-Lhasa route of the railway, the research group identified communications towers approximately every 6.7 km (Tibet).

THE RESEARCH TEAM

Siocon Subanon Association Apu' Manglang Glupa Pusaka Save Siocon Paradise Movement (SSPM)

Pigsalabukan Bansa Subanon - Subanon Federation (PBS)

The Legal Rights and Natural Resources Center, Inc.-Kasama sa Kalikasan (LRC-KSK/Friends of the Earth-Philippines)

The DIOPIM Committee on Mining Issues (DCMI)

Philippine Indigenous Peoples Links (PIPLinks)

MiningWatch Canada (MWC)

Tebtebba

In 2005, the Canadian company TVI Pacific Inc. officially opened the Canatuan mine on the island of Mindanao in the Philippines, although the company had a presence in the area for several years before. Producing gold, silver, copper, and zinc, the openpit mine has created some jobs in an impoverished area and generated revenues for the indebted national government. However, it has also displaced many families;

divided the local indigenous people, known as the Subanon; deprived thousands of small-scale miners of their livelihood; and negatively affected rice farmers and fishers living downstream. Because of increased levels of sediment and metals in local rivers and creeks. One of the most controversial aspects of the mine is that it is located on the peak of Mount Canatuan, which the Subanon living in the area consider to be sacred.

Mindanao has been the site of a sustained conflict between various Muslim groups and the Philippine government for the last three decades. TVI Resource Development (Philippines) Inc., the subsidiary operating the mine, has hired personnel from the Philippine army to provide security. These security forces have cleared people from the area, including indigenous peoples and small-scale miners, and confronted local demonstrators. Some confrontations have been violent. Members of the Subanon have repeatedly complained about the mine and related human rights issues to the Philippine government.

They also brought their case to the UN Working Group on Indigenous Peoples. A coalition of local and international organizations, including indigenous, church-based and community groups, conducted a human rights impact assessment of the mine, piloting the draft methodology provided by Rights & Democracy.1 Several of the local groups involved have been clear in their opposition to the mine for some time.

This caused tensions during the assessment because the company and some local groups questioned their credibility. The coalition tried to canvass all points of view, including those of TVI Resource Development, which co-operated with the assessment.

The central finding of this report is that the investment has had a negative impact on the ability of the Subanon to enjoy the human right to self-determination, to human security, to an adequate standard of living, to adequate housing, to work and to education.

3

WOMEN HUMAN RIGHTS IN PHILIPPINES

SCOPING

The Philippines is an island nation located in the Malay Archipelago in Southeast Asia. It was colonized by Spain (1521-1898) and the United States (1902-1936), and was occupied by the Japanese during World War II before becoming an independent country in 1946.

Ferdinand Marcos was president and then dictator of the country from 1965 until 1986, when he was forced from power by a popular movement. Governments have since been elected democratically, although corruption has been a persistent problem. Gloria Macapagal-Arroyo, the current president, took power in 2001 when Joseph Estrada resigned due to allegations of corruption. She won re-election in 2004, but her government has since been undermined by a series of scandals.

During the Marcos regime, the military was used to protect the economic and political interests of the country's elite, resulting in grave abuses of human rights. People considered to be opponents of the regime were subject to torture, arrest, and detention.

Many disappeared. The current government has also been criticized for its human rights record. Many activists, journalists and community leaders have been killed or declared missing. In 2006, the Philippines was tied with Afghanistan as the second most dangerous country in the world for journalists, after Iraq. Few perpetrators are caught and brought to justice. The population of the Philippines is estimated to be about 90 million people. One quarter of them live on the large, southern island of Mindanao, where many of the richest mineral deposits are found. Despite this resource wealth, many of the people of Mindanao live in abject poverty. This is especially true of those living on the peninsula of Zamboanga, where the mine operated by TVI Resource Development (Philippines) Inc. is located.

Mindanao, with a mainly Christian population, is the site of a conflict which began in 1970 between Muslim separatists and the Philippine government. Groups involved in this armed conflict include the Moro Islamic Liberation Front, the Abu Sayyaf Group, and the New People's Army. In 1995, the Abu Sayyaf Group torched the town of Ipil on the Zamboanga peninsula. In May 2003, the Moro Islamic Liberation Front attacked the town of Siocon, where the TVI mine is situated, killing 22 people and injuring many more. An estimated 120,000 people have died and millions more have been displaced in more than three decades of fighting.

Economic growth in the Philippines has lagged behind that of its East Asian neighbours. Foreign debt is estimated to be 3.96 trillion Philippine pesos (US $77 billion). This does not include sizeable domestic debts. About half of the existing debt has been incurred under President Arroyo.

The Philippines is rich in mineral resources, including gold, copper, nickel, and chromite which is used in the manufacture of steel and certain chemicals. However, these resources have not been well developed for a variety of reasons, including continuing political unrest and opposition from farmers and fishers concerned with the environmental impact of mining. Heavy seasonal rains and frequent seismic activity (the Philippines is in a zone prone to earthquakes and volcanic eruptions known as the Pacific Rim of Fire), have also affected mining activity.

In an effort to improve economic growth and increase revenues (which it needs in part to pay debts), the government has liberalized the legal regime for mining, passing the Revised

Philippine Mining Act in 1995. The legislation was drawn up with the help of the World Bank. In 2002, a new national mineral policy was implemented by executive order. It streamlined government procedures to grant mining permits to foreign investors. A 2004 ruling by the Philippine Supreme Court allowed foreign companies to own 100% of mining operations, eliminating the previous limit of 40%.

The Chamber of Mines of the Philippines says that large-scale mining will provide additional revenue for the government and jobs in isolated mining areas.

However, much of the mining and exploration is taking place in sensitive areas, provoking local opposition.

One such place is on the Zamboanga Peninsula on the island of Mindanao. The peninsula is home to approximately 350,000 indigenous people known collectively as the Subanon (also known as Subanen, Subanan, and Subanun). They are mainly farmers or fishers and revere a common ancestor called Apu Manglang. Their highest traditional council in the region of the mine is the Council of the Seven Rivers, a group of traditional leaders.

For the Subanon of the southern peninsula, Mount Canatuan is a sacred place and they want the area to remain untouched. Historically, it was where leader Apu Manglang made a covenant with the Apu Sanag, an immortal being, to save the people from a disease that was ravaging the community. It is also where the boklog, the highest ritual for Thanksgiving, is performed every seven years. The peak of Mount Canatuan, according to the Subanon was not for occupation, flamboyant use, or architectural manifestations.

However, they have had difficulty protecting the area because laws governing land use and land ownership have not been respected, allowing multinational firms to establish a presence in the area.

Small-scale miners began working in the area in the 1980s, against the wishes of some of the local Subanon. By the 1990s, when TVI Resource Development arrived, there were thousands of small-scale miners working in the area.

HUMAN RIGHTS IN PRINCIPLE

The Philippines has ratified the following UN human rights treaties: the International Covenant on Civil and Political Rights (1986); the optional protocol to that covenant (1989); the International Covenant on Economic, Social and Cultural Rights (1974); the Convention on the Elimination of all Forms of Racial Discrimination (1967); the Convention on the Rights of the Child (1990); and the Convention on the Elimination of all Forms of Discrimination Against Women (1981).

Regarding the protection of indigenous people's rights, a major step was taken at the international level when members of the UN Human Rights Council adopted the UN Declaration on the Rights of Indigenous Peoples in June 2006.

Among other things, the declaration recognizes the urgent need to respect and promote the inherent rights of indigenous peoples, especially their rights to lands, territories and resources, which derive from their political, economic and social structures, and from their cultures, spiritual traditions, histories and philosophies. It is important to mention that a national Philippine law, the 1997 Indigenous Peoples Rights Act, is based on the same principles as the UN declaration.

Resource law in the Philippines has its roots in the Regalian Doctrine, imposed by the Spanish, under which all natural resources belonged to the state.

When the United States became the colonial power, it imposed land laws that discriminated against non-Christian native people. The 1987 Philippine constitution formally recognized the rights of indigenous peoples. It says that the state is obliged to protect the right of indigenous cultural communities to their ancestral land and to ensure their economic, social and cultural well-being. The constitution also says that the state should apply customary laws governing property rights or relations, especially in determining the ownership and extent of ancestral domain.

The Mining Act of 1995 includes a provision stating there should be no mining on ancestral lands without the prior consent of the indigenous people. The act also states that agreement must be reached with indigenous communities on a royalty from the mining, which will be used for their socioeconomic wellbeing. A 1996 TVI's mining activity caused the deforestation of the top of Mount Canatuan. revision said this royalty must, at a minimum, be equivalent to 1% of the gross revenue of the mine.

The Indigenous Peoples Rights Act stipulates that the state should guarantee respect for the cultural integrity of indigenous people and ensure that they benefit equally from rights and opportunities that national laws and regulations grant to other members of the population. The act also says that the right to ancestral domains includes the right to ownership, the right to develop lands and natural resources, the right to stay in the territories, the right to redress in case of displacement, the right to regulate entry of migrants settlers and organizations, the right to safe and clean air and water, the right to claim parts of reservations, and the right to resolve conflict. There are special protections for political systems and decision-making processes. The constitutionality of the provisions on ancestral domain in the act was challenged in the Supreme Court of the Philippines on grounds that the provisions contravene the Regalian Doctrine. However, the Supreme Court dismissed the case in 2000.

RESEARCH ON THE INVESTMENT

The Company

TVI Resource Development (Philippines) Inc. was incorporated in the Philippines on January 18th 1994. It is a subsidiary of the Canadian mining company, TVI Pacific Inc., which has its headquarters in Alberta and is listed on the Toronto Stock Exchange. The Canadian company owns 40% of TVI Resource Development (Philippines) through two wholly owned subsidiaries based in Hong Kong and Anguilla, in the Caribbean.

At least 19 other companies from Canada, the Philippines, and elsewhere own the remaining 60%.

TVI Pacific, the Canadian company, was incorporated in Alberta in 1987 and spent several years exploring for minerals in Canada before looking abroad. Clifford M. James is the president, chairman and chief executive officer of TVI.

The Canadian company began looking for opportunities in the Philippines in 1993 and set up corporate offices in Manila that year. The Canatuan mine, which is operated by its Philippine subsidiary, TVI Resource Development, is its only operating mine. The mine contains deposits of gold, silver, copper, and zinc. TVI Pacific owns a drilling company and a mineralprocessing firm in the Philippines. It is also exploring for minerals elsewhere in the Philippines and in China.

The Contract

The history of the Canatuan mine contract begins with Ramon Bosque, a small-scale miner who moved into the area to prospect. Mr. Bosque, who is not a Subanon, registered a mining claim and then applied for a prospecting permit in 1990 for a large area within the Central Zamboanga Forest Reserve that included Mount Canatuan. In 1991, he teamed up with Benguet Corp., a Philippine gold mining firm established in 1903, and was given the prospecting permit. Together they applied for a Mineral Production Sharing Agreement in 1992. Under such an agreement, the government grants a company the right to conduct mining operations in exchange for a share of final mine production.

In 1994, TVI Pacific set up the Philippine subsidiary that signed an agreement in Canatuan with the Benguet Corp. for an option to explore the area and to purchase the Mineral Production Sharing Agreement, which was still making its way through the government approval process. The Philippine government approved the Mineral Production Sharing Agreement with Mr. Bosque and Benguet Corp. in 1996. They then assigned it to TVI Resource Development in 1997. The government approved this transaction in 1998. Under the terms of the assignment, Mr. Bosque receives a 1% royalty and Benguet Corp. has the option of buying back into the project.

Under the Mineral Production Sharing Agreement, which has a 25-year term, the company is obliged to protect the environment, assist in the development of local communities, and also help the development of mining technology and the geosciences in the Philippines. In terms of community development, the company agreed to respect local rights, customs and traditions; allocate funds for community development; improve local education, water, electricity and medical services; and give preference to Filipino citizens in the area when it hires employees for the mine operations. The agreement also says the company will pay a royalty equivalent to 1% of the market value of minerals and mineral products produced by the mine to the indigenous people who had a valid ancestral domain claim. The indigenous community in receipt of the royalty must draw up a management plan.

In 2003, TVI Resource Development followed up on the commitments made in its agreement with the government by signing a memorandum of agreement with the Siocon Subanon Association Inc. Under this second agreement, the company committed funds for the preparation of a plan to protect the ancestral domain. It agreed to provide additional school buildings and a vocational building for the local community. As well, it agreed to pay the legally required royalty to the Siocon Subanon Association Inc. In return, the association promised to use all its efforts to ensure that the company could conduct its mining operations free of harassment and interference.

TVI Resource Development did not begin operations immediately after taking over the Canatuan site because it had difficulty raising money, due in part to opposition from the local community. In order to raise money, the company increased its authorized capital stock in 1997 and also registered with the Board of Investment of the Philippines as a preferred pioneer enterprise engaged in mineral exploration. This gave it access to certain government incentives, including a tax exemption on the import of capital equipment and a tax credit on domestic equipment.

Operations began in 2002, when the company started processing tailings already on the site that had been produced by small-scale miners, who had been digging there since the 1980s. The processing was done at a cyanide processing plant, which had been in place since the mid-1990s, and it was done at a rate of 50 tonnes a day. This type of processing stopped in January 2004 when the tailings ran out.

In 2004, the company began open-pit mining in the area and expanded its processing plant so that it could handle 450 tonnes a day. The mine and new processing facilities were officially opened January 1st 2005. The plant has since been expanded and was processing an average of 1,800 tonnes a day by the end of September 2006.

The company said that in the first nine months of 2006, the Canatuan mine produced 34,490 ounces of gold, 453,115 ounces of silver, and 42,976 ounces of gold equivalent, a measure used when gold is found in combination with another metal such as silver. Corporate profits for the nine-month period were CDN $8.7 million. The company employs 628 people at the Canatuan project, which is expected to end in 2008.

The Canatuan mine lies within the boundaries of the town of Siocon. In 1989, the Subanon living in Canatuan created the Siocon Subanon Association Inc. and then used this group to apply for a Forest Stewardship Management Agreement. They received this agreement, which recognized their right to manage their own forests, in 1991. Two years later, individuals within the group applied for a Certificate of Ancestral Domain Claim, which was awarded in 1997 and later converted into a Certificate of Ancestral Domain Title in 2003. This certificate is held by individuals and not by any particular Subanon group. All of these moves were made to protect their rights to their ancestral lands.

When the Subanon learned that Mr. Bosque had been given a prospecting permit by the Department of Environment and Natural Resources, the Siocon Federation Subanen Tribal Council approached the Office of Southern Cultural Communities and the local town leaders for advice on how to defend their rights.

The town leaders told them they did not have to worry because they were the rightful owners of the land. In 1992, a number of Subanon groups got together and approached government officials and agencies to protest against the presence of Mr. Bosque and his band of small-scale miners on their ancestral lands.

None of the protests by indigenous people appear to have been recorded by the Mines and Geosciences Bureau, the arm of the government that issued the Mineral Production Sharing Agreement to Mr. Bosque and Benguet Corp. in 1996. Leo Jasareno of the bureau told the research team that there was little coordination at that time between his agency and the Department of Energy and Natural Resources, even though his bureau is a sub-agency of the department. It was not until 1997 that the bureau received the Certificate of Ancestral Domain Claim (that the Subanon had applied for in 1993), which recognized the land was their ancestral territory.

The fact that the certificate, which establishes indigenous rights to the land, was officially issued after the Mineral Production Sharing Agreement is a key element in this dispute. It should be noted that where there is a Certificate of Ancestral Domain Claim, the Department of Energy and Natural Resources should not issue any licence without the prior and informed consent of indigenous peoples.

The tension in Canatuan worsened during the 1990s as thousands more small-scale miners, some of the Subanon, flooded into the area in search of gold. Eventually the Subanon found common cause with some of these miners, who feared that large-scale mining would force them out of the area. Thus the situation in Canatuan was tense when TVI Resources Development entered the picture.

HOME-STATE INVOLVEMENT

Through its embassy in the Philippines, the Canadian government has supported the mining activities of TVI Resource Development. Two ambassadors have visited the site, and have praised the company as a responsible miner. Canada and the Philippines signed a bilateral investment treaty in 1996. The agreement requires that foreign investors be given fair and equitable treatment in line with international law.

In a controversial move, the Canadian International Development Agency (CIDA) channelled funds earmarked for local initiatives through the mining company between 2003 and 2005. The funds were meant to be used to buy goats for local women. The CIDA personnel in the Canadian Embassy in Manila were well aware of the long-standing conflict in Mindanao when, in June 2003, they approved the program financed by the Canada Fund for Local Initiatives. However, they did not request a Peace and Conflict Impact Assessment to assess the possible human rights ramifications of the project, as was done for other Canadian development projects in the region.

According to CIDA, the money was channelled through the mining company's community development officer because the local community did not have the capacity to administer the program. In the course of the project, the local people made embassy officials aware of the specific human rights allegations against the mining company.

In 2005, the Standing Committee on Foreign Affairs and International Trade tabled a report in the Canadian House of Commons recommending an investigation of the TVI Resource Development mine. It also called for the creation of clear legal norms in Canada to ensure its companies and residents are held accountable for environmental damage and human rights violations abroad.

The report also urged the Canadian government to make its support for companies conditional on such companies meeting clearly defined standards for corporate social responsibility and human rights. The standing committee's report argued that one way of holding companies to account is through human rights impact assessments.

ADAPTING THE METHODOLOGY TO THE CASE STUDY

A coalition of groups from the Philippines and abroad produced this human rights impact assessment. They include indigenous groups, legal experts, and nongovernmental organizations, including church-based groups with strong links to the region. The research was coordinated by a research fellow from the Mindanawon Initiatives for Cultural Dialogue program at Ateneo de Davao University. Material from the company and independent observers provided background information.

Our team modified the draft methodology designed by Rights & Democracy. We did not strictly follow the original structure of the research guide, which included a series of specific questions. Instead, we encouraged informal and open exchanges.

The coalition used the major human rights treaties that the Philippines has ratified as reference points when assessing the impact of the TVI Resource Development mine on the people in the area. The most important treaties in terms of the research are the International Covenant on Economic, Social and Cultural Rights and the International Covenant on Civil and Political Rights.

The group also refers to the UN Declaration on Indigenous Peoples because the 1997 Indigenous Peoples Rights Act of the Philippines is based on the same principles.

The TVI Resource Development mine has sparked heated debate in the Subanon community, which is now polarized on the issue. This made it difficult for our team to conduct the research. The Council of Elders, a Subanon group that supports the mine, refused to meet with the researchers at first, but later participated in a focus group discussion. The objectivity of the team was repeatedly questioned although it made an effort to canvass the full range of opinions. The team was also helped by the large volume of pre-existing materials.

The research began with a review of existing material and organized a workshop for farmers, fishers, smallscale miners and various communities, which was also attended by Rights & Democracy. The research team orally translated the research guide into language the communities would understand, solicited their ideas, and tried to gauge their understanding of human rights. They then broadened the consultations. This phase of the project involved a combination of storytelling, making maps of the area, and constructing timelines.

The research took 10 months. In that period, we conducted eight focus groups, interviewed 97 individuals from the community, and met with 35 key informants for in-depth interviews. In September 2006, we held a two-day meeting with community representatives so that we could clarify their views and add any information that had been overlooked.

TVI Resource Development participated in the research. The team visited the company compound twice during the course of this research, interviewing management and staff and reviewing documents. Unfortunately, the company recently changed management and the team found that the new staff lacked institutional memory. The company conducted its own human rights impact assessment and hired experts to conduct an evaluation. It has not yet shared its report with the research team.

The researchers also met with representatives of the key Philippine government agencies involved with the mine, including the National Commission on Indigenous Peoples, the Mines and Geosciences Bureau, and the Department of Environment and Natural Resources. They also met with officials from the Canadian Embassy.

OUTCOMES OF THE RESEARCH

The research focused on six human rights: the right to self-determination, to security, to an adequate standard of living, to adequate housing, to education, and to favourable conditions of work. These rights are enshrined in the International Covenant on Economic, Social and Cultural Rights, which places obligations on its signatories, in this case the government of the Philippines, to uphold the human rights described in the covenant. Certain of these human rights are also enshrined in various national laws in the Philippines.

The Human Right to Self-determination

In order to understand why the Subanon assert that their right to self-determination has been violated, it is necessary to understand their traditional leadership structure. A timuay, or traditional leader, heads each local territory. He is helped in his work by a soliling, who acts as his executive officer or secretary. Only Subanon who belong to the timuay or soliling lineage, which is established on a patrilineal basis, can legitimately fill these posts. Major disputes may be settled by a gathering of timuay from several local territories. This gathering is known as a gukom. The relevant gukom in the area of the TVI mine is comprised of the descendants of the seven traditional leaders of the seven rivers that flow through the area. The gukom of pito kodolongan, also known as the Council of Seven Rivers, will be referred to hereafter as the Gukom of Seven Rivers.

Under the leadership of Timuay Boy Anoy, the Subanon have been consistent in opposing large-scale mining claims on the grounds that Mount Canatuan holds spiritual and historical meaning for the tribe. However, the company has not acknowledged the sacred nature of the site. It denies that the mountain has any religious or cultural significance. However, an archeological impact assessment commissioned by the company in 2004 as part of its environmental impact assessment states that although Canatuan has no visible archaeological resources, a Subanon ritual (boklog) does exist.

TVI Resource Development has not dealt with the rightful Subanon. Instead, when it came time to reach agreement with the indigenous people of the area over arrangements for the mine and the payment of royalties to them, both of which are required by the Mining Act of 1995, the company dealt with two groups that are not recognized as legitimate by the Gukom of Seven Rivers. Those groups are the Siocon Subanon Association Inc. - which was not led by a timuay at the time of the agreement - and the Council of Elders. The members of the Gukom of Seven Rivers, who are the traditional leaders in the area, believe the government and the company have not respected their human right to determine their own political structure and status.

The Siocon Subanon Association was first created in 1989 to apply for forestry rights in the area. While the association is not a traditional Subanon political structure, its first leader was Timuay Boy Anoy, a traditional Subanon leader who opposed plans for the TVI mine.

From 1994 to 2001, company representatives tried unsuccessfully to secure the endorsement of the recognised indigenous leaders, mainly through the head of the Siocon Subanon Association. In 2001, Pablo Bernardo, the attorney for the association, organized an election without the knowledge or sanction of Timuay Boy Anoy or his soliling. During this election, a new set of officers, who supported the mine, was established. Mr. Bernardo, who also supported the mine, is a Subanon, but he is not from the Canatuan area. Timuay Anoy and his secretary, Onsino Mato, challenged the elections. They argued that Mr. Bernardo did not have the authority to hold the elections, that he had not informed all of the current officers that the elections were taking place, and that the new head of the association, Juanito Tumangkis, was not of timuay lineage.

Timuay Anoy and Mr. Mato intensified their campaign against TVI operations and took their case to court.

In 2001, Mr. Mato also went to the UN Working Group on Indigenous Peoples to denounce the violations of the Subanon's human right to self-determination, as well as other human rights violations in Canatuan. Despite these continued protests over the legitimacy of the association leadership, TVI chose to sign a memorandum of agreement with the new Siocon Subanon Association in 2003 and to transfer to that group the 1% royalty the company is required to pay the indigenous people.

That same memorandum of agreement gave certain status to the Council of Elders, another group whose legitimacy is rejected by Subanon, including the Gukom of Seven Rivers. The Council of Elders was initially formed in 2002 at the instigation of the National Commission on Indigenous Peoples. The commission wanted to end the divisions among the Subanon and get them to work together. The Gukom of Seven Rivers, after conducting a genealogical validation in 2004, rejected the legitimacy of this group on the grounds that 21 of the 30 members were not of timuay lineage and that some were not even from the Canatuan area.

As well, they said there was no precedent in the Subanon traditional culture for having such a council.

Mount Canatuan is sacred for the Subanon people. This photo shows how Nevertheless, the Council of Elders is mentioned in the 2003 memorandum of agreement the company signed with the Siocon Subanon Association. The memorandum says the council gives its authorization to the Siocon Subanon Association to collect the royalty.

It is not clear where the council's authority comes from. The indigenous claim to the land is based on the Certificate of Ancestral Domain Title, which the government awarded a named group of Subanon individuals in 2003. It is not held in the name of the Council of Elders or the Siocon Subanon Association. Some, but not all, of the individual titleholders are members of the Council of Elders.

The Gukom of Seven Rivers says the Council of Elders has no authority in this matter. In signing the memorandum without the consent of the ancestral land holders, the Siocon Subanon Association and through it the Council of Elders have allowed the company to avoid compliance with the Philippine Mining Act of 1995 and the Indigenous Peoples Rights Act of 1997.

Both acts state that ancestral land should not be mined without the prior consent of the indigenous people. The 1997 act also says that the National Commission on Indigenous People cannot issue an approval certificate for mining on ancestral land without obtaining, in advance, the free consent of the indigenous people affected.

The Commission on Human Rights of the Philippines investigated the matter of consent and concluded that the company had not obtained true prior consent from the indigenous people for the mine. A provincial officer of the National Commission on Indigenous People also said that this memorandum of agreement did not represent free, prior and informed consent, and that it was a "midnight deal" because it was executed with the wrong people. The Mines and Geosciences Bureau has stated that, "the lasting solution to the issues is for the company to come to terms with the rightful Subanon community."

While the details are complicated, the basic point being made by the Subanon of Canatuan is that the government and the company have ignored their traditional leadership structure.

In particular, the company has dealt with groups who are neither recognized as legitimate authorities by the Gukom of Seven Rivers, nor as the legitimate ancestral land holders. Furthermore, the company has deprived the Subanon of their right to maintain their traditions and cultural practices. In doing this, Subanon feel that TVI Resource Development has violated their human right to self-determination.

The Human Right to Security of the Person

Security has been a concern in the area of the TVI mine since the 1970s because of the presence of the Abu Sayyaf Group and the Moro Islamic Liberation Front.

The two groups have engaged in a low intensity armed conflict with the Philippine government for more than three decades. As well, the roads leading to Canatuan were considered risky in the 1990s because of robberies, ambushes and occasional murders.

The mining company has a security force made up of auxiliary soldiers provided by the government. These members of the Special Civilian Armed Force Geographical Active Auxiliary (SCAA) are recruited, trained, and armed by the national military and are under the direct command of the Philippine Army.

However, the company pays their salaries. One of the problems with security at the mine is the lack of clarity about whether the SCAA are accountable to the company or to the government. The company has said that the security forces are there not just to protect the mine, but also to protect the surrounding area against activities by the Moro Islamic Liberation Front.

In 2005, TVI Resource Development signed a memorandum of agreement with the 1st Infantry Division, Philippine Army. The agreement states that the army will provide auxiliary forces "to render security guarding services, maintain peace and order, guarding and protecting the installations and properties of the company... and such other places that may agreed upon... from theft, pilferage, robbery, arson and other unlawful acts by employees and or other threat groups." At the time this report was written, the company had 628 employees, including the 160 members of its security force. They are armed with a variety of high-powered weapons.

Canatuan was not an empty space when TVI bought its rights from Benguet Corp. in 1994. The construction of a logging road and the fear that loggers and, later, miners would despoil the area led to the construction of houses by some of the local Subanon during the 1980s to guard their lands and sacred places. By the early 1990s, thousands small-scale miners had moved into the area. From the beginning, TVI faced opposition from the community and from small-scale miners, who say they have prior rights to mining the area.

When it first arrived in the area, TVI immediately erected checkpoints at all the entry and exit points to Canatuan. Three checkpoints were erected on the road leading to the mining complex. At that time, employees of Golden Buddha Security Agency, a security firm based in Zamboanga City, manned these checkpoints, assisted by the SCAA.

The security forces at the checkpoints were ordered by the company to control the passage of all travellers and to impose an economic blockade, especially on small-scale miners. They also prevented some people from entering the area. Anyone passing through the checkpoint was stopped. Some packages belonging to small-scale miners were confiscated.

Local people have filed numerous complaints with the Commission on Human Rights of the Philippines, the Armed Forces and other authorities about the conduct of the security forces. The complaints cited the existence of the checkpoints themselves, as well as travel disruptions, a food blockade, acts of violence and intimidation, and delays in construction of buildings, including a school. After the Mineral Production Sharing Agreement was approved, abuse at the checkpoints appeared to worsen. Some checkpoints are now situated beyond the boundaries of the mining concession.

There have been many violent incidents in the area of the mine. In particular, in September 1999, members of the 903rd Philippine National Police Mobile Group violently dispersed a human barricade formed by Subanon attempting to prevent the company from bringing drilling equipment into their ancestral domain. The participants were beaten with sticks, tied and dragged on the ground. A criminal suit filed against the police was dismissed for want of probable cause.

In December 2002, unknown assailants ambushed a company vehicle travelling to Siocon. Thirteen people, mostly local Subanon, were killed and 12 were injured. The dead included three SCAA, a mine employee, and nine civilians. The company beefed up its security following that incident.

The Commission on Human Rights of the Philippines has conducted at least four investigations into incidents at the TVI Resource Development mine. In one of its reports, the Commission recommended that "the petition for the cancellation and/or revocation of MPSA No. 054-96-IX, now pending before the Office of the Secretary of the DENR be closely monitored." Despite the investigations and recommendations, the situation has not changed and the company still holds its Mineral Production Sharing Agreement. Most of the related legal challenges have not made it through the courts because the Subanon and small-scale farmers cannot afford the legal fees.

The company has recently reduced the number of checkpoints and has conducted a series of training courses on human rights for its security forces.

The human right to an adequate standard of living Siocon, the area where the mine is located, is the rice granary of Zamboanga del Norte. Eighty percent of the workforce is involved in agriculture or fishing. The mining company says its activities affect only 1% of the Siocon River watershed and thus contribute little to its degradation.

However, the Canatuan and Lumot creeks, which run through the mining area, are tributaries of the Lituban River, which drains into the Siocon River. A 2005 company report on the environmental impact of its activities said that 95 hectares of the Canatuan Creek watershed were directly affected by the mining operation due to the construction of the three tailings dams, ancillary facilities and other mining related activities.

The same report said that three hectares of the Lumot Creek watershed were directly affected.

Farmers and fishers in the area surrounding the mine say that changes in water quality and the environment have had an impact on their lives and on their ability to make a living through farming and fishing. For example, farmers on the Litoban and Siocon rivers say increased sediment in the water has caused their irrigation equipment to break down. They also blame the rise in sediment for new rice diseases, which have forced them to move their crops to less fertile areas. The Mines and Geosciences Bureau said the mine alone should not be blamed for the increase in sediment because a logging firm, David Consunji Logging Local reports of violence and intimidation Eusebia Rago, a small-scale miner, was with her husband and children on November 9th 1996, when armed men in military uniform arrived in the area where the family was mining. The men, whom Ms. Rago knew by name, pointed guns at them and ordered them to stop what they were doing because the area was owned by TVI.

"We are just working a living here," Ms. Rago told them. "We did not steal. We work hard to survive even if it causes us pain." The men, who were members of the company's security force, fired their guns in response. "If you will not stop what you are doing, something will happen to you," one of them told her.

Pedro Bolong, Toto Sumala and Boy Canga were at a canteen in Canatuan on November 10th 1996, when six SCAA approached them. The SCAA started drinking. After one hour, one of them, who was identified by the three men, drew a hand grenade and ordered them to leave.

Anita Ansani was carrying vegetables she planned to sell in a village where small-scale miners lived when she was stopped at a checkpoint. She was turned back and warned not to return to the village.

Macario Salacao, a Subanon traditional leader, was taking part in a picket line to prevent the mining company from bringing equipment into the area on March 17th 2004. A SCAA fired on the picketers, wounding four, including Mr. Salacao. Timuay Boy Anoy, a Subanon traditional leader was prevented by TVI's SCAA from entering Canatuan in 1999. As one of the ancestral domain holders, he has the right to enter his ancestral domain when he so wishes. Nevertheless, a similar incident happened again in 2004.

Company, is also operating in the area. The mining company has built facilities in an attempt to resolve the problem. These include a mine waste dump close to the open-pit mine. However, the banks of this dump have been eroded by water. During a visit to the area, the research team noticed that erosion was taking place, even though the walls of the waste dump had been terraced to stabilize the embankment.

The company also built 18 sediment ponds between 2004 and 2005 to reduce siltation in the water. Eight ponds were due to be built in 2006. Unfortunately, most of these ponds are already full, while some were abandoned because of massive bank erosion. A 2005 report by the Multipartite Monitoring Team (composed of representatives from the company, non-governmental organizations, the indigenous community and the government), said that despite company efforts, sediment was still increasing in local creeks and rivers.

Communities living along the coastline, especially in the area where the Siocon River flows into the sea, complain of high levels of sediment and a bitter taste in the water. It is unclear what is causing the bitter taste. The company has not yet built a treatment plant for this ore. The fishers say there are fewer fish close to the coast and they have to go farther out to sea to catch fish. This means they have to spend more money on fuel for their boats. Owners of fish farms, where prawns and milkfish are raised, report a higher mortality rate for their fingerlings and smaller harvests. They believe this is caused by poor water quality.

An increase in trace metals in water consumed by humans can have a negative impact on human health. Water sampling by the Mines and Geosciences Bureau in 2002 found that mercury in some local waterways exceeded the government standards. Small scale miners operating in the area before the arrival of TVI were using mercury and TVI has been processing their mine tailings. A 2005 report by the Multipartite Monitoring Team also reported high mercury levels in lower Canatuan Creek.84 That part of the creek also had arsenic, cyanide and lead levels that exceeded standards.

The farmers, fish-farmers and fishers who have constantly opposed the mine say that they were not adequately consulted about the project, or about its potential impact on water quality. The Local Government Code of 1992 states that community consultations should be conducted prior to implementation of such projects. When the company held a series of information campaigns from 1996 onwards, it was primarily in response to local resolutions and petitions opposing the mine. The human right to an adequate standard of living entails the right to full and equal participation in developmental and environmental planning and decision making, and in shaping all policies affecting one's community and living conditions, at the local, national and international levels.

TVI operations have also had an impact on the livelihoods of 8,000 small-scale miners who were already in the area when the company arrived and who had developed an informal economy based on subsistence mining.85 Despite efforts to obtain legal recognition, these small-scale miners are still working without official permits". Nevertheless, their activities had generated a myriad of associated small businesses and provided direct and indirect employment for people living in the area, including a multi-purpose cooperative and a store selling food and general Downstream communities living along the coastline suffer from changes in supplies.

The small-scale miners have complained of intimidation and harassment carried out by TVI's security force. They say that the security force has engaged strategies such as bulldozing mining tunnels, enforcing a food blockade, and intentionally interrupting the cooperative's supply routes. The miners have filed a series of related complaints. The small-scale miners feel that the Government of the Philippines has failed to protect them from company actions that eventually led to the loss of their livelihoods.

THE HUMAN RIGHT TO ADEQUATE HOUSING

The Committee on Economic, Cultural and Social Rights, which monitors and interprets the covenant, concluded that forced evictions are incompatible with the requirements of the covenant. The 1987 Philippine constitution also stipulates that "urban or rural poor dwellers shall not be evicted nor their dwelling demolished, except in accordance with law and in a just and humane manner". Resettlement must be done with "adequate consultation with them and the communities where they are to be relocated."

When people are resettled, they can be exposed to increased risks, including poverty, homelessness, landlessness, food insecurity, increased morbidity and mortality, unemployment, marginalization, loss of access to common resources, loss of access to public services, and loss of social cohesion. As well, resettlement can lead to increasing risks to host populations.

In the case of indigenous peoples, displacement from traditional territories also means loss of cultural identity and is a threat to their existence as a people. In addition to indigenous peoples, women, children, and the elderly are most vulnerable to resettlement.

There have been forcible evictions in Canatuan since mid-2003, when the mining company secured support from the Philippine government to forcibly demolish the facilities of the small-scale miners and to remove the miners from the area. The company said that it paid people to leave, offering compensation that it said was many times higher than what was legally required. Those receiving the compensation say the process is neither transparent nor equitable. Some Subanon who have been displaced complain that their farmlands have been bulldozed without proper compensation.

As well, the people who received eviction notices issued by the company perceived them as threats. Harassment of small-scale miners and incidents of violence by security forces destroying the miners' facilities for the mining company have been documented. These include an incident on May 22nd 2006, when the family of a small-scale miner was forcibly removed and their home destroyed by the security forces, working with Subanon who supported the company.

When mining started in mid-2004, the company estimated there were still 150 families living on land in the path of the growing open-pit mine. In June 2005, 50 families near the pit staged a vigil to prevent the company's security forces from demolishing their homes. At first, the vigil was successful. But several days later, the security forces returned in greater number. A bulldozer was used to destroy the gardens in which the miners grew their food, including root crops and bananas. By June 2006, the company estimated that 30 families remained of which five were indigenous Subanon.

THE HUMAN RIGHT TO FAVOURABLE CONDITIONS OF WORK

The human right to work is enshrined in the Universal Declaration of Human Rights, Conventions of the International Labour Organization and in the International Covenant on Economic, Social and Cultural Rights. Article 7 of the covenant describes the human right to work as the right to fair wages, equal pay for work of equal value without discrimination, and a safe and healthy working environment. Article 8 refers to the right to form trade unions and the right to strike.

National legislation in the Philippines also protects the human rights of workers. The constitution directs the state to protect these rights and to promote the welfare of workers. It affirms the right to association, collective bargaining, and the right to strike.

TVI Resource Development has created salaried jobs in an area where such jobs did not exist (although thousands of small-scale miners were already in the area). However, there have been complaints made against the company for some of its labour practices. An attempt to form a union in 2005 failed and workers told organizers from the National Federation of Labour that the company had not paid overtime to some workers and had terminated others without due process and without paying social security premiums.

The union organizers said the company workers were difficult to organize because the area is guarded by security forces and meetings had to be held many km away.

Several workers told the research team that people were afraid that the creation of the union would cause the company to close the mine. "It is a good thing that there is no union, because at least we still have a job," one worker said.

There is also a continuing disagreement over whether the 160 SCAA at the mine are employees and could therefore join the union. A 2003 contract signed with the members of the SCAA asserted that they were employees of the mine. However, the 2005 memorandum of agreement between TVI Resource Development and the Philippine army said they were not. The company still pays their salaries, provides uniforms and equipment, but does not provide housing.

THE CASE OF THE GALVES FAMILY

In June 2006, the home of the Galves family, located in the mining area, was destroyed. On this point everyone agrees. There are conflicting accounts of who demolished the home, whether anyone was in it at the time, and whether private property was confiscated. This case indicates the confusion that often prevails when eviction precedes commercial development, especially when the evictions are carried out by local people. Those affected say company security forces participated in the destruction of the home, wounding a number of people, and confiscating private property. The company said the home was not destroyed by its security forces but by people belonging to the Siocon Subanon Association.

Erdulfo Comisas, an official with the Siocan Subanon Association and a member of the Council of Elders, said he mobilized a team of Subanon to dismantle shanties owned by non-indigenous people. No one was home, he said, when the home was destroyed. However, a SCAA who monitored the incident said at least 20 members of TVI's security force were there. He thought the demolition was poorly done because there was no official from the local community present to observe and it had been done at night.

When we discussed this incident during our consultations with the Siocon Subanon Association and the Council of Elders, they denied that the security forces were present.

This has created a great deal of confusion about their status. A large number of the workers supporting the creation of the union in 2005 were SCAA.

Dionison Jubilan, the assistant security manager for the company, said the majority of the security forces believe they are company employees. The research team asked SCAA about their status. "We have become TVI's private army," an unnamed SCAA told the research team. "We took part in demolitions and have sacrificed a lot." He said the security forces did not want to return to army duties because they feared that rampant corruption in the army meant they would not be paid. The company is now conducting seminars for its security forces to explain their role.

TVI Resources Development created a labour management council in 2005 where employees can air their grievances, discuss other problems, and talk about areas where the company could improve its performance.

Discussions at the council have led to better working conditions, wages and benefits. However, in terms of housing and work opportunities, some discrimination still exists towards indigenous people. In early 2004, Subanon workers lived in what the locals called chicken cages in an area known as Manokan. These shelters were about two metres tall and had room for only one person. Non-indigenous workers lived in a bunkhouse, which was more solidly constructed than the huts. Later in 2004, the indigenous workers were moved to better quarters in an area called Manhattan.

But their housing is still of poorer quality than that of non-indigenous workers. Mila Corpuz, former manager of human resources for the company, said she hopes to make further improvements. In terms of working conditions, the company has four types of employees: managers, technical supervisors, skilled workers and unskilled labour. In the last two categories there are temporary and regular workers. The workers told the research team that the unskilled, temporary jobs are mostly filled by indigenous people. Usually, workers start out on a casual status, become probationary workers after three months and can apply for regular status after six months.

Regular employees receive benefits and privileges that are not available to casual and probationary workers. They receive a salary of 220 pesos a day, plus 15 days of vacation leave and 15 days sick leave a year. They are eligible for a bonus if they work a full month without taking any leave. In addition, regular workers enjoy an extra month of pay each year (the so-called 13th month). They must be given 15 days notice of termination and receive a month's pay, plus unused sick and vacation leave when they go. In December 2005, the company started a health insurance plan for regular employees, but not their families. The company plans to extend the coverage to family members in 2007.

Apart from these benefits, every employee interviewed confirmed that once they became regular staff, they were provided with steel boots, rubber shoes, a t-shirt, and a raincoat. They also receive free meals. The workers interviewed by the research team believe that the company paid better wages than other companies in the region.

THE HUMAN RIGHT TO EDUCATION

The Philippine government, which is heavily indebted, has repeatedly cut spending on education and health.

Since 1997, real per capita spending by the national government on education has fallen 19%. Health spending has dropped 43% in the same period. Between 1997 and 2003, government spending on education has been only 3.2% of gross domestic product, a broad measure of the economy. In the Siocon area, there are no government education services, except for primary schools.

The Canatuan community built its own school in 1998 and then expanded it over the years with support from local government officials. Materials for the school had to be smuggled past company checkpoints. By January 2003, it had 182 students attending grades one through five.

More students were expected to register in June 2003, the beginning of the new school year, necessitating an expansion of the building. The provincial governor donated the necessary construction materials. The material arrived in Canatuan in August 2003 and was placed at the Canatuan Primary School. Later that year, TVI, through its chief security consultant, confiscated the material. The company said the materials were damaged. It replaced them at its own expense.

The company used these materials to build a two-room primary school about six kilometres away, near a security post manned by SCAA. It did this without consulting the local community. It also provided three schoolteachers, school supplies and other facilities.

Residents complain that the new school is too far away, inaccessible due to landslides caused by mining, and too close to the armed security post. Parents are concerned for the safety of their children, who must now walk a long way on roads used by heavy equipment.

The distance, bad weather, and security risks have significantly reduced school attendance. The company attempted to address some of these complaints by providing vehicles and raincoats on rainy days. Local critics of the company said that by seizing the materials and building the school where it wanted, the company was obliterating an existing community and creating a new one.

The company said it relocated the school for safety reasons. There is an open-pit mine above the community where the previous school was located and the company was worried about boulders falling on the school and community below. The company promised to provide a school bus by January 2007.

There are currently 182 pupils in elementary school and 32 students in a high school, which started this year. The majority of the students are Subanon, whose parents are employed by the mining company. There is no special curriculum for the indigenous Subanon. The company has developed a special summer job program for Subanon students so that they can gain work experience while being paid.

CONCLUSIONS AND RECOMMENDATIONS

The presence of TVI Resource Development has created some jobs in an impoverished area and generated revenues for the indebted national government.

However, the arrival of the mining company in Canatuan has also divided the Subanon people. This in turn has had a negative impact on their right to self-determination and on their system of governance.

Security measures implemented by the mining firm have contributed to militarization of the area. This militarization has had a negative impact on the ability of the Subanon to enjoy the human right to security and the human right to housing. Mining activity appears to have increased the levels of sediment and metals in some local waterways, threatening the human right to an adequate standard of living.

The Philippine government holds the primary obligation to protect the human rights of its people. In the Canatuan example, there has been a clear gap between the existing legal framework and its application. By not enforcing national laws enacted for this purpose, the government has allowed the company to engage in activities that have violated the human rights of local communities.

Elementary school built by the Subanon and small-scale miners. It has now been transferred by TVIRD six kilometres away from the community and near a SCAA security post.

Recommendations

For the Government of the Philippines

The Government of the Philippines should assume responsibility for investigating the current conflict in Canatuan and for adopting procedures that would ensure such examples do not reoccur in future. The purpose of such a process would be to determine the legality of the company's current activities as well as its proposed expansion of activities in the area. Attention should be given to equal access to justice, the creation of appropriate complaints mechanisms, access to information, and controls over military and paramilitary security forces. In addition, an independent body should be created to monitor and report on the implementation of these procedures and to actively solicit the views of the local communities.

Local communities should be given capacity training in the principles of human rights so that they can identify abuses and assert their rights. This training should include the provision of the appropriate documents outlining human rights. The Philippine system of Barangay Human Rights Action Centres should be strengthened and their locations expanded. There are about 14,406 such centres in the country, but they are concentrated in only a few regions. The Philippine government should endorse the UN Declaration on the Rights of Indigenous Peoples and ratify the International Labour Organization Convention No. 169. The use of human rights impact assessments should be institutionalized and these assessments should be used whenever licences and permits are issued or renewed.

For the Company

The company should make all efforts to resolve the many issues and conflicts in Canatuan before proceeding with expansion of its operations in adjacent areas. This will require participation in an independent monitoring procedure and an agreement to work directly with affected communities who might oppose their investment. Until such processes are in place, TVI should halt its operations in Canatuan, as well as its expansion plans. TVI should, at least temporarily, ensure that paramilitary security forces are disarmed, and it should ensure that community claims of damages are investigated and resolved without delay.

4

WOMEN AND HUMAN RIGHTS IN TIBET

SCOPING

The history of Tibet can be traced back to the early 7th century when various tribes and clans who lived on the high plateau united as a confederation. Through the centuries, the Tibetan people have maintained a shared identity and territory, although a central authority has not always existed. In 1949, Chinese troops entered eastern Tibet claiming to bring modernization while offering guarantees that internal governance and cultural and religious systems would remain under Tibetan administration.

These guarantees of autonomy quickly proved illusory. In March 1959, following a series of protests and rallies, Chinese forces suppressed an uprising in which more than 10,000 people died. The Dalai Lama and some 80,000 followers fled across the Himalayas and were given sanctuary by the Government of India. It is estimated that since 1959, approximately 1.2 million Tibetans have died as a result of the Chinese occupation, either through harsh prison conditions, summary execution or starvation. Meanwhile, the Dalai Lama has campaigned for a peaceful resolution of the conflict. He has received several international peace awards for his efforts, including the Nobel Peace Prize in 1989.

Before the People's Republic of China became a member of the United Nations in 1971, the General Assembly passed three resolutions in support of the Tibetan people, citing various violations to their fundamental rights and freedoms, including their right to self-determination. In 1991, the UN Sub-Commission on Prevention of Discrimination and Protection of Minority Rights (now the Sub-Commission on the Promotion and Protection of Human Rights) passed a resolution expressing concern at the continued violation of the human rights of the Tibetan people.

Today, the status of Tibet as an autonomous region within China is protected by national legislation entitled the Law on Regional Ethnic Autonomy. This law, revised in 2001, is meant to implement a system of regional autonomy based on constitutional provisions that allow for the creation of administrative regions with their own governance systems. The law includes the right to enjoy self-government, to manage internal affairs, to formulate separate regulations, to protect language and religious freedoms, and to independently manage economic development. Theoretically, it enables autonomous areas, including Tibet, to enact local legislation and to modify state laws and policies in the interests of local priorities and needs. In practice, these rights are not used, possibly because they must be approved by the Standing Committee of the National Peoples' Congress or because state ministries enjoy an effective veto which is not part of the law. Further, the law does not permit actions deemed "harmful to the state."

In addition to national laws, there are a number of regulations that apply specifically to the Tibet Autonomous Region and the other autonomous prefectures that are part of historical Tibet. These include regulations designed to enhance the role of women and workers, and to manage the environment and natural resources. In practice however, efforts to apply affirmative action policies based on these regulations would likely be viewed as controversial by authorities because of a general distrust of Tibetans and the role of the Party at all levels of policy development and implementation. Despite increasing prosperity across China, poverty continues to plague the majority of Tibetans.

According to the United Nations Development Program, Tibet is the poorest and least developed region of China. This disparity is not merely regional but takes on an ethnic dimension when looking at Tibetan and Chinese populations within Tibet itself, where discriminatory social and fiscal policies have entrenched a two-class social and economic system. In was in this context that in June 1999, Chinese President Jiang Zemin announced a vague new program entitled China's Western Development Strategy (sometimes referred to as the Go-West Campaign), describing it as a means to strengthen national unity, safeguard social stability, and consolidate border defence.4 To be successful, the strategy required an ambitious plan of infrastructure development and foreign investment.

HUMAN RIGHTS IN PRINCIPLE

The People's Republic of China became a member of the United Nations in November 1971, replacing Taiwan and occupying a seat on the UN Security Council.

Since then, the government of China has ratified more than 20 human rights treaties, including five of the seven core human rights treaties: the Convention on the Elimination of All Forms of Discrimination Against Women in 1980; the Convention on the Elimination of Racial Discrimination in 1981; the Convention Against Torture and Other Cruel, Inhuman or Degrading Treatment or Punishment in 1988; the Convention on the Rights of the Child in 1992; and the International Covenant on Economic, Social and Cultural Rights in 2001.

In addition, China has signed, but not ratified, the International Covenant on Civil and Political Rights and the Convention on the Protection of All Migrant Workers and Members of their Families.

China regularly submits reservations when it ratifies treaties, meaning that it does not accept all obligations included in the documents. For example, China maintains a reservation with regard to labour rights protected in Article 8 of the International Covenant on Economic, Social and Cultural Rights, and similarly it has withdrawn from provisions for monitoring procedures contained in Article 20 of the Convention against Torture and Other Cruel, Inhuman or Degrading Treatment or Punishment. Despite the ratifications however, the domestic status of international treaties remains unclear. Although the Government of China explicitly recognized human rights in its constitution in 2004, this does not have the same implication for domestic legislation as it does in countries where the constitution is a legal document rather than a statement of principles. Moreover, China argues that international law does not apply to individuals but only to states.

It therefore continues to emphasize the principle of non-interference in internal affairs whenever questions about its domestic human rights compliance are raised. Nevertheless, in its relations with western agencies and other governments, the Government of China talks about human rights and this discourse is reflected in the release of numerous White Papers published since 1991.

The UN treaty bodies - committees that monitor State Party compliance with various human rights treaties - have issued reports that include specific mention of the situation in Tibet. Most recently, in 2006, the Committee on Economic, Social and Cultural Rights reviewed China for the first time. It noted with concern "reports regarding the discrimination of ethnic minorities by the State party, in particular in the fields of employment, adequate standard of living, health, education and culture."

Such observations point to the exclusion of Tibetans from their own development process.

Railway communication towers appear approximately every 6.7 km along the route of the railway.

RESEARCH ON THE INVESTMENT

The railway from Gormo to Lhasa is a flagship project of China's Western Development Strategy. The railway was originally conceived during the 1950s, but it wasn't until 1994 that surveys and feasibility studies were conducted.

The total length of the track is 1,118 km, of which more than 960 km is at or above 4,000 metres above sea level. More than 560 km of track is built on permafrost. The railway travels across a vast untouched plateau from Gormo, once the centre of the Tibetan salt trade and now a bustling Chinese city, over the Tungla Pass and through Nagchu and Damshung to Lhasa, Tibet's capital city.

Many Tibetans object to the railway because they believe it is a political project aimed at quelling dissent in the restive region. A secret 1970 report released in 1993 by the Government of the United States cited the lack of a railway as the primary reason why Beijing had so far failed to fully assimilate Tibet into China. Tibetans argue that the railway will facilitate the movement of military troops into and within the region, that it will encourage the influx of Chinese entrepreneurs and workers eventually making Tibetans a minority in their own land, and that it will provide the infrastructure needed to export Tibet's resource riches to the industrialized eastern regions of China.

The first train arrived in Lhasa on July 1st 2006, after research for this report was completed. An official opening ceremony took place under heavy security. At the ceremony, the chairman of the Tibet Autonomous Region, Champa Phunstok, dismissed allegations about the purposes of the railway, telling assembled dignitaries and western journalists that the central government would not deal with Tibet's government-in-exile unless the Dalai Lama conceded that both Tibet and Taiwan have always been part of China.

Authorities have since announced that three new extensions to the railway will be constructed: one to Nepal via Shigatse; one to the Indian border at Nyalam in Sikkim; and one to southeast China via Chengdu.

The Company

Nortel is a Canadian company, headquartered in Brampton, Ontario. It develops and manufactures communications and information technology and in 2005, reported more than US $18 billion in total assets and more than US $10 billion in sales.11 Nortel's 35,370 employees12 work in Canada, the US, Europe, the Middle East, Latin America, Africa, the Caribbean and Asia.13 By the end of 2005, Nortel had helped install more than 300 wireless networks in more than 50 countries.

In the 1990s, the internet revolution presented an opportunity for the company to shift its focus from telecommunications equipment to information technology.

By 1998, more than 75% of internet traffic in North America was carried on Nortel's high-performance optical networks.15 The end of the dot-com boom however signalled the beginning of financial and legal troubles for Nortel. Its stock plummeted and its workforce was cut in half.16 Between 2001 and 2004, Nortel and certain of its former officers and directors were named as defendants in 27 class action lawsuits in the US and Canada.17 In 2005, the company agreed to pay US shareholders US $2.25 billion. The Canadian suits have yet to be settled.18 At the end of 2005, Nortel reported a loss of US $2.6 billion.

Tibet

The word Tibet is often used in reference to the Tibet Autonomous Region of China. In fact, the autonomous region comprises only one administrative region of the three that comprised historical Tibet. The western mountainous parts of present-day Sichuan, with the northwestern tip of Yunnan, once made up the Tibetan province of Kham (Dhomey), while most of Qinghai, with a western part of Gansu, was once known as the Tibetan province of Amdo (Dhotoe). Most of what comprises the present day Tibet Autonomous Region was formerly known as Central Tibet (U-Tsang) province.

With a population of about 2.6 million,6 the Tibet Autonomous Region includes only about half of the total ethnic Tibetan population in China and it does not include many of the regions of historical Tibet.

For the purposes of this report, the word Tibet will be used in its broader sense and Tibet Autonomous Region will indicate only central Tibet. This report uses location names in Tibetan-English transliteration. Despite Nortel's shaky performance on the home front, it has steadily increased its presence in emerging markets, especially in China, where it has two research and development centres and four manufacturing plants. Nortel has won a series of contracts to construct, expand or provide equipment for telecommunications networks in China. They include deals with China Railcom, a national telecommunications operator; SINOPEC, China's largest producer and marketer of oil products; and PetroChina, a subsidiary of the stateowned China National Petroleum Corporation.

Nortel has said that it is not collaborating with any government to repress human rights and that it has contributed to communities in the form of donations and technology training programs. However, at the annual general meeting of Nortel shareholders on June 29th 2006, the Vancouver-based Ethical Fund submitted a resolution proposing that the company prepare a report about its policies with respect to human rights in China and Tibet, and that it cooperate with a human rights impact assessment of its investment in Tibet. Nortel's board of directors recommended, in a written statement to shareholders, that they vote against the resolution. The resolution nevertheless received 32% of votes cast.

The Contract

In 2001, Nortel announced that it had concluded a deal to provide China Railcom with a nationwide, multiservice ATM (asynchronous transfer mode) backbone network. ATM is a cell relay, circuit-switching network and data link protocol that encodes data traffic into small fixed-sized units. It facilitates the connection of two end-points before any data has been exchanged between them. The agreement included provision of both equipment and services.

China Railcom (formerly the China Railway Communication Co.) was transferred to state ownership in January 2004 and is one of the six primary telecommunication service providers in China. China Railcom is now administered by China's Ministry of Railways and enjoys related preferential policies. On March 16th 2005, Nortel announced its contract with China's Ministry of Railways to provide a digital wireless communications network for the Gormo-Lhasa railway. According to the Nortel press release, it would be the first commercial use in China of the Global System for Mobile Communications for Railways (GSM-R). The contract followed a year-long trial of the technology by Nortel China's research and development team along 186 km of the track. Deployment required three types of sub-systems: the base stations (towers), the mobile stations (on board the train) and the network subsystem.

Nortel has denied that this contract constitutes an investment, but the provision of services within the contract, coupled with the company's substantial commercial presence in China, would likely characterize it as investment under international law.

Dual-use Technology

China's Ministry of Railways assigned researchers at Beijing Jiaotong University with the task of developing an overarching management and planning system for the railway. The researchers designed what they call the G3 system, integrating Nortel's GSM-R with a Geographic Information System and a Global Positioning System to create a new standard for railway Tower and station under construction at Damshung. communications.

The Geographic Information System (GIS) is a suite of software and hardware tools designed to combine relational databases with satellite maps of the earth's surface. For rail transportation applications, spatial data which graphically represents the geometry of the rail network is visually cross-referenced with related attributes, for example, the location of bridges, stations and rolling stock, or socio-economic data to support decision making.

The Global Positioning System (GPS) is a satellite navigation system operated by the United States Department of Defence. It consists of a constellation of 24 satellites orbiting the earth and six ground stations. The satellites transmit a signal that allows the user to determine with some accuracy the precise location of their GPS receiver. GPS receivers are accurate to within less than 15 metres.

The G3 system integrates these three technologies (GIS + GPS + GSM-R) to create a state-of-the-art information planning system for the railway. Nortel's GSM-R system provided Beijing Jiaotong University with all the services it required to successfully deploy the G3 system: remote train control, voice communications for all users, emergency call handling, data message exchange, communication recording, and integration capacity with other existing (or future) systems. Once integrated, the G3 system provides, in the words of its engineers, "an extremely accurate location-tracking system."

Military Implications

There is a reasonable expectation that the Gormo-Lhasa railway and the communications technology that supports it, will result in the permanent militarization of the Tibetan plateau. The Jamestown Foundation, a US-based think-tank, says that the Tibet railway will provide, "previously unrealized strategic, tactical, and conventional possibilities for the People's Liberation Army to direct military firepower toward South Asia and beyond." Journalists invited to travel on the first train in July 2006 reported that military camps and bases were seen along the tracks and that convoys of military vehicles were often visible, even though much of the route was uninhabited. The Military Area Commands of the Tibet Autonomous Region and Qinghai Province and the Qinghai Armed Police Force have reportedly deployed up to 10,000 soldiers and civilians along the route of the railway and according to media reports, their tactical communications are supported by Nortel's GSM-R technology.

In the name of national security, governments are turning increasingly toward security and surveillance technologies that are often derived from hi-tech, military research programs originally designed to track the movement of troops on the battlefield. These surveillance and C4I technologies (command, control, communication, computers and intelligence) cover a wide range of components, subsystems, products and software. They are used by the military, law enforcement, and emergency services, but also by commercial and private organizations. (The term C4I generally refers to military and police systems while civilian systems are more commonly referred to as information and communication technologies.) Most civilian communications technologies have surveillance and control facilities that mirror and are derived from military applications.

Modern military, security and police organizations rely on sensors to yield intelligence, surveillance and reconnaissance, and they use networks to integrate and share the information that is gathered. Once the sensors and networks are integrated, they collectively comprise what William Owens, former chief executive officer of Nortel, once called a "System of Systems." The technology transfer that the Government of China is most actively seeking from Nortel and other western companies is precisely this - sensors, networks and the ability to integrate them. Sensors and networks are the key components for both modern-day security systems and modern-day warfare. While they are not in and of themselves weapons, they can be used as such when they are integrated and combined with real time, operational intelligence.

Beyond Tibet, the railway, its communications system and its planned extensions will form a key part of China's new security infrastructure, with implications beyond the plateau to central Asia. Chinese Vice-Premier Zeng Peiyan has said that East Turkestan (ch. Xinjiang) on Tibet's northwest border will become China's main source of energy in the next five to ten years. To counter any threat of insurgency, Chinese security forces have invested heavily in updating their command and control systems to ensure a rapid response to any protest. The Xinjiang military region has hosted a series of exercises in the Taklimakan Desert where it incorporated a C4I local area network in an area 1,000 km long, integrating intelligence, command and control, automated artillery fire support, airspace surveillance and control, and logistics re-supply. This has significant consequences for high-altitude "infowar" allowing security forces to rapidly respond to any perceived threat.

None of this has been lost on India.

A July 6th 2006 announcement that the Gormo-Lhasa railway would be extended to the Indian border for trade purposes prompted expressions of concern from India's security experts. The retired joint director of India's Federal Intelligence Bureau said that China would now be able to "monitor troop deployment and movement along the disputed border". Military intelligence officials have reportedly objected to opening of the trade route based on security concerns. The Chinese army has intercontinental ballistic missiles (ICBMs) designed for rail transport. The railway thereby provides Beijing with the potential of operating missile trains, with hiding places across the plateau, and threatening India with ballistic weapons in the same way it currently threatens Taiwan.

RAILWAY COMMUNICATIONS AS PART OF CHINA'S GOLDEN SHIELD PROJECT

The railway and its communications systems will also have security and surveillance uses in Tibet itself. Railway communications are part of China's Golden Shield, a project that links national, regional and local security and surveillance agencies. The Golden Shield is a gigantic online database, incorporating speech and face recognition, closed-circuit television, smart cards, credit Military barracks are frequent along the Ghormo-Lhassa railway track.

records and internet surveillance, offering immediate access to the registration records of every citizen in China. It was the subject of a major study by Rights & Democracy in 2001. The Government of China has described the Golden Shield as a means of strengthening central police control and improving efficiency.

Surveillance systems can range from closed circuit television surveillance, to local, regional or national traffic control, and to global systems for the monitoring of telephone, internet and fax communication. Such systems have legitimate military, police and civilian uses but they also have inherent capabilities that facilitate human rights violations when unfettered by the checks and balances taken for granted in most democratic states. It is this state of the art technology and communications equipment that enables the security apparatus of a single-party state to identify and arrest human rights defenders, pro-democracy campaigners, trade union organizers and political dissidents.

In September 2001 Agence France-Presse reported that the Public Security Bureau had set up a closed-circuit television network along China's national railway network. This surveillance system allows officers to compare the faces of the public against a central database. In October 2001, following trials of the system installed in Beijing station, China Railcom announced that it had placed an order with Nortel to build a nationwide data network, which presumably will carry the closedcircuit television images.

The Public Security Bureau has built up a national data bank that records information and data on about 1.25 billion of China's 1.3 billion people. Last year, 330,000 criminal cases, or 20 percent of the total, were broken with the help of the data bank and the internet.

According to Beijing Youth Daily, the network allowed the police to apprehend 39 suspected criminals within five days. Today, rail passengers have to negotiate numerous checkpoints throughout Beijing station, a process likely to be replicated in stations across China and along the Tibet railway.

HOME STATE INVOLVEMENT

The Government of Canada denies any involvement in the Tibet railway project, either through participation in negotiations between Nortel and the Chinese Ministry of Railways or through the provision of funding to the project. Similarly, Export Development Canada denied in 2001 that it had provided any support in terms of insurance or loan guarantees to any Canadian company interested in pursuing projects related to the Tibet railway.

The Canadian government has, however, provided substantial support through its suite of trade promotion services to Canadian business, including to companies interested in investment opportunities in Tibet and specifically related to the information and communications technology or railway sectors. In addition, a series of high profile trade missions to China, one ministerial visit to Tibet, luncheons Canada hosted for senior Chinese officials, and conferences in both Canada and China promoted and endorsed China's Western Development Strategy.

Canada has also been one of the countries to provide training programs for Chinese engineers, specifically related to railway construction and operation on permafrost. Chinese Vice-Minister of Railways, Sun Yongfu, told journalists that Chinese experts "had been sent to Russia and Canada to study permafrost rail construction."

Numerous other memoranda of understanding and bilateral agreements have promoted co-operation, investment, and technology exchange between Canada and China. They include an agreement on science and technology, a memorandum of understanding on information and communication technology, and a 2005 memorandum of understanding on railway development. Researchers could not find a single reference to human rights concerns in any of these documents.

Privacy regulations prevented researchers from finding out whether Nortel had submitted its technology to Canada's export control review process, which oversees the export of military and dual-use technologies. The Government of Canada maintains strict control over dual-use technologies and reviews them from a human rights perspective. However, any item that is not listed on the Export Control List would be exempted from the process. Although the current list includes telecommunications systems, equipment, components and sensors, there are interesting exceptions.

For example, systems and modules or integrated circuits for information security are exempted from the dual-use category and some technologies are broken down into individual components for assessment.

The Government of Canada is currently negotiating a Foreign Investment Protection Agreement with China based on a standard model. The agreement seeks to guarantee protection for Canadian investors, in part by defining dispute settlement processes. The model makes no reference human rights and provides no dispute settlement process for individuals or communities who might experience a human rights violation as a result of any particular investment project.

It is interesting to note here that the United States, in part to deal with concerns about economic development projects in Tibet, passed the Tibetan Policy Act of 2002.

Its provisions apply to the Export-Import Bank (export credit agency), the Trade and Development Agency, and other US entities.

The act establishes a number of conditions to be met before projects in Tibet may proceed. For example, projects should be implemented only after a thorough assessment of the needs of the Tibetan people has been conducted, through field visits and interviews; be preceded by cultural and environmental impact assessments; neither provide incentive for, nor facilitate the transfer of ownership of Tibetan land or natural resources to non-Tibetans; be implemented by agencies prepared to use Tibetan as the working language of the projects.

DIFFERENT INVESTMENT GUIDELINES

Chinese Government: The Government of the Tibet Autonomous Region published its Guidelines for Investment in Tibet. They explain a range of incentives for investment, but contain no suggestions for the protection of local people or their culture. Among the preferential policies offered to investors are:

- o Special provisions for investors in Nagchu (a key stop on the Gormo-Lhasa railway), including the use of local farmland, forests, grasslands;
- o First priority authorization to develop land and underground resources for those investors involved in the construction of railways or rail stations;
- o Funds to purchase land at 50% of its value, with associated fees waived for high-tech and infrastructure investors;
- o Fee waivers for investment above US $10 million;
- o Special treatment of investor requests for long-term or resident visa applications;
- o Exemption from income and operating taxes for projects such as infrastructure, transportation and energy development.

Tibetan government-in-exile: With foreign capital set to stake a claim in Tibet, the Tibetan government-in-exile issued its own guidelines for foreign investment and bilateral development assistance projects. The Guidelines for International Development Projects and Sustainable Development in Tibet set out basic principles for ethical investment in Tibet. They also provide sector-specific criteria for ethical investment, including in areas prioritized by China's Western Development Strategy, such as agriculture, energy, environmental services, healthcare and education. Specific recommendations encourage:

- o Hiring Tibetans in management positions;
- o Provision of loans and credit to Tibetan entrepreneurs;
- o Use of the Tibetan language for public and educational documentation;
- o Skills training and other forms of technical assistance;
- o Conservation of Tibet's extensive, fragile resource base and the environment;
- o Reversal of the process of marginalization of Tibetans and empowerment of Tibetans to take control of developing Tibet.

ADAPTING THE METHODOLOGY TO THE CASE STUDY

The research team faced a number of challenges as it sought to apply the human rights impact assessment methodology in Tibet. This case study is fundamentally different in nature from the others because the research took place before the railway was operational. Whereas the other case studies in the project sought to identify the actual impact of operational projects, the Tibet case study placed greater emphasis on the collection of contextual information in order to identify the potential future impacts of the investment project.

There were other reasons that necessitated a substantive revision of the research methodology for this case study. The prevailing climate of fear meant that no single community was able to follow our process from beginning to end and it precluded an open and transparent site visit. The railway is 1,118 km in length and the impact of its communications technology will be felt far beyond communities located along the track. Communications technology itself is intangible, difficult to identify as a precise entity and has multiple purposes - civilian, police and military - that are difficult to separate from each other. Finally, Nortel did not agree to collaborate with the research and therefore we had no access to contract details or to the company's perspective on the investment.

Nevertheless, during the site visit, researchers travelled the entire length of the railway and interviewed individuals in several communities along the way. In total, the research team interviewed more than 75 individuals over a three-week period. Among Tibetans, we spoke with monks, nuns, students, business people, taxi drivers, teachers, tour guides, shop owners, hotel workers, farmers, nomads, sex workers, beggars, employees of nongovernmental organizations and one Public Security Bureau official. Among Chinese, our conversations included railway workers, shoe shiners, taxi drivers, tour guides, sex workers, petty merchants, as well as one journalist and at least one government official. Security concerns prevented prolonged visits with any one community or group. We were constantly aware of the threat to the personal security of our sources and guides and therefore exercised a good deal of restraint in pursuing sensitive lines of questioning. We documented no names and took no photos of anyone interviewed.

Before and after the site visit, we collected data from external sources including media reports and academic studies, and we conducted interviews within the Tibetan refugee communities in India, Nepal, Canada, the United Kingdom, the United States and Australia, as well as with western journalists in China, with Chinese activists in Hong Kong, and with representatives of nongovernmental organizations who were campaigning against the railway during the time of our research.

We would note here that despite numerous efforts by Rights & Democracy since 2005 to engage Nortel in this case study research, the company has consistently refused to participate. We contacted chief ethics and compliance officer, Susan Shepard, in August 2005 and subsequently invited her to participate in a seminar on the export of surveillance technology to China in

October 2005. Later, Nortel's vice-president for international relations, William Neil, informed us by telephone that Nortel would not participate either in the seminar or in this research. We requested the response in writing but never received it.

In May 2006, Rights & Democracy sent a formal letter addressed to Mr. Neil, describing the preliminary findings of our site visit to Tibet and requesting a meeting to discuss them. On June 12th 2006 we received an email communication from Richard Dipper of Nortel, promising a response before June 23rd 2006. On June 23rd 2006, we received a second email from Mr. Dipper, again declining to participate in the project. Rights & Democracy then suggested that even without formal collaboration on the research, Nortel might agree to answer specific questions related to its investment in Tibet. There was no response and no further communication, despite our leaving phone messages which were not returned.

OUTCOMES OF THE SITE VISIT RESEARCH

The research guide requests two types of data when looking at the enjoyment of human rights in the project area: general context and actual impact. For this case study, because the site visit research took place before the railway was operational, the emphasis is on general context as already explained. The data collected includes information from external sources but emphasizes first-hand information obtained by the research team during its site visit in March 2006.

In presenting the research results here, we have focused primarily on the human rights that would be directly affected by communications technology introduced via the railway: the right to security of the person; the right to privacy; the right to freedom of opinion and expression. However, in the course of our research we also made a number of observations regarding other human rights that are significant in terms of the general context in which the technology is being deployed. These include the right to self-determination; the right to freedom of thought, conscience and religion; and the right to development understood here as the progressive realization of economic, social and cultural rights.

Discrimination was a cross-cutting issue that had an impact on the enjoyment of all rights. Although our experience did not allow strict adherence to the methodology and research guide, the material gathered does faithfully reflect the opinions expressed in interviews conducted by researchers during the site visit. As such, it is a fair reflection of community views and the general context in which Nortel is deploying its communications technology in Tibet.

THE HUMAN RIGHT TO SECURITY OF THE PERSON

On a visit to China and Tibet in 2005, the UN Special Rapporteur on Torture reported "a palpable level of fear and self-censorship which he had not experienced in the course of his previous missions." There can be no doubt that the Tibetan people live in a "climate of fear", a phrase first coined by an inspection panel sent to Tibet by the World Bank in 2000 to assess the proposed resettlement of 58,000 Chinese farmers into Tibetan areas of Amdo province.52 The panel report was important because it was a mainstream affirmation of what Tibetan refugees have long claimed - that exercising their human rights could threaten their personal liberty and security.

In fact, the research team experienced that same climate of fear. Each time we initiated a conversation with individuals, we worried that our purpose would be exposed. As we self-censored, the responses from interviewees were similarly guarded. If we were able to develop a degree of trust, some subject areas remained taboo, such as the Tibetan government-in-exile, political prisoners, the Panchen Lama and human rights.

While most people were happy to talk about the railway in a casual conversation, it was difficult to obtain their views about the potential impact of the railway or the new communications technology associated with it. In some cases, people just walked away.

In others, heads bowed but no verbal response was offered. One woman told us that when westerners ask such questions, the responses often end up in public reports back in their countries. Chinese authorities have been known to track down sources even months later, she said. In fact, the research team found significant documentation by credible human rights agencies attesting that Tibetans remain in prison for offences that were deemed to threaten state security or promote counterrevolution.

The threat to personal security extends also to western development organization representatives working in Tibet. Special permits are required to work in the Tibet Autonomous Region and these must be negotiated with the government in Beijing. One westerner, who had been working as a teacher for several years, refused to meet with us. He reportedly feared losing his residence permit or being harassed by the authorities.

THE HUMAN RIGHT TO PRIVACY

The Chinese constitution stipulates in Article 40 that all citizens enjoy the "freedom and privacy of correspondence".

Other national laws purport to protect the right to privacy in China. Nevertheless, numerous reports have been written describing the negative impact of China's Internet Information Services Regulations, and China employs more than 30,000 internet police to implement the regulation.

The fear of surveillance is palpable among both Tibetans and Chinese living in the Tibet Autonomous Region. Cameras are ubiquitous in public spaces such as train stations, market squares, and tourist sites. We were warned repeatedly to limit our conversations in restaurants, monasteries and even in our own hotel rooms. Individuals felt most comfortable speaking with us outdoors. Our team considered these experiences to be indicators of endemic breaches of the right to privacy. Both Tibetans and Chinese we interviewed were convinced that every private communication could potentially end up in a Public Security Bureau office, with dire consequences. By extension, the research team understood that those same communications would likely enter the Golden Shield database, soon to be supported in part by new communications technology introduced via the railway.

Everyone we met in Tibet - Tibetans, Chinese and westerners - operated on the assumption that all email and telephone communication is monitored. Even when the research team purchased local subscriber identity module (SIM) cards for their cellphones, the government vendor required personal information, including passport details, home address, hotel address, visa number, tour guide number and travel dates. Although some of the same information is required when purchasing a SIM card outside of China, the significance for privacy and personal security is quite different in Tibet, where there are no democratic checks and balances, as we might commonly understand them in Canada.

FORCED DENUNCIATIONS

While visiting one of Tibet's three major religious institutions, we encountered a young monk who spoke openly about three fellow monks who had recently been expelled from the monastery for refusing to denounce the Dalai Lama. He told us that they had been forced to return to their home village where they are kept under close surveillance. To leave their village even for a day requires prior permission from local authorities and they must report back to police upon return. Local businesses are reluctant to hire them, fearing repercussions from authorities. Once expelled, the monks will never be able to return to the monastery.

There was very little one could do to help people in this situation, the monk explained, adding that they fully understood the consequences when they refused to denounce the Dalai Lama. The level of tension in the monastery was extremely high, the monk added, and he cautioned us about speaking to anyone inside the monastery because there might be hidden microphones. When the research team interviewed representatives of western non-governmental organizations, they insisted we meet outside of their offices. One agreed to meet us in the office but quietly pointed to a microphone mounted high on the wall. His responses to our questions were qualified by repeated gestures towards the microphone. Chinese residents in Tibet also expressed concerns about privacy. During a discussion with a group of Chinese business people and one party official in a restaurant in the Chinese part of Lhasa, we were asked not to repeat or record any of the conversation, even though much of it concerned non-political issues. When the discussion turned to the railway, the group immediately got up and left the room. Both police and army are highly visible in public spaces and around monasteries. They sit on chairs, drinking tea and taking notes. Columns of police march through public spaces so regularly that they rarely receive a second glance from local people. Nevertheless, the constant atmosphere of surveillance has a distinct impact on the sense of personal security and on other human rights, particularly the human right to freedom of opinion and expression.

THE HUMAN RIGHT TO FREEDOM OF EXPRESSION

The right to freedom of opinion and expression is the flip side of the right to privacy and it is dependent in large measure on the right to receive information. From the moment we arrived in Tibet, people constantly warned us about the impact our conversations might have on our own security and on the security of those we spoke with. Everyone in Tibet engages in selfcensorship. From pilgrims to bank managers, caution and suspicion characterized all of our encounters. It was in this context that we sought to evaluate respect for freedom of expression and the impact that modern communications technology might have on it.

We were advised not to identify ourselves as representatives of a human rights organization and not to take photos of anyone we interviewed. We were told too much questioning might raise suspicion. While many people declined to engage conversations about sensitive issues, others opened up. The rationale for these leaps of faith seemed to be desperation. Conversations often ended with the request, "people outside Tibet please help us".

Numerous individuals reported that the number of internet cafés in major towns has significantly decreased in the past two or three years, particularly in Nagchu and Lhasa. There was no apparent reason. We observed mirrors facing the screens of some computers in some internet cafés, perhaps for surveillance or intimidation.

We also noted a sign in a Lhasa internet café reminding users to provide full identification to the café owner before using the internet. Access to western internet sites was intermittent. One never knew, we were told, when any particular site would be available. The Rights & Democracy site, including its China's Golden Shield report, was available each time we tested it, while others such as the Tibetan government-in-exile site, were never available. One businessperson interviewed told us that he had once mistakenly accessed a website that included the Dalai Lama's travel itinerary. A few days later, he said, officers from the Public Security Bureau visited his workplace asking who had accessed the forbidden site. Although there were no repercussions from the incident, it does provide an example of the extent to which surveillance is ubiquitous in Tibet. The research team was often asked to provide proxy server information and to urge Tibetans in western countries to post more information on websites using Chinese text because, they explained, regrettably many young Tibetans are unable to read Tibetan but they all read Chinese.

Freedom of the media is non-existent anywhere in China. State-run news services exist, but access even to these is limited in Tibet. We were unable to obtain even one copy of a Tibetan language newspaper, although we were told that such a publication exists. Tibetans in Lhasa told us not to bother because it contains no information. We were told repeatedly that radio signals from foreign news agencies such as the British Broadcasting Corporation, Voice of America and Radio Free Asia are frequently jammed. Others complained that the information provided by foreign news agencies was not reliable. Informal systems of communication operated on a fairly sophisticated level.

Primary among these, especially for older Tibetans, are the traditional tea houses where information is shared on issues ranging from politics to housing costs. Younger Tibetans were experimenting with new communication technologies in order to receive information and discuss politics. Many were beginning to use Skype, a voiceover- internet protocol that allows any individual with internet access to speak with others around the world without charge or for a very small cost. Although much of our follow-up research took place using Skype, its degree of security remains unclear and conversation was therefore limited.

THE HUMAN RIGHT TO SELF-DETERMINATION (RESPECT FOR NATIONAL SOVEREIGNTY)

In 1997, the International Commission of Jurists published a major study on human rights and the rule of law in Tibet. It concluded that Tibetans are a "people under alien subjugation, entitled under international law to the right of self-determination, by which they freely determine their political status. The Tibetan people have not yet exercised this right, which requires a free and genuine expression of their will."55 During the course of our research it became clear that inequality in power relations obliterated any pretence that Tibetans had participated in any of the decision making related to the railway.

Interview questions about land rights and community consultation were met with incomprehension. We were not able to find anyone who had been consulted about construction of the railway or about the introduction of modern communication infrastructure along its route. Even the idea that such a consultation might take place was viewed as amusing. Given this reality, there was no reason to ask about compensation or recourse mechanisms; none are available.

Clearly there have been no negotiations with nomadic herders, for example. Nor had the state or company sought any semblance of free, prior, informed consent with regard to the introduction of Nortel's communications technology across the plateau. There was a stark lack of understanding amongst communities along the railway about the implications it could have for their cultural or political rights. Most did not realize that Nortel's towers, placed approximately every 6.7 km along the railway track, were related in any way to the functioning of the railway. Nomadic families we encountered told us that the railway had dissected traditional migratory paths, that yaks feared moving through tunnels created for them beneath the rail tracks, and that the number of people able to maintain the traditional lifestyle was rapidly decreasing. Many had been forced to find work in urban centres. One man explained that he became a taxi driver and now sees his family only occasionally. He worried that Tibetans are increasingly denied access to grazing land on the plateau, including the official nature preserve through which much of the railway travels, while industrial development and infrastructure construction is promoted, and illegal mining by Chinese migrants is tolerated by authorities. This last point was later confirmed by non-governmental organizations interviewed in Lhasa.

The research team heard numerous allegations of so-called modernization programs imposed by state authorities to move people off their traditional land and into small clusters of cement block housing. We were told that the pace of settling nomadic communities in this manner, accompanied by fencing of pastures, has accelerated significantly in the past three years. The impact experienced is loss of traditional livelihoods, devastation of communities, and social disenfranchisement.

THE HUMAN RIGHT TO FREEDOM OF THOUGHT, CONSCIENCE AND RELIGION

China's constitution, in Article 46, protects freedom of religious belief, but qualifies the right by stating, "no one may make use of religion to engage in activities that disrupt public order ...". No one can visit Tibet without being struck by the deep conviction and reverence for the Buddhist faith shared by all Tibetan people. Wherever we travelled and whatever the situation, prayer wheels turned, incense burned and mantras were chanted. But religion in Tibet is often associated with its political struggle. Photos of the Dalai Lama were revealed hidden behind walls, pictures, mirrors and in the hems of clothing. Devotion to the Dalai Lama is closely associated with concern about the 11th Panchen Lama, whose whereabouts have been unknown since he was abducted by Chinese authorities in May 1995 at the age of five.

Monks and nuns spoke passionately about the current challenges confronting the traditional monastic system in Tibet: insufficient numbers of Buddhist scholars and qualified teachers; restrictions on the numbers of monks and nuns; and forced reeducation in monasteries, including forced denunciation of the Dalai Lama. Monasteries have become little more than tourist sites. Many featured signs congratulating the government for renovations, but in general the research team found they were poorly maintained, with only some sections open and suitable for tourism. Nunneries were in worse shape than monasteries. This was all the more disturbing given the incredible wealth of art contained within these buildings, much of it dating back as far as the 7th century and constituting not only a national heritage, but also a unique part of art history of value to the international community.

As our research group joined an official tour group in a monastery near Lhasa, the Chinese tour guide explained the meaning behind Buddhist statues, mandalas and scriptures as "this shows that Tibet was always part of China" or "this Tibetan king was loyal to China" and other similar statements. We were told that most tour guides now are Chinese, not Tibetan, and a number of examples were cited of Tibetan guides having been arrested for giving inappropriate responses to questions asked by clients. "Our history is being rewritten," one monk told us. "Please don't forget us."

THE HUMAN RIGHT TO DEVELOPMENT (ECONOMIC, SOCIAL AND CULTURAL RIGHTS)

In its Declaration on the Right to Development, the United Nations reaffirmed the importance of the right to self-determination as an underlying principle of development, and it preconditioned development on the elimination of human rights violations resulting from racial discrimination, foreign domination or occupation. In 2006, the UN Committee on Economic, Social and Cultural Rights released a report expressing concern that disparity in income is widening between the eastern and western provinces of China. In fact, endemic poverty amongst rural Tibetans was impossible for the research team to ignore. The vast majority live without electricity, running water, permanent housing, health care, schools, or even motorized transportation. They live as they have for centuries, walking across frozen expanses with their sheep and their yak, seemingly untouched by the incredible pace of development taking place all around them, save for the occasional solar panel. The recent construction boom, including construction of the railway, does not appear to have had positive implications for Tibetans' right to work. Infrastructure projects such as the railway require high levels of capital inputs and skilled labour. These come primarily from outside of Tibet, either from China's eastern provinces and/or from partnership with western companies.

A single construction company from Chengdu constructed almost all of the numerous bridges along the railway track, relying mostly on migrant labour from China's eastern provinces. As a result, the benefits of development accrue outside of Tibet. Media reports estimate that of the 38,000 jobs generated by construction of the railway, only 6,000 were given to Tibetans.59 We could not find figures specific to the number of workers employed to install the communications infrastructure. The practice of importing labour into Tibet is based on the claim that Tibetans themselves do not have the skills required, and therefore they can carry out only manual tasks, for the lowest pay. This would appear to contradict China's autonomy regulations, which require training and technical capacity development for minority groups in minority areas.

We observed workers doing unskilled manual labour, such as track maintenance or cement mixing for stations, platforms and access roads, along the railway route. But none of those we approached were Tibetan. We interviewed six Chinese workers who were shovelling cement into moulds. They told us that they had been recruited through an agency in Wuhan province and that they had come to Tibet because wages were good. A few hundred feet away stood a group of young Tibetan men from the area. Even as their traditional livelihoods were undermined by the railway's disruption of migratory paths, they were excluded from the temporary, unskilled work provided by the railway.

We were told numerous stories about non-existent health care in much of Tibet, and about ethnic discrimination in the health care system, where it did exist. Western development workers explained that Tibetans are increasingly the victims of scams perpetrated by Chinese pharmacists who diagnose ailments and write prescriptions, sell the medicine (often at hugely inflated prices), and even lend patients money to buy that medicine. At brothels which proliferate along the route of the railway, the sex workers we spoke to did not use condoms. Many of the truckers who form the core of their clientele come from parts of China with significant levels of HIV/AIDS. Without any facilities for testing or treatment, one can only assume that HIV infection will certainly spread beyond the railway route to villages and nomadic communities across the plateau.

Tibetans often expressed worry about the status of Tibetan language in all areas of life. Commercial signs feature Chinese script, while Tibetan script appears in much smaller size and is often rife with spelling and grammar errors. We were repeatedly told that Tibetan language "has no purpose" or "is not important" or "has no value in obtaining work". We met many Tibetans who could speak their language but could not write it. Our interviews revealed significant despair among Tibetans confronting the decision to send their children to Chinese schools. One asked, "Why would we send our children to Tibetan school when they need to speak Chinese to get a job and to live?"

THE HUMAN RIGHT TO BE FREE FROM DISCRIMINATION

Tibet today is defined by its political relationship with China. On the ground, systemic discrimination is painfully obvious. It permeated all interviews and observations during our mission. The issue is further complicated by the rapidly increasing number of Chinese migrants enticed to Tibet by the assortment of government incentives and a lack of opportunity for Tibetans in their own communities.

The site team observed many specific examples of ethnic discrimination in Tibet. For example, in industries where one might expect Tibetans to be visible, such as tourism, they are rapidly being replaced by Chinese entrepreneurs taking advantage of subsidies not available to local people. In support industries, such as taxi driving, Tibetans have been almost completely excluded. A Chinese driver told us that Chinese people are simply "harder working" than Tibetans who are "too backwards" to be driving taxis. He added that he would never have a Tibetan person in his taxi because "they smell bad". He explained that he didn't like living in Tibet, but that the money was good. He acknowledged that it is important to keep monasteries and other tourist spots in operation because they attract tourist dollars - a view we often heard expressed. We also observed indicators of discrimination at the site of a Canadian mining investment in Shadthongmon, approximately 90 km northwest of Shigatse. At the time of our mission, the mining operation consisted of 10 drilling rigs, with tents for workers and operations.

A smelter was under construction. Interviews we conducted in Shadthongmon revealed that local communities had not been consulted and had almost no idea of what all the activity was about. Our research team encountered a group of western business people in Shigatse, and a tense interaction between them, their Chinese hosts, and a member of our mission revealed that advocating for the rights of the Tibetan people would be a definite deterrent to obtaining contracts and licensing rights in the area. One official threatened to take our passports if we did not acknowledge that Tibet is part of China.

A NUN'S VIEW OF WESTERN INVESTORS

In one of our most emotional and memorable encounters, an elderly nun responded to questions about the benefits of western investment in Tibet. She said that westerners accompany their investment with good public relations. Many, she said, have knowledge of Tibetan language or Chinese language. They promise that their particular project will bring development to Tibet and to the Tibetan people. Once the project becomes operational, however, it benefits the westerners themselves and their Chinese counterparts. Tibetans remain marginalized and are used in glossy publicity photos for the project. What Tibetans actually need, according to the nun, is improved access to health care, Tibetan language education, and freedom of religion. Western investment never extends to these areas, she said.60 Subsequent announcements that the railway would be extended to Shigatse appear to lend credence to the view often expressed by Tibetans that one of the railway's primary purposes has always been to facilitate the exploitation of Tibet's mineral riches. It was the conclusion of the research team that any positive impacts of modern communications technology introduced via the railway would accrue disproportionately to Chinese government officials and entrepreneurs who form the majority of urban populations in Tibet, while for Tibetans, potential advantages would be undermined by constraints such as surveillance, poverty and inappropriate policies.

CONCLUSIONS AND RECOMMENDATIONS

Surveillance systems have legitimate military, police and civilian uses, but they also have inherent capabilities that facilitate human rights violations when unfettered by the checks and balances taken for granted in most democratic states. It is this state-of-the-art technology and communications equipment that enables the security apparatus of a single-party state to identify and arrest human rights defenders, pro-democracy campaigners, trade union organizers and political dissidents. In Tibet, the introduction of modern information and communications technology along the Gormo-Lhasa railway is part of a politically motivated, two-track development model that contributes to human rights violations. Specifically, the GSM-R technology provided by Nortel for use on the Gormo-Lhasa railway is part of China's surveillance architecture and thereby underpins the capacity of the state to monitor dissent and maintain political control in Tibet.

Nortel cannot claim that it lacked prior knowledge about China's human rights record in Tibet because such information is widely available in Canada. In selling advanced communications technology to the state, the company failed to conduct adequate due diligence, even when shareholders requested that it do so. There is no observed effort on the part of Nortel to assess the potential impact of its investment on human rights. The technology sold by Nortel to China's Ministry of Railways is integral to the modernization of China's military capacity and therefore to the consolidation of its military control in Tibet and more broadly in Central Asia. Increased militarization of the Tibetan plateau constrains the ability of Tibetans to claim their right to self-determination and violates the development guidelines issued by the Tibetan government-in-exile.

Since 2001, the Government of Canada has been aware of civil society concerns related to the Gormo- Lhasa railway and has expressed its own concerns to the Government of China about continued restrictions on freedom of expression, including those resulting from the state's use of controls and censorship.61 At the same time, however, the Government of Canada has allocated public funds for the promotion of Canadian investment interests in Tibet without assessing the potential impact that specific types of investment could have on human rights.

As a result, the government is unable to provide adequate guidance to Canadian companies wishing to invest in Tibet, and it does not condition the provision of government services on respect for human rights. It may not be possible to conduct a thorough and comprehensive impact assessment in an authoritarian or occupied state. This conclusion naturally brings forward the question of ethics in relation to any foreign investment in such situations. However, it is the view of the research team that even a limited survey provides some valuable insight into the general context for a potential investment.

This insight should enable the company and the home state to make decisions about probable future impacts on human rights and to take the appropriate steps to address them or to withdraw from the project.

Recommendations for the Company

Nortel should conduct human rights impact assessments for its investment projects in China and Tibet. The use of human rights impact assessments should become an integral component of the company's efforts to ensure corporate accountability in general but specifically when shareholders demand that such a step be taken. Nortel has taken the important and positive step of creating a position within the company to deal specifically with corporate social responsibility. The responsible employee should be encouraged to co-operate with civil society organizations that request collaboration and to engage with affected communities in a way that is relevant to the local context. Nortel should initiate an effort to develop a best practice approach to corporate accountability within the company. For example, it should launch an immediate investigation into its research and manufacturing operations in China, with special attention to the possible dual-use of the communications technology its sells and transfers to the Government of China. Nortel should also endorse international initiatives that provide a guiding framework for corporate social responsibility, for example the UN Global Compact.

For the Government of Canada

The Government of Canada should impose temporary restrictions on the export of information and communications technology to China until appropriate steps have been completed to evaluate their potential impact on human rights.

The Government of Canada should encourage a review of its export control legislation, specifically in relation to the international trade in dual-use technology. Such a review might be best undertaken in partnership with other countries, perhaps adopting a model based on the successful campaign to ban landmines, in which Canada initiated an informal process built on the strength of civil society movements and governments from the Commonwealth and La Francophonie.

The Government of Canada should take steps to ensure that its economic relationship with China does not inadvertently support violations of human rights. For example, it should link China's compliance with human rights law to continued negotiation of the Canada-China Foreign Investment Protection Agreement. The issue of state surveillance and human rights should become a regular discussion topic at all levels of the Canada-China bilateral relationship, including the Canada-China Bilateral Dialogue on Human Rights.

As part of its trade and investment promotion activities in Tibet, the Government of Canada should provide Canadian companies with the development guidelines issued by the Tibetan government-in-exile and it should withdraw trade and investment services, including export credit, when the spirit and intent of those guidelines are not respected.

5

WOMEN AND HUMAN RIGHTS IN ZAIRE

SCOPING

Formerly known as Zaire (until 1997), the DRC is the third largest country in Africa. Despite its vast potential with its abundant natural resources, the DRC is one of the poorest countries in the world. A former Belgian colony that gained independence in 1960, the DRC has not experienced development that benefits its population. DRC's successive governments have had a dismal human rights record. Under Mobutu's dictatorship, fundamental human rights guaranteed by national and international laws were violated, and the Congolese people were subjected to violence and extrajudicial executions.

The sad events of this period include the student massacre at Lubumbashi University (1990) and ethnic cleansing against Kasaians in Katanga (1991 to 1992). Then, in 1997, fighters from the Alliance of Forces for Democracy and Liberation (coalition of Congolese rebel movements fighting Mobutu's regime), with the support of the Rwandan army, overthrew Mobutu Sese Seko, ending his 30-year dictatorship and bringing Laurent-Désiré Kabila to power.

The following year, in July 1998, Kabila tried to drive out the Rwandan army, which ignited a second war in the DRC, this time involving Zimbabwe, Angola, Namibia, Chad, Libya and Burundi. Often termed "Africa's first world war," the conflict directly and indirectly caused the deaths of three to five million people, many of whom died of famine, exposure and disease. Laurent-Désiré Kabila's human rights record went from bad to worse, from his ban on party activity to summary executions of both civilians and military personnel by the Military Court. Pressure from the international community, particularly South Africa, the United States and Belgium, led to the signing of a ceasefire in 1999 in Lusaka, and the creation of the UN Mission in Congo (MONUC). Following the assassination of Laurent-Désiré Kabila in 2001, his son, Joseph Kabila, took power. A second peace agreement was signed the next year in Sun City. Rwandan and Ugandan troops formally withdrew that same year and 2003 saw the creation of a transitional government.

The Inter-Congolese Dialogue and the establishment of a transitional government led by Joseph Kabila marked the end of hostilities between the main rebel factions. However, insecurity continued to reign in both Kivus, in northern Katanga and, especially, in Ituri. MONUC's presence failed to prevent massacres and war crimes from being perpetrated, as well as the widespread use of rape as a weapon of war and the recruitment of child soldiers.

THE MINING SECTOR IN THE DRC

The DRC is extremely rich in natural resources, particularly cobalt, copper, diamonds and gold. After independence and the nationalization of businesses, particularly the Union Minière du Haut-Katanga which became the Générale des Carrières et des Mines (GECAMINES), the mining sector became the largest source of revenue for the state, and a means of rapid enrichment for the political elite. But plunging copper prices in 1980 and a number of failed attempts to rehabilitate the sector with World Bank support virtually bankrupted GECAMINES, the regime's cash cow. As a result, the DRC has been unable to pay back its US$14 billion debt.

In 1995, international financial institutions started pressuring the country to privatize its entire mining sector. The outbreak of war in 1996 delayed this process and it was not until the establishment of the transitional government that foreign companies started arriving in the DRC to negotiate contracts, often with authorities that had no legitimacy or jurisdiction to do so. Several joint venture contracts signed with Canadian and South African juniors represented the first step toward the random dismantlement of GECAMINES. With the bankruptcy of this State company, many services that had once been provided by GECAMINES, including healthcare, education and housing, were abandoned and, in many instances, never replaced by the State. The abandonment of GECAMINES concessions has put many miners out of work and into debt.

Moreover, access to natural resources, in particular mining resources, is one of the key factors that prolonged the armed conflict. Three reports by the Group of Experts on the Illegal Exploitation of Natural Resources and Other Forms of Wealth in the Congo, appointed by the UN Security Council in 2000, documented the direct connections between neighbouring countries exploiting these resources including by the rebel groups they supported, and the extreme violence perpetrated against local communities. These reports also identified elite networks that were selling these products of war on the world market through the intermediary of unscrupulous transnationals.

Today, the mining sector abounds with players and operators who took advantage of war conditions to stake their claim, often with the consent of state authorities. This sector includes many Congolese who work as diggers or traders. Artisanal diggers sell ore to Congolese traders who, in turn, sell it to transnationals or export it mostly to South Africa or China. The Lutundula Commission, a parliamentary commission created by the transitional government to investigate contracts signed during the war, concluded that the state does not benefit a great deal from this trade because many of these products are concealed by transnationals from tax authorities-with the complicity of government officials. In fact, the DRC arbitrarily granted tax exemptions to several joint ventures for a period of 15 to 30 years. It is important to keep in mind that the DRC is ravaged by endemic corruption affecting all of its institutions (it ranks 156 according to the Corruption Perceptions Index 200611).

It should also be pointed out that much of the country's natural resources, besides copper and cobalt, have not been responsibly managed for several decades. Instead, informal, artisanal or semi-industrial exploitation have prevailed until very recently. Today, much of the resource exploitation continues in the same way, without any form of regulation. Despite the large number of deposits in the DRC, natural resource management lacks transparency, depriving the country of an important means for its national development.

Many studies have shown the dangerous nature of mining in the DRC in terms of armed conflict, massive human rights violations, the destruction of the mining sector overall and the difficulty of implementing the Mining Code. These studies also denounce the lack of transparency of mining operators, for example by hiding revenue from the state in order to avoid payment of taxes.

The Lutundula Commission exposed some of the factors that led to large-scale "abusive exploitation" in the mining sector, namely the absence of a state with real authority over the entire territory, the war and the political instability in the DRC. All of these factors contributed to transforming the DRC into a "self-serve economy where diverse networks intersect and businessmen of all stripes and horizons work together to exploit copper, cobalt and related metals, diamonds, gold, cassiterite, coltan, wood, coffee..."

International financial institutions identified the restructuring of the DRC's mining sector as a priority and lent their support, in 1997, to the first stages of economic liberalization in the country after Mobutu's fall. Like all other developing countries with significant mining potential, this assistance targeted primarily the definition of a new mining code to attract foreign investment as the motor of development, according to the World Bank. Replacing the 1981 Mining Act, the new Mining Code, adopted in July 2002, provided the DRC with an investor-friendly regulatory framework.

The new code promotes "the reduction or elimination of 'tariff barriers,' such as royalties, import and export taxes or custom duties that would interfere with the flow of money.

Fiscal measures designed to benefit mining company shareholders (dividend taxes), have tended toward lowering levies that would likely paralyse or simply reduce investors' mining revenues." The role of the state is profoundly transformed under the new code. Under the 1981 code, the Executive Council had to ensure that mining activities would respond to "national development objectives."

In contrast, the new code defines the role of the state as follows: "Assuming mining development will be ensured by the private sector, the state's role is essentially limited to promoting and regulating the mining sector."

Under the previous mining code, companies could receive tax exemptions for a period of 10 years, which sometimes exceeded the lifespan of the enterprise. Under the new tax and customs system, which applies to all mining investment projects, exemptions have been eliminated. There can be deductions, however, if justified.

In addition, the new code imposes environmental protection obligations on mining rights holders, a stipulation that did not exist in the previous regulation. The Ministry of Mines is the sole responsible authority for environmental inspection and control measures. Yet the public institutions charged with ensuring that national standards in the mining sector are respected lack the necessary resources to accomplish this task. A shortage of qualified personnel and insufficient resources to pay them,20 along with the absence of synergy between the various services, has largely handicapped their ability to act.

Until January 2004, the World Bank oversaw a series of reforms in the mining sector, describing them as a driving force for rapid economic recovery. In addition to the development of the new mining code, the reforms also included launching or restructuring key companies like GECAMINES and developing a mining registry.

HUMAN RIGHTS IN PRINCIPLE

The DRC is a signatory of the main human rights treaties, namely the International Covenant on Economic, Social and

Cultural Rights (1977) and the International Covenant on Civil and Political Rights (1977). It has also ratified many international conventions, including the Convention Against Torture and Other Cruel, Inhuman or Degrading Treatment (1996), the Convention on the Elimination of all Forms of Discrimination against Women (1986), the Convention on the Rights of the Child (1990), the Rome Statute of the International Criminal Court (2002) and the African Charter of Human and Peoples Rights (1982).

In addition to these international commitments, the Democratic Republic of Congo has developed various national laws to establish mechanisms to implement and respect human rights. It is regrettable, however, that the many commitments made by the DRC remain unfulfilled and serious human rights violations experienced by its citizens on a daily basis.

RESEARCH ON THE INVESTMENT

The Société Minière du Katanga Sprl (SOMIKA) operates in the province of Katanga, one of the wealthiest copper and cobalt regions in the world. Created by deed in Lubumbashi in December 2001, this is a US$5 million investment with a US$15 million expansion plan in the works. Initially divided among three associates, the shares belonging to the two Congolese associates were sold in 2003 to VIN MART Canada, while the shares of the third associate were sold to MIN MET UAB. Since then, the capital has been divided between the two associates, with MIN MET UAB holding 90%, and VIN MART Canada the remaining 10%.

From the outset, SOMIKA has concentrated its activities on processing heterogenite, which is composed of copper and cobalt. SOMIKA does not have its own deposits and instead it processes ore that it has purchased from various regional sites. The ore is extracted by artisanal miners who are hired as day labourers by local entrepreneurs. SOMIKA also processes ore obtained from GECAMINES.

The SOMIKA site comprises two separate installations: a hydrometallurgy facility and a pyrometallurgy facility. Upon receipt of the ores, one sample per bag is sent to the laboratory for analysis. The results of these tests determine if the ore is directly exported or kept at the site for hydrometallurgical or pyro-metallurgical processing.

Liquid tailings basin. Workers are hired to collect tailings that still contain commercially valuable ores.

SOMIKA recently began operating a few mining sites in "partnership" with GECAMINES, however extraction is still carried out by artisanal miners. According to the Lutundula Commission, GECAMINES' installations and concessions have been overrun by artisanal diggers. These diggers are often children with no schooling who depend on Congolese traders and primarily foreign purchasing agents.25 The Commission adds that GECAMINES "lacks the necessary material resources for its industrial installations and consequently turns to artisanal mining overseen by expatriate companies (BAZANO, CHEMAF, SOMIKA) that profit from "abnormally lucrative collaborative" contracts.

Moreover, "the GECAMINES concessions have been overrun by uncontrolled elements of the army who also participate in artisanal mining and have caused insecurity for GECAMINES as well as diggers who are often forced to work for free for these new overlords." SOMIKA's processing plant, built against a backdrop of administrative confusion and political transition, is located in what is considered a green zone by local authorities (a non-construction zone). It is also located over a major water table eight kilometres from the city of Lubumbashi. The choice of location sparked several popular opposition movements that demanded SOMIKA's operations be relocated to a more appropriate location, to be determined after public consultations. In addition, successive ministerial decisions ordered the suspension of the company's activities, its relocation and, finally, the reopening of the plant. Despite the controversy, SOMIKA entered an expansion phase while trying to calm the population of Lubumbashi.

SOMIKA employs some 550 permanent workers and 1,500 day labourers.28 Its partner company MUKAT, a labour broker that supplies the day labourers, is present on the site of the processing plant. As part of its social programs, the company plans to purchase a pump to increase the capacity of the water distribution station in Ruashi, to open a "SOMIKA Social Works" account to support schools and orphanages, and to purchase computers for an Internet learning project for school children. In addition, the collective agreement stipulates an education allowance of US$50 for all permanent workers, regardless of the size of their family. This sum covers the education cost of one child.30 SOMIKA has also committed to rewarding, each year, the 10 children with the best grades by providing their school supplies.

ADAPTING THE METHODOLOGY TO THE CASE STUDY

All of the suggested stages of the human rights impact study were implemented from November 2005 to August 2006 by our research team, composed of representatives of four Congolese organizations and led by CRONGD. This committee was made up of members of organizations selected on the basis of their experience, interest and commitment to mining issues. To begin with, the strategy proposed was based on the cooperation and participation of all the stakeholders, with the objective of meeting representatives of the company targeted in the case study. Despite some difficulties during the research, SOMIKA did eventually agree to participate in the study.

We then proceeded with "scoping" and collecting data on the investment project. It should be noted that it was very difficult to access information. At this stage, steps were taken to adapt the methodological tool developed by Rights & Democracy to the Congolese and, more specifically, Katangan context. In January 2006, we held a training session with future researchers to familiarize them with human rights issues and the draft methodology. Note that several companies working in the mining sector, including SOMIKA, were also invited to this training session, but none responded to our call. In total, researchers from the five member organizations of the steering committee received training to conduct the necessary interviews for the project. They were deployed on three sites:

Lubumbashi, Likasi and Kolwezi. Meetings were held with the company, local government, labour and community representatives in order to develop as accurate a portrait of the situation as possible.

While the study went smoothly outside the company's sites and in area communities, the lack of cooperation from public administrators and the impossibility of obtaining access to the SOMIKA installations during the first part of this research (even though it had promised its full cooperation) made the process much more complex. It should be noted that SOMIKA had previously been involved in disputes concerning pollution of the water table with some of the civil society members on the steering committee and/or the researchers. It should also be pointed out that an international audit on the issue of water, monitored by the DRC government in collaboration with the World Bank, was initiated and implemented in this same period by SOMIKA which, according to its representatives, limited the company's availability. In fact, SOMIKA managers asked that our study be delayed until after the international audit, given the "decisive nature of this audit for the future of the company." Lastly, it is of note that during the first cycle of the study, contact was established with the "political and administrative" and customary authorities of the target sites, who responded positively to our call.

In July and August 2006, a strategy was developed to restore dialogue with SOMIKA. After a great deal of negotiation, the team managed to renew contact with the company and begin new research involving SOMIKA representatives and agents. The company also provided a series of critical documents to complete the study. SOMIKA's cooperation at this stage should be acknowledged.

OUTCOMES OF THE RESEARCH

This section uses the main international instruments ratified by the DRC, particularly the International Covenant on Civil and Political Rights, International Covenant on Economic, Social and Cultural Rights and International Labour Organization conventions. We also refer to the Constitution of the DRC in order to document certain potential impacts of SOMIKA's activities on the population of Katanga. While the research indicates that a larger number of rights should really be studied, the preliminary results presented here address primarily labour rights.

The preliminary results also reveal possible impacts on additional human rights, including the human rights to health, to water and to development. More extensive research would be required to make any conclusions about the full impact of SOMIKA's activities on these rights.

THE HUMAN RIGHT TO FAVOURABLE CONDITIONS OF WORK

As a member of the International Labour Organization (ILO), the DRC is obligated to respect the ILO Declaration on Fundamental Principles and Rights at Work. In addition, the DRC has ratified the ILO's eight core conventions on labour standards. Among these instruments ratified by the DRC are Convention 98, the Right to Organise and Bargain Collectively (1949) that provides that workers shall enjoy protection against actions of anti-union discrimination. The Convention also prohibits "any acts of interference by each other, in particular the establishment of workers' organizations under the domination of employers or employers' organizations..." Moreover, the DRC guarantees in general the respect of fundamental human rights on its territory without discrimination. The second title of the Constitution promulgated by the President of the Republic on February 18, 2006 confirms this commitment.

Fair Wages

With respect to working conditions, we observed discriminatory practices in the mining companies in general and SOMIKA in particular. During the interviews conducted with the workers, it was determined that discrimination affects primarily Congolese workers, especially in terms of wages. More specifically, for equivalent work, Congolese workers earn 10 to 20 times less than their foreign counterparts. Working conditions and social benefits are distinctly superior for expatriate workers than for nationals. With respect to access to employment, interviews with SOMIKA workers revealed that only those with ties of family or friendship with recruiters were hired. The company nevertheless insists that candidates are selected on the basis of merit and must undergo grading and skill testing.

The company recognizes two categories of Congolese workers: permanent workers and day labourers. According to Congolese labour standards, the company must ensure that the wages and social benefits of permanent workers are negotiated prior to hiring. Day labourers, however, are not hired directly by SOMIKA. Instead, SOMIKA has a number of agreements with various entrepreneurs responsible for meeting the company's constant labour needs. This arrangement provides SOMIKA with a loophole that enables it to protect itself from labour surpluses. Congolese law stipulates that any person hired by a company for more than 22 days a month automatically becomes a permanent employee under the charge of that company.

The company MUKAT is responsible for the wages and social benefits of the day labourers in SOMIKA's plant in exchange for a commission. The average wage of a day labourer is 2,000 CDF. Day labourers do not have the right to any of the benefits enjoyed by permanent workers.

SOMIKA recognizes several categories of permanent workers. They are paid in cash on a monthly basis and day labourers on a daily basis. The interviews conducted by the research team revealed that in the past, the workers received a payslip detailing remuneration and deductions.

However, since the last strike in May 2006, payslips which previously detailed deductions have been replaced by lists without details. The workers are no longer provided with any specifics concerning the final sum received. In some cases, workers are informed of their wage conditions and social benefits only once they have started to work.

A Decent Living

The DRC's transitional Constitution guarantees the human right to adequate food. This right, however, is difficult to exercise when the majority of Congolese live on less than US$1 a day.

In a context of generalized poverty, companies provide social benefits in kind, in the form of flour or various types of provisions so that their workers can meet their food needs.

Consequently, the social benefits provided by SOMIKA to its workers include lunch for day labourers and permanent workers. The workers interviewed, however, stated that these meals were inadequate both in terms of quantity and quality. Permanent workers also receive a 50-kg bag of flour each month, irrespective of family size. The size of the bag of flour increased from 25 kg to 50 kg, following the adoption of a new wage and social benefits classification. Many workers stated that their wages did not permit them to provide a steady and sufficient quantity and quality of food for their families.

While SOMIKA does not board its workers, it does provide a rental allowance. Yet the workers interviewed indicated that this allowance was insufficient to pay for decent housing.

Safe and Healthy Working Conditions

Despite significant efforts by SOMIKA to offer a healthy and safe working environment, the situation is still not perfect. The most common problems are injury, burns, accidents and poisoning. These accidents are reported to the National Social Security Institute for compensation.

Moreover, the company's management of ores and tailings (dust) and its chemical storage system, which is located very close to the dispensary, pose a danger to the work environment. The plants are virtually brand new and in excellent condition, but the company's heterogenite products are still stored in the open air. In addition, our study revealed inadequate safety equipment for the workers. According to a number of people interviewed, the company does not provide all workers with protective masks, gloves and boots.

There is also a major inequality in the working conditions of permanent workers and small operators, particularly those working on artisanal extraction sites. Artisanal diggers (estimated to number over 150,000 in 2005 in Katanga alone) include thousands of young unschooled children paid by traders or purchasing agents, a system that benefits certain mining companies. A study conducted in Katanga by the Nouvelle Dynamique Syndicale in 2004 revealed that "nearly 60,000 diggers extract heterogenites in Katanga Province. Of this number, 40% are children under 18 years of age and 5% are women who perform various tasks. The mining of cobalt and copper requires a lot of expensive equipment as well as specific individual and collective safety measures that are lacking in artisanal mining. Major companies, including EGMF, CHEMAF, SOMIKA, GROUPE BAZANO, purchase, process and market these products, which can sometimes contain uranium, derived from artisanal mining."

Research revealed that while SOMIKA does not directly hire this captive and cheap labour force, it turns a blind eye to the practices of its subcontractors. As one of the largest trading companies, SOMIKA purchases products from the artisanal mines. However, a SOMIKA representative stated in an interview with Global Witness that the company does not have any responsibility toward the diggers and that it is unaware of their working conditions.

Heterogenite products are stored in the open air, exposed to rain and wind. The storage site is located close to the dispensary. The human right to freedom of association At the national level, the right to form a free and independent union is enshrined in Article 38 of the Constitution and ensured through regular elections in the workplace. Most large mining companies in the region have union delegations elected and overseen by recognized unions, although employers commonly manipulate them.

While the collective agreement at SOMIKA specifies that the parties "agree...to not exercise any direct or indirect pressure that would prevent the expression of union freedom or individual freedom at work," research revealed that the company does not presently respect all of its obligations in terms of freedom of association and the effective recognition of the right to collective bargaining. In fact, SOMIKA has no independent union but rather a system of worker representatives from various departments. These representatives are chosen by the employer despite circulars from national authorities that ordered all companies and other establishments to organize social elections by June 30, 2005. The employer justifies its violation of this order by pointing to the political instability in the country. Meanwhile, workers cannot understand why the company does not organize elections and does not consult them about issues related to wages and the collective agreement. Negotiations take place on an ad hoc basis, at the request of the employer or worker representatives. The workers can, however, exercise their right to strike to bring the employer to the negotiating table.

THE HUMAN RIGHT TO DEVELOPMENT

Given the general mining context in the DRC, it is important to address the compatibility of the investment project targeted in the study with the full realization of the human right to development "by virtue of which every human person and all peoples are entitled to participate in, contribute to, and enjoy economic, social, cultural and political development, in which all human rights and fundamental freedoms can be fully realized." (Declaration on the Right to Development, Article 1) Since we were unable to access data on the exact economic spin-offs from this investment for the DRC, it was difficult to measure the impact of the project on the human right to development. In the DRC, the mining code and regulations also introduced clauses pertaining to the obligation of all mining companies to contribute to the development of the communities by implementing related activities.

Related activities refer to socio-economic activities that are not directly related to mining, but largely contribute to the development of the community where these ores are mined. This would include the creation of roads, hospitals, schools and so on. Given that the company's social actions are not the outcome of a concerted social policy or program in collaboration with the state or the communities, it is difficult to assess them as a contribution to the realization of the human right to development. While we can report that the company provides assistance in the form of school supplies, payment of school fees for one child per family, and the provision of mattresses, beds and medication for area health clinics, these tend to be sporadic rather than part of a long-term course of action.

According to Article 9 of the DRC's Constitution, "the State exercises permanent sovereignty, particularly over the soil, subsoil, waters and forests, Congolese airspace, rivers, lakes, and maritime space as well as over the Congolese territorial ocean and continental shelf." The state can therefore dispose of these resources as it sees fit. However, customary law, which governs village populations, establishes the village chief as the owner of the lands occupied by the peasants. This confusion has caused a great deal of conflict between the state and communities as well as between communities and mining companies.

Bolstered by this constitutional principle, the government as well as mining investors do not tend to consult affected communities when establishing mining operations in a given location. Research revealed that SOMIKA did not consult local communities when it established operations. In fact, it generated a lot of controversy between various government departments.

Several contradictory notices from local and national authorities were issued to the company, demanding the closure, relocation and reopening of the plant.

THE HUMAN RIGHT TO HEALTH

The human right to health guaranteed by the DRC is inaccessible to the majority of the population. Public hospitals are in disrepair, without medication, and sometimes without qualified personnel, while private hospitals provide consultations and treatment that are beyond the ability of most Congolese to pay. According to Article 93 of the DRC's Mining Regulation, companies must, during mining activities, provide medical care facilities with the necessary equipment, medication, vaccinations and medical personnel along with a disease and epidemic prevention program.

SOMIKA's installations include a 24-hour emergency dispensary, consisting of one examination bed, one observation bed, two chairs and two cylinders used to sterilize and store sterile medical equipment. All nonmanagerial workers are required to undergo an annual examination. However, the workers interviewed lamented the state of hygiene in the dispensary, which is located beside a depot with elevators that emit toxic gas.

Permanent workers are covered by medical insurance. Managers can therefore obtain care at the Polyclinique Le Jourdain, while non-managerial workers receive care at the Centre Ste-Bernadette, and foreign workers go to the Centre Martin Luther King.

The research also revealed that workers suffering from occupational diseases cannot obtain their medical test results. Day labourers are not covered by any health insurance, although the company does cover the cost and treatment of workplace accidents and occupational diseases.

THE HUMAN RIGHT TO WATER

In the DRC, the Régie de distribution de l'eau (REGIDESO) is the only state company that treats and distributes water. In order to fulfill its obligation to provide the population with drinking water, it must guarantee the quality and regular distribution of water.

Meanwhile, the Ministry of Tourism and the Environment is responsible for environmental protection and public sanitation. However, it lacks the resources and equipment necessary to ensure law enforcement.

The fact that SOMIKA set up its operations above the Kimilolo water table generated a lot of public concern. While SOMIKA's operations have not yet affected access to water, we can confirm that there is a hydraulic interconnection between the company's site and the water-catchment area at Kimilolo. It is important to stress that the site in question was zoned "green" by the Lubumbashi urban plan in 2000 and previously by a statute that dates back to the colonial period, in order to protect groundwater that supplies 70% of the drinking water to the city's population.

In December 2003, the Minister of Mines dispatched a team of three experts who concluded that the "fractured underlying rock shows permeability that could lead to significant infiltration" and that "if protection measures are not taken, SOMIKA will contaminate the Kimilolo waters in the long term."

The report concluded that "to date, there has been no contamination however, given that SOMIKA is a hydrometallurgical plant, the risk of contamination will persist until protective measures are put in place (see the Mining Regulation)." The Ministry also issued a series of recommendations, some of which were implemented by SOMIKA. Several groups criticized this report, however, insisting that the relocation of the installations was the only viable alternative.

A meeting was held on July 29, 2004, under the auspices of the Deputy Minister of Energy, between several levels of government and SOMIKA. In September 2004, members of parliament mandated to study the SOMIKA affair concluded that the site should be relocated. The members of parliament heard the results of an Agri-Food Research Centre (CRAA) water quality analysis that it conducted for REGIDESO.

Their study revealed the presence of metals that could be toxic, including cadmium, lead and zinc in the water, as well as an annual increase in the levels of these metals. In addition, the head of the Urbanism and Habitat division explained that the site occupied by SOMIKA is reserved for tree planting and is not zoned for industrial processing activities.

SOMIKA acquired this site before the creation of the development plan in 2000. Lastly, the head of the provincial division of the environment denied having given his approval to the project, explaining that the authorization came from Kinshasa and that a letter from the Ministry of the Environment prohibited him from managing the issue.

The new mining legislation requires companies to conduct an environmental impact assessment and produce an environmental management plan prior to commencing activities. SOMIKA established its operations before the new mining code entered into effect and therefore was not subject to this obligation.

However, in order to conform to the provisions of the new code, the company presented an environmental adjustment plan to the relevant departments of the Ministry of Mines, which received favourable responses from the authorities in charge of these departments, and built settling basins to collect the effluents and all of the cleanup water from the plant.

According to SOMIKA, these measures would prevent the infiltration of contaminated waters into the water table.

The various sources of possible contamination identified by SOMIKA include, in particular, the risk posed by liquid effluents. Wastewater from hydrometallurgical processing (approximately 80 cubic metres of effluent a day) is directed by pipeline to a quarry.

This abandoned quarry is located 1.5 km from the plant and 2.4 km from the water catchment area at the Kimilolo River. According to SOMIKA, most of the metals that could be contained in the ore are removed during the copper and cobalt extraction process. As for the acid solution, it is neutralized using caustic acid before being discharged.

A study commissioned by SOMIKA concluded that it was very unlikely that quarry waters could infiltrate toward the Kimilolo pumping station due to the impermeable nature of the subsoil (clay shale) located beneath the water table in this location. The report also concluded that the risk was even further reduced by the fact that the quarry was located in a different catchment area from the Kimilolo station area.

SOMIKA uses two types of drains to manage runoff water. Rainwater falling within the installations is collected by a brick-sided concrete drain system and directed to a 2,500 cubic metre tank. Rainwater falling outside the installations on the upper portion of the catchment area toward the SOMIKA site is redirected through a drain dug directly in the ground.

SOMIKA also addressed the risks related to solid waste. After leaching, the ore is kept in a storage area located some 100 metres from the plant.

The area is protected by geomembranes. In addition, lime is added to reduce the acidity of the waste (primarily silicon dioxide). SOMIKA states that this measure prevents infiltration into the subsoil. Note that an earthen drain, without any brick or concrete, surrounds the waste area. According to the hydrogeologist, Mr. Ilunga, this drain should be made out of concrete. Mr. Ilunga also stressed that geomembrane is never 100% effective and only has a lifespan of a few decades.

Faculty from the School of Public Health were interviewed and confirmed that many contamination risks exist. They stated that through osmosis, contaminants could, over the long term, infiltrate the water table, which would contaminate the drinking water of area residents.

The results of two new environmental studies are eagerly awaited. The first is an environmental impact assessment that was conducted by a delegation of European experts led by Boris de Handschutter. This study addresses the impact of the company's activities on the water consumed by residents.

The other is an environmental audit conducted by Canadian engineering company, SNC-LAVALIN, and commissioned by the government of the DRC and the World Bank. It is important to point out that SOMIKA has promoted access to drinking water in Kabonve through its financial support for the restoration of the Kasibisi water pumping station, which has been inactive for more than 10 years. The company's contributions to social development projects have included the purchase of a pump to enhance the capacity of the Ruashi water distribution centre.

CONCLUSIONS AND RECOMMENDATIONS

Despite the difficulties encountered throughout the study, the research team nevertheless collected information that can help to better understand the impact of SOMIKA's operations in the DRC.

First, SOMIKA's operations are located above the Kimilolo water table in Lubumbashi and several studies have established a link between the SOMIKA site and the water-catchment area at Kimilolo. This link implies a risk of potential water contamination resulting from SOMIKA's operations.

Second, research has revealed discriminatory labour practices with respect to working conditions at SOMIKA. While the team believes that it was able to test the human rights impact assessment tool, a large number of difficulties compromised completion of the study.

Furthermore, a change in the executive secretary of CRONGD, coordinator of the research group, disrupted progress of the project. Consequently, the members of the DRC team noted an "absence in managerial and scientific leadership in the implementation of this project which seriously compromised its quality and completion." As a result, it has not been possible to formulate more substantiated conclusions based on the preliminary results presented in this report. More extensive research and fact checking would be required to obtain more conclusive results.

Recommendations for the Government

It is important to raise public awareness of the Mining Code and regulations and to ensure that mining legislation is respected. It is essential that the government build the capacity of the institutions and personnel responsible for implementing its mining laws. Moreover, the government should require more transparent management of company activities, as well as of its own management of mining activities.

We therefore recommend that the international community tie any financing for extractive companies to a commitment to respect human rights, and support civil society efforts to monitor the practices of extractive companies.

For the Company

We recommend that SOMIKA ensure greater respect for the transitional Constitution in terms of fundamental rights, as well as the mining legislation and labour legislation in effect in the DRC. It is also essential that the company permit union elections to be organized. Moreover, SOMIKA should respect the Extractive Industries Transparency Initiative process for greater transparency of its activities with respect to the surrounding communities.

For Civil Society

Congolese civil society should put pressure on the government to respect the laws and regulations in the mining sector. It is important that civil society work to raise public awareness among local communities, extractive companies and political authorities of mining legislation and other international standards that promote and protect human rights. We also recommend that civil society conduct periodic studies on the activities of mining companies in the DRC and publish reports on company activities and human rights in the country. We recommend that international NGOs contribute to building the monitoring and lobbying capacity of local NGOs and to strengthen their capacity to conduct a human rights impact assessment.

CENTRO DE ESTUDIOS LEGALES Y SOCIALES (CELS)

Asociación Civil por la Igualdad y la Justicia (ACIJ) In 1993, the government of Argentina created what was then the largest privatized water concession in the world when it awarded a contract to Aguas Argentinas S.A., a consortium of European and Argentine companies, to operate the water and sewage systems in Buenos Aires and surrounding municipalities. More than seven million people lived in the concession area at the time of privatization. The population has since grown to more than twelve million.

Asociación Civil por la Igualdad y la Justicia and Centro de Estudios Legales y Sociales, two Argentine non-governmental organizations that work to promote and protect human rights, decided to investigate whether this new public-private partnership respected the human rights of the people of Buenos Aires. They selected Aguas Argentinas because of the importance of water to human existence, the size of the investment, and the fact that it was being used as a model for other water privatizations around the world. This case study is the only one in the project that focuses on one specific human right.

It draws on the International Covenant on Economic, Social and Cultural Rights and an interpretative statement on the human right to water, referred to as General Comment 15. The

General Comment provides a useful framework for monitoring state compliance with obligations to respect, protect and fulfill the human right to water. It asserts that access to water should be sufficient, safe, acceptable, accessible and affordable.

The research team studied the performance of both Aguas Argentinas and the Republic of Argentina over the life of their contract, which was terminated by the Argentine government in early 2006. During the investigation, the two main actors consulted were the company and the regulator, Ente Tripartito de Obras y Servicios Sanitarios.

It is the responsibility of the Republic of Argentina to respect, protect, and fulfill the human rights of the people within its territory and to ensure that third parties, such as Aguas Argentinas, respect human rights. The central finding of this research is that the public-private partnership had a negative impact on the ability of the people of Buenos Aires to enjoy the human right to water.

6

HUMAN RIGHTS AND WOMEN IN ARGENTINA

SCOPING

Argentina is the second largest country in South America, and has a population of about 40 million people. In the 20th century, it suffered periods of political instability, including a military coup in 1976, which ended with a return to democracy in 1983. The new democratic government struggled with a range of challenges and the country was in economic crisis when Carlos Menem, head of the Partido Justicialista, won a national election in 1989.

The Menem government rushed through a new law, Ley de Reforma del Estado, which declared a state of economic emergency in the provision of public services. The law authorized the government to privatize or liquidate public utilities and allowed it to do so by decree, without public consultation. The sweeping privatization program, which would see most of the large, state-owned enterprises sold or given to the private sector to manage, was part of a series of neo-liberal economic reforms.

The government sought to attract foreign investors, pegging the value of the Argentine peso to the United States dollar on a one-to-one basis, and negotiating a series of bilateral investment treaties with other countries that would promote and protect foreign investment.

At the time of the Menem victory, water and sewage services in Buenos Aires and certain surrounding municipalities were the responsibility of a state-owned company, Obras Sanitarias de la Nación. The government decided it would offer these services in the form of a concession to private investors. It set up, by decree, a regulatory framework in 1992 that set out the rights and obligations of the future concessionaire, the regulatory bodies and consumers. The state established a two-step bidding procedure. In the first step, bidders were assessed on how well they could meet the technical requirements of running the water and sewage concession. In the second step, bidders competed on the basis of their financial proposals, including how much of a tariff discount they would offer consumers once they took over the concession.

In December 1992, through a resolution passed by the Secretariat of Public Works, the government announced that a consortium of European and Argentine companies would be awarded the concession. The consortium included Lyonnaise des Eaux (now Suez) and Compagnie Générale des Eaux (now Veolia Water), both of France; Sociedad General de Aguas de Barcelona S.A. of Spain; Anglian Water plc (now AWG plc) of the UK; and Banco de Galicia y Buenos Aires S.A., Sociedad Comercial del Plata S.A., and Meller S.A., all of Argentina. They subsequently formed an Argentine company, Aguas Argentinas S.A., to hold and operate the concession. In April 1993, the government and the consortium signed a formal contract giving Aguas Argentinas a 30-year concession to control and manage the water and sewage systems in Buenos Aires and the surrounding area. The private company took over the public service in May 1993.

Up to this point, the public received very little information about what was happening to their water and sewage systems. It would be seven years before a public hearing was held.

At the start of the concession, more than seven million people lived in the area served by Aguas Argentinas. That number grew to more than nine million when one of the surrounding municipalities, Quilmes, was added in 1995, and is now estimated to be 12 million. When Aguas Argentinas assumed responsibility for water and sewage services in the concession area, 42% of the population was not connected to the sewage network and an estimated 30% was not connected to the water network. Those with no sewage connection used septic tanks and cesspools or dumped waste into the rivers or the ground. The majority of those without a water connection obtained their water from wells. Water and sewage services were not uniform in the concession area. The more affluent neighbourhoods were better served than those of the poor. Thus, it was the most vulnerable groups in the capital and the surrounding area that had the most to gain if the new public-private partnership lived up to its promises.

HUMAN RIGHTS IN PRINCIPLE

When the concession contract with Aguas Argentinas was signed in 1993, Argentina had already ratified most of the international human rights treaties that are in effect today. Since the 1994 constitutional reform, most of these instruments have gained constitutional status, including the International Covenant on Economic, Social and Cultural Rights.

The Committee on Economic, Social and Cultural Rights, which was created to monitor and interpret this covenant, has determined that water is a human right protected under the covenant. It has also determined that the human right to water is inextricably related to the human right to the highest attainable standard of health, to adequate housing and to adequate food, and that it must be seen in conjunction with other human rights enshrined in the International Bill of Human Rights, foremost amongst them the human right to life and human dignity.

The committee also said that when the state decides to privatize water provision services, as it did in Buenos Aires, it must still comply with its human rights obligations. Even as one of the parties to the concession agreement, the state must protect equitable access to water as a human right obligation.

The state is responsible for the functioning of the concession as a whole, including the regulatory body, the company, and itself. If the body of control created under legislation is not efficient, if it does not respond to recommendations, if it delays the resolution of important issues, or if it does not apply remedial measures to remedy breaches, the state is not complying with its obligations.

It is worth mentioning the UN Norms on the Responsibilities for Business and Other Transnational Corporations with Regard to Human Rights (the Norms). These Norms, adopted by the UN Sub-commission on the Protection and Promotion of Human Rights in 2003, set out the obligations of corporations in respecting human rights. They include sections on consumer protection and environmental protection although they remain a work in progress and are not binding on corporations.

When Argentina reformed its constitution in 1994, Article 42 was added to protect consumers. Among the consumer rights referred to in this new article was the right to adequate and truthful information. The article stated that authorities were obliged to control the quality and efficiency of public utilities and to create consumer associations. The article also said that regulations for public utilities would be established by legislation and would involve consumer associations and the relevant provinces.

Argentina is party to a significant number of treaties aimed at protecting the environment. Those worth highlighting include the Convention on Biological Diversity (Rio de Janeiro 1992), the Declaration of the United Nations Conference on the Human Environment (Stockholm 1972), and the Rio Declaration on Environment and Development (Rio de Janeiro 1992).

Many of the people affected by inadequate access to water in Buenos Aires come from neighbouring countries such as Bolivia and Peru. They have no access to justice in Argentina.

RESEARCH ON THE INVESTMENT

The Company

While Aguas Argentinas was a new company, created to take over the water and sewage concession in Greater Buenos Aires, its main European shareholders all had experience in running such systems, either in their home countries or abroad. Lyonnaise des Eaux, which later became Suez, and Compagnie Générale des Eaux, which later became part of Vivendi Universal and then Veolia Water, both had more than a century of experience in water and sewage systems in France and around the world. Between them, these two companies dominate the global private water industry. Anglian Water, part of the AWG plc, was created in 1989 when Margaret Thatcher, then the British prime minister, privatized the UK water industry. The company used its British experience to expand internationally.

It is worth noting that Suez was one of the first companies to join the Global Compact, a set of voluntary guidelines governing corporate social responsibility promoted by Kofi Annan, then the UN Secretary- General, in 2000. The guidelines cover human rights, labour standards, the environment, and the struggle against corruption.15 Two of the major shareholders in Aguas Argentinas, Suez and Sociedad General de Aguas de Barcelona, are parties to this UN initiative.

The Contract

Aguas Argentinas agreed to expand coverage of the sewage system to 95% of the population from 58% and to expand coverage of the water system to 100% from 70% by the end of the 30-year contract. The contract also stipulated that Aguas Argentinas would build sewage treatment plants so that the water in and near the concession area would no longer be contaminated by waste.

The company was to provide a series of five-year plans, or planes quinquenales. Each five-year plan was to be submitted to the government regulator, Ente Tripartito de Obras y Servicios Sanitarios, for approval at least six months before the previous five-year plan expired. As well, the company was to invest US $1.1 billion in the first five years, $731 million in the second, and $963 million in the third.

The company received a loan from the International Financial Corporation, the private sector arm of the World Bank that provides loans, equity, structured finance and risk management products, and advisory services to build the private sector in developing countries. There is no evidence that the lender attached any special conditions on the provision of service to its loans.17 The International Financial Corporation became a minority shareholder in Aguas Argentinas. Workers from the state water company who became employees of Aguas Argentinas also received 10% of its shares.

The contract set standards, modelled on those recommended by the World Health Organization, for water quality, including acceptable levels of chemical and bacterial content. The regulator was responsible for monitoring water quality and for auditing the company's procedures for quality control.18 Should water quality fall below the stated standards, Aguas Argentinas was to take all necessary steps to correct the situation, including interrupting service, warning users of what precautions to take, and providing other water supplies. The regulator was responsible for informing local authorities and the media.

The concession contract did not require the operator to conduct regular environmental impact assessments of its commercial activity. However, it did enable the regulator to impose penalties if the company's activities had a negative impact on the environment. There was, however, no clear responsibility for monitoring such impacts. This would later prove to be a problem.

Since it was signed, the contract with Aguas Argentinas was subject to many modifications, all of them approved through decrees and resolutions passed by the government executive, which had the effect of distorting most of the original objectives established for the concession. In this sense, it is worth noting that the mechanism established to modify the contract was drastically reformulated, losing its original properties.

As a result, the legal framework was no longer a single, coherent entity. Instead, regulation of the concession was subject to a collection of different, sometimes inconsistent, standards.

As part of its winning bid, Aguas Argentinas pledged to reduce the tariffs paid by users by 26.9%. While this appears to represent a genuine savings to residents of the concession area, it must be viewed against the backdrop of substantial increases in the tariff in the two years before the water and sewage systems were privatized. In 1991, tariffs were increased twice - by 25% in February and by 29% in April. The government cited rising inflation as the reason. In April 1992, an 18% goods-and-services tax was added to water bills. A few months prior to privatization, tariffs were increased a further 8%.

At the beginning of the concession, an infrastructure charge was levied on new users who required a connection and on existing users who required that their connection be improved. There was a separate tariff for actual service. The contract made payment of these tariffs by users compulsory and gave Aguas Argentinas the right to bill users for services provided at whatever tariff level was in effect in each stage of the concession period.

The contract also allowed the corporation to interrupt service if a user had not paid three consecutive bills. The company could continue collecting the fixed charge from consumers, even if water and sewage services had been cut or were not effective (for example, if water pressure was too low).

A series of mechanisms was introduced to enable the company to collect outstanding amounts. These included phone and written payment claims, extrajudicial action, interruption of the service, and legal action.

To resume service, the user had to pay the outstanding debt, plus a fee for interruption and reconnection of the service.

Over the life of the contract, tariffs were raised five times. According to Alexandre Brailowsky, Manager of Sustainable Development for Aguas Argentinas, the tariff increases were made under the regulatory framework and remained among the lowest in Latin America. These claims have been disputed by a users' commission set up by the government regulator and an economist who analyzed the performance of Aguas Argentinas.

The government of Argentina set up a regulatory framework in 1992. It detailed how various public services would be sold to the private sector and the rights and obligations of the concession holder, the regulatory bodies, and the users of the service. More detailed regulations specific to the water and sewage systems were contained in the 1992 Water Decree. In order to examine the impact of water and sewage privatization on human rights it is important to understand the roles and responsibilities of the private investor and the government in providing this essential public service.

The government created a regulator, Ente Tripartito de Obras y Servicios Sanitarios or ETOSS, to regulate the concession holder and the service provided. The regulator was to "ensure the quality of the services, the protection of community interests, and the control, inspection, and checking of compliance with valid regulations and with the contract of concession".

The board of the regulator consisted of six members representing the government executive, the province of Buenos Aires and the city of Buenos Aires. Members were appointed by the government executive for a term of six years and could be reappointed for another term. The regulator's managers were selected from the board. There were no formal procedures for their appointment and they could be removed for just cause. The regulator was financed through a 2.67% charge on the service fees collected by the company.

The regulator could impose penalties on Aguas Argentinas for non-compliance with the contract. The criteria used to determine noncompliance and the amount payable for each penalty were fixed in the concession contract. In the course of the concession, the regulator imposed a number of such penalties. The concession contract stated that penalties derived from non-compliance that directly affected the rights of users should be returned to users through discounts in their service bills. Penalties derived from delays in the improvement or the expansion of the system were to be returned to the state.

Everyone living in the concession area had a right to water and sewage services. However, in those parts of the concession where the corporation provided services, people could not use alternative water supply or waste services. The corporation was responsible for the construction, operation, and maintenance of facilities to collect and purify water. It was also responsible for sewage treatment, including the treatment of spills, and it had responsibility for the water distribution network and the sewage collection network, including underground rivers, large sewers, water pipes, and pumping stations.

The connection between the water and sanitation networks and individual homes was the responsibility of the user, who was also responsible for the construction and maintenance of sanitary facilities within their home. In connecting to the network, users had to ensure the work did not disturb the functioning of the network, cause contamination, or cause sewage or water to leak. If any of these events occurred, it was up to the user to correct the situation. These obligations were placed on users, regardless of their economic status.

Both the concession contract and the regulatory framework include an annex referring to the rights and obligations of users. There is also a regulation handbook for users, which the contract stipulated would be prepared by the corporation, but which was in the end produced by the regulator, Ente Tripartito de Obras y Servicios Sanitarios.

In 1992, Argentina signed bilateral investment treaties for the promotion and protection of investment with France, Spain and Britain. These treaties are meant to increase economic cooperation among states and to protect foreign investors. All of them were in force when Argentina signed the concession contract with Aguas Argentinas. As stated above, Argentine law gives foreign investors the same rights and obligations as national investors.

The government terminated the contract with Aguas Argentinas in March 2006, citing the presence of nitrates in the water supply. Inadequate trash collection increases health risks in the community.

ADAPTING THE METHODOLOGY TO THE CASE STUDY

Our investigation looked at both the performance of a private company in its delivery of a public service and at the performance of the state in ensuring that its people had access to one of the most basic requirements of life: water. The research guide provided by Rights & Democracy was considerably modified during the course of this research. Large parts of the guide were dropped, and other parts were expanded with questions we felt were more appropriate to our investigation. We used as our starting point the International Covenant on Economic,

Social and Cultural Rights, an international treaty that identifies a number of human rights emanating from and indispensable to an adequate standard of living. We built the framework for our research on the levels of state obligation identified in General Comment 15 on the human right to water, namely that access to water should be sufficient, safe, acceptable, accessible and affordable.

We had a large area to cover - the concession area is home to twelve million people - and six months was not long enough for the community consultation the original methodology had envisaged. In order to obtain more representative conclusions, it was necessary to reformulate questions and develop new ones that would provide statistical and objective information.

Those results enabled us to identify the primary types of problems faced by most people in the sample. We completed our information gathering by interviewing people in affected communities. These interviews supplied representative examples of common problems. Obtaining public information was difficult at times.

Many of the public bodies we consulted took a long time to give us the information we requested. Some never replied to our requests. The main actors consulted - the corporation and the regulator - were reticent when answering questions and failed to openly collaborate with the research. Both took many months to arrange meetings and neither completed the questionnaire designed by our team within a reasonable amount of time. The corporation wanted to sign a mutual collaboration agreement that would allow the company to add its comments to the final report.

The company also questioned the impartiality and credibility of the organizations conducting the research. Many of the people consulted within the office of the regulator did not want to speak on its behalf, preferring to give only their personal views. Finally, the cancellation of the Aguas Argentinas contract by the Argentine government in early 2006 introduced a new complication. People we had been communicating with were either replaced or their attention was diverted to new issues.

This research became even more relevant after the government replaced Aguas Argentinas with a state-owned body, Agua y Saneamientos Argentinos Sociedad Anónima, in which the state holds 90% of the shares (the corporation's workers hold the remaining 10%). A new legal framework to regulate water supply has been created.

We used the results of this research to promote a regulatory framework that ensures access to water for all, thus respecting this basic human right. We have also won standing as a friend of the court, amicus curiae, in the legal proceedings initiated by Aguas Argentinas against the Republic of Argentina at the International Centre for the Settlement of Investment Disputes in Washington, which is part of the World Bank.

This research was used to prepare our brief for the proceedings. The community has improvised solutions to address inadequate infrastructure resulting from poor company/ government coordination.

OUTCOMES OF THE RESEARCH

The research presented in this section is organized according to the levels of state obligation as they are identified in General Comment 15 on the human right to water. In this way we illustrate the impact of the public-private partnership, Aguas Argentinas, on the human rights of the people of Buenos Aires. The quotes following each level of obligation are taken from General Comment 15.

THE OBLIGATION TO PROVIDE EFFECTIVE REGULATION

In order to protect the human right to water, the Argentine government had an obligation to establish an effective regulatory system, which included independent monitoring, genuine public participation, and the imposition of penalties for non-compliance.

The government did create a regulatory body, Ente Tripartito de Obras y Servicios Sanitarios. However, its members were appointed by the government executive, which affected its independence. The regulator's independent oversight was further compromised by the fact that it was financed through a 2.67% charge on the service fees collected by the corporation. This meant the regulator had a conflict of interest when it considered requests for fee increases, because a fee increase would also mean more money for the regulator.

A 2003 report by the National Ombudsman, Defensor del Pueblo de la Nación, said that the regulator did not function effectively.

The report cited "delays in response to requests for reports, lack of response to recommendations, and use of the extension mechanism to delay responses to highly important matters". The same report added that "the entity has established norms straying too far from its own functions, or has ignored on many occasions the principles of the National Constitution, thus not complying with the defence of the users' rights".

The National Auditor General, Auditoría General de la Nación, also expressed reservations about how Aguas Argentinas was regulated. In a letter sent to the Ministry of the Economy in 2004, the auditor general said that the practice of the regulator of using the company's annual reports to identify breaches (a practice set out in the original concession contract) meant that the regulator was not addressing problems in a timely manner. This was especially worrisome, given that the annual reports indicated that the quality of service had deteriorated over time, according to the auditor general.

The auditor general also expressed concern about changes to the treatment of information supplied by external auditors. In the beginning, the external auditors were supposed to make recommendations, based on their findings, on how management of the service could be improved. A government resolution later prohibited the external auditors from using the information they gathered to make such recommendations.

Instead, they were to restrict themselves to reviewing the mechanisms for information gathering. The result, according to the auditor general, was that the regulator was no longer receiving the independent information it needed to regulate effectively.

The penalty regime was modified over time.

According to the regulator, the modifications led to a decrease in the amount of penalties and weakened the regulator's control. In some cases, it was cheaper for the company not to comply with the contract provisions and pay the penalty than it was to comply. The penalties imposed by the regulator up to July 2003 amounted to 40 million pesos (about US $11.8 million). The majority were for non-compliance with water quality standards or with expansion plans. The corporation paid 42.1% of these fines (about 17 million pesos or about US $5 million).

The original contract stipulated that the corporation produce a regulation handbook for users. In the end, the regulator produced the handbook. Emilio Lentini, a manager with the regulator, said the government should have created the regulations. "For the corporation, the best regulations are those that do not exist," said Mr. Lentini. "Hence, it did not do anything."

To ensure effective regulation, the state had an obligation to involve the public in both the regulatory process and the formulation and implementation of national water strategies. In an analysis of the Buenos Aires water privatization,46 economists Daniel Azpiazu and Karina Forcinito of the Facultad Latinoamericana de Ciencias Sociales (Latin American School of Social Sciences) in Buenos Aires said there was public support for the privatization because the water and sewage systems had deteriorated over a long period of time.

However, the government did not consult with civil society groups about the privatization. Clemente Etchegaray, head of the users' commission at the regulator, agreed. "When the privatization took place, users' associations had no participation whatsoever.' The regulator did not set up its users' commission until 1999. It was the formal venue for civil society participation and it made non-binding recommendations to the regulator on issues concerning users' rights.

The users' commission, however, did not have direct contact with the corporation. Dr. Alexandre Brailowsky, manager of sustainable development at Aguas Argentinas, said there was no express will on the part of the corporation or the state to exclude civil society from the process. He said the lack of participation was due to a lack of interest on the part of civil society. Civil society groups tried to participate in subsequent contract renegotiations, but met insurmountable obstacles. For instance, despite a presidential decree establishing that board meetings of regulatory entities shall be open to everyone, Poder Ciudadano, an organization that promotes transparency, reported that exceptional, albeit legal, mechanisms were used to limit the participation of civil society groups in board meetings. These included conducting meetings on an urgent basis. In order to attend a board meeting, civil society groups had to register with the regulator the day before. When board meetings were called on an urgent basis, it was difficult for groups to learn of them in time to meet the registration deadline. In the second half of 2005, one third of board meetings were held on an urgent basis.

At one point, the government set up a special commission to renegotiate the public service contract, the Comission de Renegociación.48 It was to include representatives of various sectors, including users and consumers. However, after Nestor Kirchner became president in 2003, he replaced the commission with a new body, Unidad de Renegociación y Análisis de Contratos de Servicios Públicos, which limited the participation of users. Civil society groups were not the only ones that had trouble participating in decisions about the water and sewage systems. The national ombudsman asked the government for permission to participate in contract renegotiations and was turned down.

Finally, the regulator noted that Aguas Argentinas displayed "constant reticence to comply with ETOSS' resolutions". Of the total amount of penalties applied, the corporation paid about 42%. Most of the penalties were imposed for non-compliance with water quality standards or development objectives.

THE OBLIGATION TO PROVIDE ACCESS TO WATER WITHOUT DISCRIMINATION

In the concession area, there are 700 poor neighbourhoods in which two million people live. The original contract did not contemplate any specific regulations about shared responsibilities between the state and the company in these vulnerable areas. Even though there is no restriction placed on extending water services to families without clear title to their homes, some were nevertheless deprived of access to drinking water for this reason. There is an implied violation of human rights in this situation because General Comment 15 states that, "no household should be denied the human right to water on the grounds of their housing or land status." The General Comment also asserts that the state is obliged to adopt effective measures to realize the human right to water, including "facilitating improved and sustainable access to water, particularly... in rural and deprived urban areas."

Over the course of the contract, the water and sewer networks were extended into higher income neighbourhoods primarily and at a faster rate than into poor neighbourhoods. Dr. Américo García, who speaks for a group that represents the interests of users and consumers, Unión de Usuarios y Consumidores, said an analysis indicated a correlation between service and income levels. In some of the richer, northern districts of the concession, coverage reached almost 100%, whereas in the poorer southern districts, it was as low as 10% in some areas. "Evidently this has to do with investment recovery," he said.

The company said this pattern of expansion was done for technical reasons and not because residents in the areas receiving the new services had higher purchasing power. Speaking in a personal capacity, Mr. Lentini said the company did what was most convenient, rather than what the people needed. In a report published in 2005, the International Institute for Environment and Development (IIED-Latin America), an independent, non-profit organization promoting sustainable development, criticized the regulator for being too weak to control the fulfillment of the contract and to address the needs of poor neighbourhoods.

In 2002, the company, the regulator and some municipalities set up El Programa Barrios Carenciados, a program to help expand water and sewage facilities in lower income areas.56

Under the program, a plan was developed through which residents participated in making the connection between their homes and the water and sewage networks. This plan, called the Modelo Participativo de Gestión, had mixed results (see Box on this page). Under El Programa Barrios Carenciados, another plan was developed called Plan Agua + Trabajo, but it was only implemented in one district, La Matanza.

The Obligation to Ensure Water is Affordable

Tariffs posed a particular problem to vulnerable groups during the life of the concession contract. Initially, concession tariffs were determined by variables, which included zoning and the state of the construction, and there was no special provision for disadvantaged groups. Shortly after assuming control of the network, Aguas Argentinas asked for and received a series of tariff increases, which put the cost of the service beyond the reach of the poorest users.

Problems with Access to Water

Under the Modelo Participativo de Gestión, residents of the poor neighbourhoods of Hardoy and San Jorge in the municipality of San Fernando were invited to help make connections between their homes and the water and sewage networks. The main characteristic of this program was that the residents supplied the manual labour for the extension of water supply. Aguas Argentinas would supply assistance and training and the regulator would monitor the process. Residents wishing to be connected would have to pay a fixed amount and would be charged service fees once the connections were made. This program was offered only in the poorest neighbourhoods.

Marta, a resident of Hardoy, said the training provided by the company consisted of three meetings with technical staff. Most of the people being trained were women. They were to dig ditches, transport materials and make the pipeline connections. The corporation did not supply medical services in the event that any of the residents were injured on the job. There have been many claims filed since by residents of the Hardoy neighbourhood over a lack of water pressure and poor sewage drainage, caused by improperly installed connections.

A similar situation occurred in the nearby neighbourhood of San Jorge. Susana and Brenda, both residents of San Jorge, said sewers were blocked, pipes were broken and the water coming out of household faucets had an unpleasant smell. Children in the neighbourhood suffered from stomach problems, perhaps caused by contaminated water.

Because an important part of the population could not pay the different charges related to access to water supplies, a special tariff for low-income users was introduced in 2001 by mutual agreement between the company and the regulator. The Programa de Tarifa Social had many problems with its application. An analysis of the special tariff by researchers María Cristina Cravino and Silvina Susana Sánchez noted that there was little information provided about this special tariff or about the compliance of the corporation. The researchers also noted that the tariff did not amount to a universal social policy because groups had to exert pressure in order to qualify.

The concession contract allowed Aguas Argentinas to cut water service if a user did not pay three consecutive water bills. It also allowed the company to continue charging the fixed premium for connection to the network while services were suspended and to take legal action in cases of non-payment. High tariffs and the ability of the corporation to cut services and sue for payment constitute violations of the human right to water.

In 2005, 17,372 users had their services cut because of lack of payment. Dr. Brailowsky of Aguas Argentinas said the service cuts were necessary in order to preserve public order. It was policy not to cut services for those who could not pay, only for those who would not pay, he said. However, it was up to the regulator, not the corporation, to identify those users who could not pay. The burden of payment fell unevenly on poor households. This can be considered discriminatory in human rights terms because poorer households should not be disproportionately burdened with water expenses. In their analysis of the Buenos Aires water privatization,62 economists Daniel Azpiazu and Karina Forcinito noted that between 1994 and 2001 the profits made by Aguas Argentinas were large compared with those of other companies in Argentina. They said that the company's profit on net assets was 20.3%, compared with the average profit of 3.5% made by the 200 largest firms in the country. Looking at companies that were not involved in privatization, the average profit was only 0.5% in the same period. As well, they said that amendments to the contract over time reduced corporate risk. Usually, high profits accompany high risk, but in the case of Aguas Argentinas, the risks were reduced while the profits remained high.

The Seré Neighbourhood Case

In 1994, Aguas Argentinas started to extend water supplies to the Seré neighbourhood. Residents were obliged to pay the direct cost of the work. They thought it was unfair that they should be asked to do this work. Some refused to pay to be connected and continued using water from their wells. However, the concession contract gave Aguas Argentinas the right to require that residents connect to their networks and then pay an infrastructure charge and service fees. Roberto Diaz, president of the Sociedad de Fomento del Bario de Seré (The Seré Neighbhourood Association) said the model was not well suited to the middle-class neighbourhood. Some people who were connected to the water network could not afford to pay their bills and so their service was cut off. As anger mounted, the neighbourhood created a group that went out and stopped corporation workers from cutting water services. Neighbours phoned each other to warn them when work crews were in the area.

The corporation responded by suing those who had not paid their bills, which they were allowed to do under the terms of the concession contract. In the 1997 renegotiation of the Aguas Argentinas contract, the infrastructure charge was replaced with another charge. Mr. Diaz said replacing one charge with another did not address the core problem.

The conflict continued for ten years, during which the residents continued to press their case with authorities and held public demonstrations. "When one has economic troubles, one is left aside and excluded from water," concluded Mr. Diaz.

The Obligation to make Water Available

One of the most widespread problems in the concession was a lack of water pressure. The national ombudsman estimated that almost 70% of the network suffered at some point from a low pressure. The ombudsman noted that the corporation continued to bill users, even when water pressure was low, and that despite numerous complaints, the company did not solve the problem.

The corporation said the problem with water pressure was caused by increased water consumption and also because the pipes in some neighbourhoods could not withstand high pressure. A company spokesman also said that some users were compensated with either lower tariffs or other supplies. The regulator maintained that pressure problems were mainly due to a lack of investment in the distribution system. In 2005, 37,205 complaints were filed related to low water pressure, mostly in the southern area of the concession where many of the poor neighbourhoods are located. The pressure problem was particularly acute in the summer. Community leaders in some of these areas said that on many summer days almost no water came out of household faucets. Water users filed a lawsuit against Aguas Argentinas in 2001, citing low water pressure. It has yet to be resolved.

The regulatory framework gave users the right to submit complaints to the company about service or billing and to resubmit these to the regulator, if the company did not deal with the complaint to the satisfaction of the user. The regulator said it received tens of thousands complaints over the period of the concession, although the volume diminished in later years as service improved. Users could also file complaints with the national ombudsman. Mariana Grosso, a spokesperson for the ombudsman, said the office filed a number of legal suits against the corporation. One case involving a lack of water pressure is underway. Another, involving billing, was decided in favour of the ombudsman.

According to the regulator, Aguas Argentinas breached the terms of the contract numerous times in the first five-year phase of its contract. Only 58% of the investment planned for the period in the water and sewage systems was made. Dr. Brailowsky of Aguas Argentinas said the company does not agree with these figures.

Another ongoing problem in the concession was a lack of emergency water supplies. Failure to assign explicit responsibility for emergency supplies, especially in the poorest neighbourhoods, resulted in insufficient quantity of water delivered. As well, water tanks were too small and had to be replenished several times a day.

This created hardship for families, especially women, who had to carry the water every day. To access emergency water supplies, residents must install their own connections to water tanks.

The Obligation to Provide Safe Water

The concession contract identified acceptable levels for bacteria and chemicals in the water supply, based on standards recommended by the World Health Organization. The contract also stated that if tests indicated the water quality was not acceptable, Aguas Argentinas would correct the problem, arrange for other supplies, eliminate the contaminated water, and advise users on what precautions to take. The corporation was obliged to inform the public about quality problems.

In the third year of the contract, it was found that nitrate levels in some water samples were higher than normal. These problems have persisted. Between 4% and 5% of people using water supplied by the corporation risk consuming more nitrates than are considered acceptable. In those areas of the concession where the water network had not yet reached, the state was supposed to conduct a bacteriological analysis of well water and to provide emergency supplies where there were no alternative water sources. In many cases, trucks were sent to pour water into community tanks. But often there was not enough water provided, or the community tanks were in poor condition. As well, it was difficult for women and children using improvised containers to get enough water for domestic use.

In none of the cases has a study been done to determine what effect drinking the water would have on people's health.

Only in exceptional cases did the company or the government provide information about water quality problems.

Sanitation has an enormous impact on water quality. Without an effective sanitation system, water safety can be compromised. During the contract period, the sewer system was not as extensive as the water network. The company fell short of its target for sewer coverage. Instead of covering 74% of the population, as the original contract stated, the sewage network reached 63% at the time this report was written. Dr. Brailowsky of Aguas Argentinas said the decision to put a priority on water access was a government decision and not a corporate one.

Four Hundred Poor Families without Access to Water

Villa 31 is one of the oldest shantytowns in Buenos Aires. It is in the city centre, surrounded by more affluent neighbourhoods. Neither the water nor sewer network has reached it. Yet it was not until the middle of 2005 that the neighbourhood began receiving emergency water supplies from trucks that filled community tanks three times a day.

Jesús, a community leader, said this was not a solution because there was not enough water and distribution was badly organized. As well, the tanks had no covers, leaving them open to the air. Some residents drank directly from the tanks. "Summer was a real headache," said Jesús. "To obtain water, one had to wait until 4 a.m., when there was some pressure . . . They had to make lines, rise very early and sometimes the amount of water was not enough for all."

Many residents used cesspools, which were emptied by trucks. But there were too few trucks to do the job, which meant the cesspools often overflowed. Community leaders asked the city housing authority and the regulator to fix the problem. The regulator told them that it had done a needs assessment of the neighbourhood and that work would begin in 2006. This response provoked angry demonstrations.

Aguas Argentinas said that if the residents could not pay for network construction, the city housing authorities would have to pay. However, the housing authority did not have enough money. At the moment, the work is suspended and 400 families do not have water or sewage service.

He also said that the biggest technical problem facing the sewer system was that the city had postponed infrastructure renewal for too many years. However, some critics of this approach contend that the company made this argument because it was cheaper to expand water infrastructure than it was to expand sewage infrastructure.

Poor neighbourhoods in particular were affected by the lack of sanitation facilities. In some poor areas, people with no technical expertise made their own connections to the sewer network. The result was often broken or leaking pipes. In April 2006, the Ombudsman of the City of Buenos Aires released a report denouncing the health risk posed by broken or collapsed sewer networks, particularly in poor neighbourhoods in the southern area of the city. The report said waste was entering rainwater networks and rainwater was entering sewer networks, causing the system to collapse. It warned that the resulting water pollution could spark epidemic outbreaks of cholera, hepatitis and other diseases.

The contract included construction of a wastewater treatment plant at Berazategui. In 2000, the municipality of Berazategui took legal action against Aguas Argentinas to stop water pollution in the Rio de la Plata. The municipality asked that the company remedy the environmental damage and provide compensation.

Three years later, the court ordered the corporation to build a sewage treatment plant. It has not been built. The delay in constructing sewage treatment plants led to increased contamination in the concession area and in the waters nearby.

A report by the auditor general noted that: "Aguas Argentinas transports through the sewer network, the waste liquids generated by 5,744,000 inhabitants. Out of this amount, only the waste produced by 696,000 inhabitants is finally treated; i.e. 12% of the total. The rest is presently discharged into the Rio de la Plata at the point of Berazategui, without receiving any adequate treatment to achieve the quality levels set up under the regulatory framework." A similar situation occurred in the Rio Matanza Riachuelo watershed, where sewage waste was discharged without treatment.

The original contract stipulated that 74% of waste would be treated by this time. Extending the water network at a faster rate than the sewage network caused the water table to rise in parts of the concession. The combination of higher water levels and more wastewater generated by households with access to the water system led to increased pollution of the water aquifers and increased contamination of coastal waters.

In order to ensure water will be safe to drink in the future, the state must ensure that the environment is protected today. The concession contract did not require Aguas Argentinas to conduct regular environmental impact assessments of its operations.

The corporation never detailed the environmental impact of its activities in a comprehensive manner, which would have meant identifying, mapping, and monitoring areas at risk of flooding, and identifying possible side effects its activities would have on the water system.

The regulator should have taken action and forced the company to change its approach to environmental damage. It had the power to impose penalties for water contamination.

However, there was no clear responsibility for public monitoring and management of environmental impact. Alejo Molinari, quality manager at the regulator, said that the regulator had no control over the company when it came to the environment.

The city, the province, and the state had jurisdiction, but the obligations of these overlapping authorities were not clearly defined. When Aguas Argentinas did modify its behaviour because of adverse environmental impacts, it was generally prompted to do so by judicial action. Neither the state nor the corporation took the measures needed to reduce or prevent contamination of water sources. Mr. Molinari said hospitals on the periphery of the city noticed that most of the diseases they were treating were water-borne. "What does that mean? That a huge amount of resources is spent on public health," he said. As well, in none of the cases of contaminated water was there any effort to register and report on the potential effects on people's health. "There are no records, or statistics, and there is not one official in charge of such work," said Andres Napoli, director of a non-profit organization that promotes sustainable development, Fundación Ambiente y Recursos Naturales. "It is terrible."

THE OBLIGATION TO PROVIDE INFORMATION ON WATER ISSUES

Most of the people consulted for the purposes of this report said that there had been hardly any dissemination of information relating to the negotiation process that concluded in granting the concession to Aguas Argentinas. Dr. García of the Unión de Usuarios y Consumidores said that while information on the privatization process was public, it was only relevant to people who understood the privatization process. The concession contract, the regulatory framework, and the users' handbook on regulation did not compel the parties to the contract to publish information about negotiations or modifications to the tariff structure. In fact, the users' handbook said that tariff changes would be released ten days after they were approved, limiting any public input into the process.

Even the national ombudsman had trouble getting information on changes to the contract. It took three years for the ombudsman to get access to some of these changes, despite repeated requests. A public hearing was finally held in 2000, seven years after the contract had been awarded, to discuss changes to the plan for extending and improving the water and sewage networks.

The company defended its information procedures, saying that they complied with state requirements. Dr. Brailowsky of Aguas Argentinas said financial results were made available on the company's website. They were also distributed to creditors and to people and institutions that requested the information.

On matters of water and sewage service, Aguas Argentinas had a contractual obligation to "inform users on the level of current service quality, on appropriate levels and on the programs in place to reach them". However, the amount of information provided by the corporation was insufficient to comply with this obligation.

LOMAS DE ZAMORA CASE

On January 28th 2006, a notice published in Clarín newspaper raised great public consternation.

Aguas Argentinas inserted a notice in the bills sent to residents of Lomas de Zamora in Greater Buenos Aires, that read: "In the face of an increase in water consumption due to high temperatures, well water reserves could start to be used, which can lead to findings of nitrate levels slightly higher than those allowed . . . As a precaution, it is recommended that pregnant women and babies less than six months of age avoid consumption.

They will be provided with alternative water in sufficient quantities . . ." In the area affected by the presence of high nitrate levels in the water, there are 160,000 persons who learned, through their service bills, about poor water quality.

Juan Walter, member of the Seré Neighbourhood Association denounced the fact that the company was still charging the same fees, even though the emergency supplies did not show up. He also cited many problems with the claim mechanism. "We have to phone the company but the lines are always busy. Once we reach them, they have to check if alternative water supplies are available in our area. The alternative supplies are insufficient."

The case of Lomas de Zamora raised diverse reactions from governmental bodies and users' organizations.

However, when information was requested from the regulator and the company about the effect on public health of high nitrate levels, and the measures being taken to solve this problem, it was clear there were no policies to remedy this situation.

CONCLUSIONS AND RECOMMENDATIONS

Our research found that the public-private partnership established to provide water and sanitation services to Buenos Aires and surrounding municipalities failed to comply with a number of obligations set out in General Comment 15 on the human right to water.

An effective regulatory system, which included independent monitoring, genuine public participation, and the imposition of penalties for non-compliance, was not established. Access to water was not provided without discrimination. For some groups in the concession area, water was not affordable. There were problems with water supply.

It was neither sufficient nor continuous for everyone. Water was not uniformly safe, meaning free of microorganisms, chemical substances, and radiological hazards which constitute a threat to a person's health. Finally, not enough information was provided to the public on water issues. In having a negative impact on the ability of the people of Buenos Aires to enjoy their human right to water, the publicprivate partnership did not respect and protect their human right to an adequate standard of living.

Recommendations for the Government

The existing regulatory framework should be revised to reflect human rights standards and obligations. All members of society should be guaranteed access to clean water and sanitation services, without discrimination. Priority should be given to the most vulnerable people who were excluded by the concession contract and who were not in a position to obtain access to clean water by other means. Direct and indirect charges associated with the water and sewer services must be affordable and should not compromise or endanger the exercise of other fundamental rights.

Services should not be cut when someone is unable to pay and has no adequate alternative source of water. The presence of nitrates in the water is not a new problem and it is not the only problem affecting water quality and threatening the health of the population.

There should be a guaranteed standard for water quality. The government should develop policies to prevent, treat, and control water-borne diseases. There should also be a system to register cases of water-borne disease. Without such a register, it is impossible to develop a national policy.

The government must undertake the necessary work on infrastructure to prevent contamination of water sources and the environment. Contaminated water has caused severe health problems in the The government should empty the improvised septic tanks each day, but does not.

As a result, they overflow concession area. In communities where clean water is not available, the government must guarantee regular delivery of emergency water supplies.

Congress must debate the new regulatory framework for public services. The original contract signed with the Aguas Argentina and its subsequent modifications were decided by decree, without the required participation of Congress.

Civil society must also participate in both the definition of the new regulatory framework and its application. Holding secret negotiations to decide a course and then bringing civil society in once the decision has been made, as is currently planned, does not meet the minimum standards of transparency and participation.

The government must guarantee access to information on all aspects of the design and implementation of water and sanitation services. Users have not been informed about how the service will be provided and controlled.

It is crucial that the plans for the improvement, expansion, and maintenance of water and sewer services be drawn up and executed in a transparent, participatory, and public manner. This means that the procurement process should also be transparent.

Finally, the regulator for water and sewage services, which also handles complaints, should be accessible to everyone involved, including users and civil society organizations. At the moment, there are no specific provisions governing how the existing regulator will be improved and what its role will be in the new system.

Centro de Promoción y Estudios de la Mujer Andina "Lulay" (CEPEMA)

In 1997, Doe Run Peru S.R.L. purchased a state-owned smelter complex in La Oroya, a Peruvian town in the Andes Mountains. The complex, in operation since 1922, produces copper, lead, zinc, silver, gold, and other products, which emit a mix of pollutants.1

In 2006, La Oroya was named one of the 10 most polluted areas in the world by the Blacksmith Institute, an environmental organization in New York. As part of its purchase agreement, Doe Run Peru agreed to implement an existing environmental remediation and management program (PAMA in Spanish), which included important investments in technology improvement over a ten-year period.

While the company has taken some steps to reduce some pollutants, it has not built the promised sulphuric acid plant which would significantly reduce sulphur dioxide emissions.

It has requested and received four extensions from the Peruvian government to meet the deadlines contained in the original environmental remediation and management agreement.

The Centro de Promoción y Estudios de la Mujer Andina "Lulay" (CEPEMA) is a civil society association based in Huancayo, Peru. It has worked on the human rights of women since 1995.

Its mission is to achieve recognition for women's rights, especially those of women in rural areas. This group began looking into the impact of Doe Run Peru following conversations with women in the Mantaro River valley, who felt that pollution from the smelter complex was damaging their crops and animals. Focusing on women, the group looked at the human right to health, housing and water, as well as the human right to work, to information, and to freedom of expression.

CEPEMA initially wanted to study the impacts in these rural areas, but they later decided to start by looking at the city where the company is located. This study is therefore only a first step.

The group intends to increase its scope to the Mantaro River valley at a later date. The key finding of this case study is that the operations of Doe Run Peru have had a significant impact on the ability of the people of La Oroya, especially women, to enjoy their human rights. Both the company and the state are responsible: the company, because it has not honoured the terms of its original environmental agreement, and the state, because it has not enforced that agreement nor taken other necessary steps to protect the human rights of the people of La Oroya.

7

WOMEN AND HUMAN RIGHTS IN PERU

SCOPING

The land that is now Peru was once part of the Inca Empire, which at its height also included Bolivia and Chile to the south and southeast, Ecuador to the north, and the northern part of Argentina. The Inca Empire fell to the Spanish in 1533 and Peru became an important Spanish colony because of its mineral wealth. After independence in 1821, Peru was run by a series of military leaders known as caudillos. Throughout the last century, the country had a mix of democratic and military leaders. A constitution passed in 1979 marked the transition from military to democratic government. The current constitution was adopted in 1993.

Almost one third of the population of 28 million people live in or around the capital of Lima. In spite of low unemployment according to official statistics, underemployment is high. The Human Development Report, which uses a range of economic and social indicators to gauge the health of a country and its people, placed Peru 82nd out of 177 countries in 2006.

The Peruvian economy is heavily dependent on minerals and metals. In the last decade, mineral exports have consistently accounted for the most significant portion of Peru's export revenue, averaging around 50% of total earnings. The mining sector accounts for 15% of direct foreign investment, 6% of gross domestic product and 8% of the annual growth rate in the economy. Peru is the world's second-largest producer of silver, sixth-largest producer of gold and copper, and a significant source of the world's zinc and lead. Peru has significant oil and gas reserves.

Like many of its Latin American neighbours, Peru increased the role of the state in the economy in the 1960s and 1970s. Public companies were created, private companies were expropriated, and others close to bankruptcy were bought by the state. During this period, state investment in important basic services, such as infrastructure, education and health, was almost nonexistent. State-owned companies, which enjoyed a monopoly on goods and services, eventually suffered as a result of excessive bureaucracy and inefficient leadership.

With a downturn in the world economic situation and the start of the "lost decade" in the 1980s, Peru was severely affected.

A dramatic change in economic philosophy swept the region at the end of the 1980s. In 1990, the newly elected government of Alberto Fujimori began structural reforms to curb state intervention in the economy.

The government eliminated all of the monopolistic privileges of the state companies, lifted restrictions and prohibitions on foreign trade, and established non-discriminatory treatment for foreign and national investment. It passed a Privatization Act in 1991, to encourage both national and foreign private investment; set up the Commission for the Promotion of Private Investment to identify and implement privatizations; and passed new laws to facilitate and protect private investment.

The 1993 Peruvian constitution further encouraged private investment and free markets by putting national and foreign investment on an equal footing and by requiring the state to support and defend free trade and free markets. These measures were followed by new labour legislation that encouraged more flexible labour relations, including arbitration for resolving disputes. At the same time, the government of Peru began signing international agreements designed to protect foreign investment. They included the UN International Convention for the Arbitration of Disputes, the Convention on the

Recognition and Execution of Foreign Arbitration Decisions (the New York Convention), several agreements with the World Bank, and 30 bilateral investment treaties with countries around the world. In 2006, the government of Peru signed a free trade agreement with the United States (this agreement is pending ratification by the US Congress).

Laws specific to the minerals and metals sector were also updated, beginning in the early 1990s, in order to encourage more exploration and development. The Peruvian mining sector is particularly attractive for foreign investors. There is much debate within Peru, however, as to whether mining activity brings major benefits. Full-time employment in the industry is estimated to be only about 2% of total employment in the country. Tax revenues from this sector are low because of tax breaks meant to encourage more activity and in fact, Peruvian taxes on mining are among the lowest in the world.

There is a high risk of pollution and displacement of people and because of this, mining and related activities in Peru are a source of continuing social conflict. The city of La Oroya grew up around the oldest smelting and refining centre for lead, copper, and zinc in Peru.

Cadmium, silver, gold and other metals are also processed at the complex, which was founded in 1922 by a US company called the Cerro de Pasco Copper Corporation. The city of about 40,000 people is high up in the Andes, about 180 km northeast of Lima, the capital of Peru.

The smelting complex at its heart has been and remains a significant source of pollution. The complex passed from private to public hands when it was nationalized in 1974 and placed in the control of state-owned Empresa Minera del Centro del Peru S.A. (known as Centromin Peru S.A.). In keeping with the Fujimori government's free market policies, Centromin was put up for sale in the 1990s.

There were no takers for the entire company so it was broken into smaller units. One of those units, the smelter complex at La Oroya, was renamed Metaloroya and sold to Doe Run Peru S.R.L. in 1997.

HUMAN RIGHTS IN PRINCIPLE

Peru has ratified the following human rights treaties: the International Covenant on Civil and Political Rights in 1979; the International Covenant on Economic, Social and Cultural Rights in 1978; and the Convention on the Elimination of All Forms of Discrimination Against Women in 1982.

In the framework of the Inter-American system, the American Convention on Human Rights was ratified by the government in 1978; the Inter-American Convention on the Prevention, Punishment and Eradication of Violence Against Women was ratified in 1996; and the Additional Protocol to the American Convention on Human Rights in the Area of Economic, Social and Cultural Rights was ratified in 1995.

On the national level, the Peruvian constitution says the state must "guarantee the full force of human rights." The constitution says that the standards for rights and freedoms are to be interpreted in conformity with the Universal Declaration of Human Rights and with the international instruments for their protection ratified by Peru. Thus, the state is obliged to guarantee the human right of people to a social order in which they can exercise these human rights and freedoms fully.

The Peruvian state also recognizes the human rights of women and the consequent obligation to guarantee the full enjoyment of all human rights without discrimination. It must therefore apply national policies designed specifically to promote women's human rights. Laws were enacted in the 1990s to protect and promote women's rights. In 2000, the government adopted a five-year plan to promote the advancement of women and their full participation in the social, cultural and political life of the country as well as guaranteeing equal treatment and opportunities for women and men and reducing existing gender gaps through affirmative action.

Important environmental regulations have also been adopted. They include the 1990 Environmental and Natural Resources Act, which recognized for the first time the human right to live in a healthy and ecologically balanced environment.

That human right is also recognized in the current General Environment Act. In the specific case of mining activity, the most important measures in this respect were taken in 1993 when environmental impact studies led to remediation and management programs (PAMAs) signed by all companies undertaking mineral and metallurgical operations. These programs, as we will see, play a key role in this case study.

The environmental remediation and management programs could be threatened by international trade and investment agreements. Indeed, there is a concern that some national laws protecting human rights or the environment could be trumped by foreign investment protection agreements, such as the one Peru has signed with the United States. This type of agreement prohibits the state from demanding performance requirements from investors, including those designed to protect human rights. Such agreements also expand the definition of what can be considered an expropriation and they place overpowering legal resource procedures at the disposal of companies if the state should impose requirements designed to protect human rights or the environment. Practically speaking, the state ends up with the obligation to protect the company against any kind of barrier its investment may face and that investors effectively decide which environmental remediation and management programs are to be implemented.

RESEARCH ON THE INVESTMENT

The Company

Doe Run Peru is ultimately controlled by the US based Renco Group, a private holding company that has interests in mining, metal recovery, automotive assembly and fleet support, and metals production and fabrication. The Renco Group owns the US firm, Doe Run Resources Corp., one of the largest lead producers in the world. Doe Run Resources owns a subsidiary in the Cayman Islands, which in turn owns 99.9% of Doe Run Peru.

Doe Run Resources, which has its corporate office in St. Louis, Missouri, describes itself as an international natural resource company focused on mining, smelting, recycling and fabrication, and as the third largest lead producer in the world. The US company traces its roots to the St. Joseph Lead Company, which began mining and smelting lead in the United States in the late 1800s.

It began recycling lead in the early 1990s and grew into the largest lead recycler in the world. The Renco Group bought St. Joseph Lead in 1994 and renamed it Doe Run Resources. Aside from mining and smelting, Doe Run Resources retrieves and recycles lead from batteries, telephone cables and other products. Doe Run is named as a defendant in several lawsuits in the US and in Peru alleging environmental damage by its operations.

The US company doubled in size when it bought the La Oroya complex in 1997, its first venture outside of the US. Shortly afterward, it bought a copper mine in Cobriza, in the Huancavelica region of Peru, to supply raw ore to the facility in La Oroya. The complex consists of a copper smelter, lead smelter, copper refinery, lead refinery, copper fabricating plants, zinc refinery, precious metals refinery, antimony plant, arsenic plant, coke, maintenance shops, and other support facilities. La Oroya is one of only six smelters in the western world (there are some in China) that can process concentrates containing more than one metal and with significant impurities. It is able to separate the various metals and impurities and use them to produce high quality finished metals and byproducts, such as arsenic and antimony. Because there are so few smelters capable of doing this, the company is able to charge a premium.

While Doe Run Resources owns almost all of the shares of Doe Run Peru, a small number of shares are owned by the present and former employees of Doe Run Peru and Empresa Minera del Centro del Peru S.A. (Centromin), the Peruvian government entity that owned the La Oroya complex before selling it in 1997. Both Doe Run Resources and The Renco Group say they are committed in environmental responsibility.

The Contract

When it bought the La Oroya smelting complex in 1997, Doe Run Peru paid US $120.5 million for 99.9% of the shares.

The company agreed at that time to spend about US $120 million over five years on improving electricity and water supply, improving health and safety services, and funding a variety of social programs and public service infrastructure.

The company also agreed to a pre-existing environmental remediation and management program, known by its Spanish acronym PAMA, which set the environmental responsibilities of the company and of the state over a 10-year period. Under this agreement, Centromin assumed responsibility for cleaning up certain toxic deposits, controlling liquid effluents, and for some part of required reforestation and landscaping. The value of this commitment was estimated to be about US $24.2 million.

The most significant commitment made by Doe Run Peru was to build a sulphuric acid plant at a cost of about US $90 million, in order to reduce the high emissions of sulphur dioxide into the community.

The contract limited the company's environmental responsibility to environmental damage done after 1998. Any damage done before that date would be the responsibility of the state. As well, it stated that disagreements about the contract would be resolved through arbitration by the United Nations Commission on International Trade Law, a multinational body that deals with commercial disputes.

One year after acquiring the installations, Doe Run Peru applied to have its environmental remediation and management program modified. Two more modifications were sought and obtained in 2002. In 2005, the company applied for and received an "exceptional extension" of the 2007 deadline (for four years) to build the sulphuric acid plant.

The state gave its agreement, despite protests from various groups that this would threaten full implementation of human rights. It is important to note that the environmental measures the company has agreed to under its environmental remediation and management program are designed to reduce emissions and water pollution to the maximum permissible limits under Peruvian law.

ENVIRONMENTAL COMMITMENTS MADE BY DOE RUN PERU

Construct new sulphuric acid plant

Construct a treatment plant for the copper refinery effluent

Construct an industrial wastewater treatment plant for the smelter and refinery

Improve the slag handling situation

Improve Huanchan lead and copper slag deposits

Construct an arsenic trioxide deposit

Improve the zinc ferrite disposal site

Construct domestic wastewater treatment and domestic waste disposal

Construct a monitoring station.

Some reports estimate that Doe Run Peru is responsible for 99% of all emissions of particles and sulphur dioxide to be found in the air, water, dust and earth in the area.24 These emissions expose the people living in the area to significant levels of lead, cadmium, arsenic and 11 other metals. People living in the old part of the city, La Oroya Antigua, suffer most because they are closest to the smelter complex.

In 2006, La Oroya was identified by the Blacksmith Institute, an environmental non-governmental organization based in New York, as one of the 10 most polluted areas in the world. The problem has been studied by a number of other reputable organizations that have highlighted the critical levels of environmental pollution in the area.

Since privatization, these levels appear to have increased.

The company has many supporters in La Oroya because it provides well-paid employment in a context of under-employment and because it has funded a series of social and health programs in the area. At the end of October 2005 (the last period for which figures from the company are available), Doe Run Peru said it had 779 salaried employees, 2,119 hourly employees and 1,185 casual worker. There are two unions with which the company signed contracts.

Doe Run Peru has spent money on social and health programs in La Oroya. It has funded vaccination campaigns and some health care, improved some of the education infrastructure, and spent money on training. Those residents of La Oroya who support the company point to these improvements and the jobs provided by the complex as reasons for their support.

ADAPTING THE METHODOLOGY TO THE CASE STUDY

Centro de Promoción y Estudios de la Mujer Andina "Lulay" (CEPEMA) is a civil society association situated in Huancayo, Peru, which has worked on the human rights of women since 1995. Its mission is to achieve recognition for women's rights, especially those of women in rural areas.

The association began looking into the impact of Doe Run Peru following conversations with women in the Mantaro River valley, who felt that pollution from the smelter complex was damaging their crops and animals. While the association wanted to pursue the environmental issues in these rural areas, it decided to start by looking at the city where the company is located. This study is therefore a first step.

The association intends to study the Mantaro River valley at a later date. The research team collected available reports and studies on the situation and interviewed relevant stakeholders including local people, regional governments and the company.

While all parts of the research guide supplied by Rights & Democracy could have been used in this case, the association wanted to focus on those parts of the guide that most strongly applied to the study group and to this particular foreign investment. Women are in greater contact with the polluted water and housing; their physical and reproductive health is more at risk; they lack access to basic services; and when their husbands are laid off, they are more vulnerable when rejoining the labour market.

From the perspective of the indivisibility of human rights, the study sought to investigate the link between the human right to health and other human rights that were either directly related, such as housing and water, or more indirectly related, such as the human right to work, access to information, and freedom of expression.

In the first stage of the research, the association put together a research team, defined principles and strategies, and compiled studies and research on the La Oroya situation. These studies and reports included information on the health sector, the energy and mining sectors, the international human rights agreements that Peru has ratified, and news reports published between 2004 and 2006 that were relevant to the study.

In the second stage, the research team decided which groups to contact, both in the public and private sector, and it adapted the questions for each group.

The team used graphic images instead of written questions in some instances, so as to allow for a better communication with the population. The findings were validated through participative workshops and interviews then systematized to facilitate analysis.

Doe Run Peru was an active participant in the process, facilitating meetings with company representatives, local authorities, workers, and community representatives, filling out the research questionnaire and providing additional information when necessary.

While this facilitated part of the research, it must be noted that participants in those meetings and workshops were all selected by representatives of the company.

Deep divisions within the La Oroya community over the presence of the smelter complex complicated the research. People realize that the smelter is the source of dangerous pollutants, yet some reject the conclusion that the company's activities are harming their health. Doe Run Peru is the major employer in the area and it has undertaken many community and social projects winning it the unquestioning loyalty of a considerable segment of the population. This could explain the sometimes violent reaction to those demanding more vigilance from the state in order to protect and promote the human rights of people in La Oroya, for example by placing limits on the concessions made to Doe Run Peru regarding its environmental obligations.

OUTCOMES OF THE RESEARCH

This research focussed on five basic human rights: the right to health, the right to adequate housing, the right to water, the right to favourable conditions at work, and the right to freedom of opinions and expression. The human right to water is related to the right to health and adequate housing. The research team chose to focus on these particular human rights because they felt that women with family responsibilities are most affected when these rights are not respected.

The Human Right to Health

The World Heath Organization defines the human right to health as a state of complete physical, mental and social wellbeing, and not only as the absence of medical conditions or illnesses. It requires not only appropriate and timely medical attention, but also the existence of safe water and secure sanitation, good nutrition, adequate housing, good work and environmental conditions, and access to relevant information. The concept of women's reproductive health should also be included, meaning "the capacity to regulate fertility without disagreeable or dangerous side effects, having a pregnancy and delivery without risk, and having and raising healthy children", among other things.

At a minimum, the state should monitor the availability of health services (a sufficient number of public establishments, goods, services, and health programs); their accessibility (an absence of discrimination in the distribution of services); their acceptability (culturally appropriate establishments, goods and services respectful of medical ethics); and their quality (satisfactory and appropriate establishments, goods and services from a scientific and medical point of view).

The Peruvian constitution recognizes the right to health and says that every individual has the right to enjoy a balanced environment, adequate for the development of life. State obligations with respect to health include "developing activities promoting assistance and public policies which fully guarantee the exercise of this right."

Peru has the same access to health services.

Workers with insurance, known as social security, can use social security clinics.

Those without this insurance use public hospitals, clinics and health centres supervised by the Ministry of Health, and pay set fees. There is also a third option for schoolage children, pregnant women, people with tuberculosis, and people judged to be indigent by the health centres. This group has access to Integral Health Insurance, which is free.

However, a report by the Ombudsman's Office concluded that a large number of people do not have full access to health services, despite a recent increase in the number of establishments. The poor are the most seriously affected by this unequal access.34 In the specific case of La Oroya, the health of the inhabitants is of particular concern because of the risks associated with the toxins emitted by the smelter complex. For example, the presence of lead in La Oroya has been observed for several decades.

Monitoring by the Ministry of Health in 1999 showed that the average level of lead in the blood of children between the ages of two and ten reached 33.6 micrograms per deciliter, more than three times the level deemed acceptable by the World Health Organization. The Centers for Disease Control and Prevention, a US research body, determined that when lead levels reach 45 micrograms per deciliter it constitutes a medical emergency. In its early stages, lead poisoning shows no immediate or obvious external signs, yet prolonged exposure to this toxin causes irreversible damage to the central nervous system.

Lead contamination is one of the main threats to health linked to the Doe Run Peru operations. But it is not the only one. A 2005 research project by the University of St. Louis, Missouri (where the headquarters of Doe Run Resources is located), indicates that there is "a critical level of environmental pollution caused by lead, arsenic, cadmium, and other contaminants produced by the metallurgical complex".

An assessment by the Ministry of Health found that 99.9% of girls and boys between six months and six years of age who were examined had higher than acceptable amounts of toxins in their blood. Mixed together, toxins may have an even more severe impact on health. The mix of toxins found in the blood of residents of La Oroya has not yet been studied to determine if this is indeed the case.

View of La Oroya Nueva showing Doe Run Peru's offices, company's The possibility that toxins are affecting the balance between the brain, the pituitary gland and the ovaries, thus causing a disruption in estrogen and progesterone levels and causing changes in the menstrual cycle, has been studied. Children younger than three years of age and pregnant women are more sensitive to toxins which primarily attack developing organisms, than other groups.

The implications that emissions from Doe Run Peru have for women's reproductive health must therefore be carefully examined. A study carried out in 1999 revealed that lead levels in the blood of expectant mothers in La Oroya ranged from 20 to 44 micrograms per deciliter indicating high exposure.

The American Academy of Pediatrics has said that lead levels over 25 micrograms per deciliter were unacceptable for children. Not only does lead interfere with the metabolism and cell function, it also leads to delays in development, impaired hearing, and behavioural problems. In the more serious cases it can produce convulsions and affect brain function.

Some of the toxins emanating from Doe Run can cause anemia.

Such anemia weakens the blood system and thus increases the likelihood of miscarriage in a pregnant woman. As well, toxins can be transmitted to the unborn child via the lymphatic system and to infants through breastfeeding. Pregnant women are therefore particularly vulnerable to toxic exposure. It is possible that the existing toxins are causing serious fertility problems in women.

Doe Run Peru signed an agreement in 2003 with the Ministry of Health aimed at gradually diminishing lead levels in people who were not employed by the company, but faced the greatest risk of exposure and sensitivity (mainly pregnant women and children).

Under this three-year agreement, the company would provide the premises for development of the program; cover the cost of logistics, materials, supplies, equipment, and publicity; and carry out in its laboratories the chemical analyses of samples. The Health Ministry would administer the health plan, designate specialized professionals for the program; and conduct quality control of the blood results.

In June 2006, the agreement was renewed and expanded in terms of both scope and the players involved. The government of Junín, the region in which La Oroya is located, signed the deal, which now seeks, among other things, to establish a culture of health among the inhabitants of the city and in Yauli province.

Under this new agreement, the company agreed to promote the participation of civil society groups and representatives of other sectors. It also agreed that the sample analysis would be carried out in laboratories that had national or international accreditation. The effect on health of the four main metals found in emissions from the Doe Run Peru complex Arsenic: Causes irritation of the stomach and intestine, a decrease in the production of red and white blood cells, a change in the skin and irritation of the lungs. It is possible that the presence of arsenic can intensify the development of cancer, especially in the skin, lungs or lymph nodes. High concentrations can cause miscarriages, infertility, skin disruptions, loss of immunity to infections, heart disturbances and brain damage.

Lead: Disruption in the formation of hemoglobin and anemia, increase in blood pressure, kidney damage, miscarriages and subtle abortions, disruption of the nervous system, brain damage, decreased fertility of the male through damage to the sperm, decreased learning ability in children, behaviour problems in children such as aggressivity, impulsive behaviour and hypersensitivity.

Fetuses can be contaminated by lead through the mother's placenta, damaging their nervous system and brain.

Cadmium: Damage in the lungs, which can cause death, damage to the kidneys' filtration system, diarrheas, stomach pain and vomiting, bone fractures, birth defects and possible infertility, damage to the central nervous system, damage to the immune system, psychological disorders, possible damage to the DNA or development of cancer.

Antimony: Eye, skin and lung irritation. Continuous exposure can cause lung diseases, heart problems, diarrhea, severe vomiting and stomach ulcers.

There are serious questions with the latest approach being taken by the company and by the government to resolve the problem of emissions. Instead of ending emissions, the strategy emphasizes hygiene. This transfers the responsibility for avoiding harmful exposure to the community members themselves. For those most sensitive to exposure, such as children, it simply moves them away from the installations during the day.

While it cannot be denied that these measures might reduce health risks, the central focus should have been to fully comply with the commitments contained in the initial environmental remediation and management agreement within its original timeframe. Furthermore, the Ministry of Health did not assume responsibility for implementing a holistic action plan to protect the right to health in La Oroya, despite an order to do so by the Court of Constitutional Guarantees in 2006.

Participants in the research workshops said that medical attention in La Oroya is not free, there is a lack of medication and specialized personnel, hospital supplies such as blankets and beds are in poor condition, and that poor women and their families are forced to wait for long periods before they are treated.

Some participants said they had to start waiting at 4 am in order to get access to public services. As well, if specialized care is required, patients must be transferred to facilities outside of La Oroya. Not only does this put the cost of care out of reach for poor people, it also makes it difficult to collect accurate statistics on the problems associated with toxic emissions from the Doe Run smelter complex.

Understanding the human right to health in terms of availability, accessibility, acceptability and quality, it is clear that the state not only failed to hold the company responsible for its initial obligations, it has also failed to provide the necessary measures to protect the population from the specific risks the smelter entails. It is therefore not fulfilling its obligations to respect, protect and fulfill the human right to health.

The Human Right to Adequate Housing

The human right to adequate housing should not be interpreted narrowly or restrictively, but should be understood as the right to live in a place of safety, peace and dignity. It should also be guaranteed for all persons, regardless of income.49 In Peru, the 1979 constitution eliminated certain economic, social and cultural rights such as the right to housing, but housing is protected in the International Covenant on Economic, Social and Cultural Rights which Peru has ratified. The Ministry of Housing, Construction and Sanitation is responsible for housing, urban development and sanitation. It shares responsibility for urban planning and development with regional and local governments.

Peru has a housing crisis. An estimated 41.9% of the population lives in inadequate housing and 1.2 million units need to be built or refurbished. The problem is worse in rural areas than in urban areas. One of the worst affected regions is Junín.

A report by the Ministry of Housing estimated that 22,804 more units are needed in the region. The report said that many existing homes were built with substandard materials, often informally, and without strong municipal supervision to ensure that technical standards were met. As well, because many people have built homes on land before getting legal title, hoping to get it later, sanitation and other infrastructure systems in many areas are inadequate.

Women are responsible for raising children, preparing food, cleaning and taking care of family health, and therefore they spend more time in the home and experience housing inadequacies more keenly. Too often, the facilities they need, such as public washing places, are located far from their homes necessitating long journeys and additional physical effort to fulfill their family obligations. The situation is worse for poor women and single mothers. Government programs such as Credit My Home and My Own Roof, which are meant to stimulate greater home ownership, carry minimum requirements for financial guarantees which women without a steady income or savings cannot provide.

In La Oroya, housing does not appear to be a problem for most Doe Run employees. The company offers employees free access to homes with basic water and sewage services. However, poor people generally rent units in La Oroya Antigua, the old part of town. Rents are low in this area because the homes are small, there are no water or sanitary services, and the area is close to the smelter complex.

Toxic exposure is high, not just because of the proximity to the Doe Run facilities but also because earth from the area, which is already saturated with toxins, is used to build adobe or brick homes.

The greater concentration of lead dust in the walls and floors increases health risks. While the problem is particularly severe in La Oroya Antigua, it is not exclusive to that part of the city. A 2004 study of samples taken from the floors of homes all over the city indicated that toxin levels exceeded acceptable amounts in 88% of units. In La Oroya Antigua, 100% of the samples exceeded international standards.

The state has remained silent and inactive about the condition of homes in La Oroya and the dangers faced by its inhabitants. The government has not paid people to relocate to safer homes in another area. To date, it has not elaborated or implemented a specific policy on this issue. As a result, residents lacking sufficient financial resources continue to experience precarious conditions.

THE HUMAN RIGHT TO WATER

The International Covenant on Economic, Social and Cultural Rights, which Peru has ratified, is an international agreement that specifies a number of human rights that emanate from and are indispensable for an adequate standard of living. The Committee on Economic, Social and Cultural Rights, established to monitor state compliance and to interpret the covenant, has determined that the human right to sufficient, safe, acceptable, accessible and affordable water clearly falls into the category of guarantees essential for an adequate standard of living.

La Oroya Antigua's housing facing La Oroya metallurgical complex. The Peruvian constitution says that water belongs to the state. The General Water Act states that it is the government's responsibility to develop a comprehensive water policy.59 Several ministries share the responsibility for water.

Peru has vast water resources, but unplanned settlement, industrial and mining growth, and the absence of adequate sanitation systems have led to the use of canals and rivers as dumping grounds for untreated solid wastes, toxic wastes, and dangerous chemical substances. This puts the health of the population at risk.

Water-borne disease is one of the main causes of illness and death in the country, especially among children. According to a 2003-2004 survey, 64.4% of Peruvian homes have access to clean water through the public network; 18% get their water from rivers, ditches and springs; 5.9% get water from a well; 4.1% use a public fountain; and 3.5% get water from water trucks.60 Whether water networks should be privatized is a controversial issue in Peru. It is not clear whether the population, or just investors, would benefit. To date, there have been no large water privatizations.

Water shortages and water pollution affect men and women differently, yet women are usually absent when this matter is debated and policy is decided. Research carried out by the United Nations Development Fund for Women noted that in developing countries, women are responsible for domestic and community water management and they are also the ones who obtain and carry water in rural areas.

Information on water resources in La Oroya is sketchy because most of the studies done in Peru have focused on the city of Lima. The research team was told at the workshops that La Oroya gets its water from the Tishgo River, the Cuchimachay Spring, and other springs and wells. Empresa Municipal de Servicios de Agua Potable y Alcantariado (EMSAPA), a municipal body, supplies water to people living in La Oroya Antigua. Doe Run Peru has its own water system for both drinking water and water used at the complex.

It provides employees with drinking water. In 2002, the company began a project to treat and recycle its industrial wastewater to mitigate the impact of dissolved zinc emptying into the Mantaro River. In its annual report, the company said it stopped taking water out of the Mantaro River in September 2005 after it determined that recycled water plus water from Tishgo River, the Cuchimachay Spring, and other springs and wells was sufficient. Doe Run Peru had also committed to reduce by December 2006, wastewater emissions below maximum permissible levels. The research indicated that women in La Oroya Antigua, in particular, have serious problems with water access. The majority of homes are not connected to the water system and women must draw water for cooking and cleaning from public fountains where they also wash their laundry. This affects cleanliness (laundry), personal hygiene, and food preparation for all of the family. Furthermore, the quality of the water cannot be trusted. Water pollution seems to have increased, particularly in the Yauli and Mantaro rivers. Studies indicate that both rivers are contaminated with mining residue and fecal matter. This affects the right to personal and collective health of every person in the area.

Participants in some research workshops said that the cost of their water was reasonable and that water is available throughout the day. They believe that the water they consume is not polluted. It should be noted, however, that participants were not from La Oroya Antigua, where the most severe problems are located.

Participants also affirmed that their criterion for evaluating water quality was the presence of chlorine (water chlorination, however, is only the first of many steps needed to ensure that the water is potable). They also noted that they are involved in decision-making through the Association of User Boards, which decides how water in each sector is administered. There is also a committee set up to monitor the municipal water body, but women's participation in this committee appears to be limited.

The research group was unable to find studies and information on water quality in La Oroya Nueva and La Oroya Antigua. The team sent a questionnaire to the municipal water body, but did not receive an answer.

THE HUMAN RIGHT TO FAVOURABLE CONDITIONS OF WORK

In addition to the International Covenant on Economic, Social and Cultural Rights, Peru has ratified 70 International Labour Organization conventions that set out the fundamental principles of labour rights. As well, the Peruvian constitution enshrines freedom of employment, the principle of equal treatment and equal opportunity, the right to a minimum salary, limits to the length of the workday, protection from arbitrary dismissal, the right to unionization and collective negotiation, and the right to strike. It also promotes social security. There are national laws and programs designed to implement these constitutional commitments.

In Peru, as elsewhere in Latin America in the 1990s, economic policies were reformed to encourage national and international investments. During this period, the Ministry of Labour was weakened by a reduction in staff. This limited its functions of inspection and control.

At the same time, in its eagerness to stimulate economic competitiveness, the government sought to make the labour force more "flexible" through a reduction in salaries and the elimination of some existing protections. One effect of these measures was the creation of firms dedicated to providing subcontracted labour to companies. While a legal framework was developed to regulate these services, in practice the measures put little responsibility on the company to whom workers were offering their labour. Furthermore, a new practice emerged in which subcontractors were governed by civil, rather than labour law. Limits were placed on unions and grounds were established for collective dismissals without severance pay. Workers found that these reforms limited their ability to organize for better salaries and conditions and had a negative impact on the quality of employment in the mining sector.

According to reports by the UN Economic Commission on Latin America and the Caribbean, the quality of employment is improving slowly in Peru. In 2005, less than 30% of Peruvians had employment that could be considered decent. The remaining 70% were independent workers in the informal sector, salaried workers in small businesses or agriculture, or were unemployed.

The job situation at Doe Run Peru in La Oroya must be seen in this context.

Much has been said about the positive impact of the company on the right to work. In 2006, the company had about 3,500 workers, of which 2,500 held permanent positions with recognized social benefits and rights. Information gathered at the workshops indicated that permanent employees at Doe Run Peru felt they had few labour problems. Permanent workers have a work contract and receive wages ranging from 1,500 to 5,000 soles a month (US $470 to $1,570), depending on their job. This is an attractive sum compared to the legal minimum living wage of 650 soles a month (US $204).

They also benefit from good safety procedures. With respect to their collective rights, workers reported having the freedom to join one of the unions at the complex but added that many of them do not actively participate in union activities despite being covered by the collective agreement. Women told us that they receive the same pay as men and that the company respects the law when they are pregnant or breast-feeding.

Those interviewed expressed considerable concern about subcontracted labour. They pointed, in particular, to low wages and long hours without overtime compensation. Women are disproportionately affected by the problems associated with subcontracted work.

While women constitute only 3.38% of permanent employees at Doe Run Peru, they constitute 7.13% of its subcontracted labour. They often accept poor working conditions and low pay if that is the only way they can earn money to support themselves and their family. Cases have even come to light in which women have hidden the fact that they were pregnant. Women make up the majority of workers providing industrial cleaning and laundry services. Women doing these jobs are at greater risk of being in contact with pollutants but the degree to which they qualify for labour protection and benefits remains unclear because they are subcontracted workers.

THE HUMAN RIGHT TO FREEDOM OF OPINION AND EXPRESSION

Freedom of opinion and expression is enshrined in the International Covenant on Civil and Political Rights and in the Peruvian constitution which states that every individual has the right to "freedom of information, opinion, expression and dissemination of ideas orally or in written form or pictorially, through any medium of social communication, without previous authorization, nor censure, nor any other impediment whatsoever, responsibly under the Law". Freedom of expression goes beyond the right to express ideas orally or in writing and includes the right to use any appropriate means to disseminate information. As for the collective dimension, this includes the right to receive any information without restriction, pressure, intimidation or violence. There are limitations on the exercise of this right in cases of national security, personal intimacy, and in cases expressly prohibited by law.

Access to information is a core aspect of the human right to freedom of opinion and expression since it contributes to knowledge and allows different points of view to be accepted and respected. The constitution therefore also guarantees that any person can request the information they need "without express cause" and receive it from any public entity within a legally stipulated period, for a fee which covers the cost such a request entails. The Ombudsman's Office has the responsibility of protecting constitutional and personal rights, among them the right to freedom of opinion and expression.

This human right was repeatedly violated during the Fujimori administration, when the intelligence service conducted campaigns to discredit journalists and members of opposition political parties. There continue to be cases of interference by public authorities and business leaders, who through censorship or indirect restrictions limit the collective right to receive information.

In the case of La Oroya, neither the company nor the state has taken an active role in providing information about the health risks posed by the Doe Run Peru operations. Most of the information available has been brought to light by non-governmental organizations and the Catholic Church. These groups have provided the impetus for debate on how pollution is affecting the people of the area and what should be done about it. It was only in 2003, six years after Doe Run Peru assumed control of the complex at La Oroya, that information campaigns were developed to reduce the risk of lead contamination among women and children. Although these campaigns were the result of an agreement between the company and the Ministry of Health, there is still insufficient public information about the precise impact of the toxic pollutants produced by the company on the health of the inhabitants of La Oroya.

The Cascabel historical bridge, formerly the main access that linked This absence of information creates tension between supporters of the company and those who believe it is violating basic human rights. These tensions were heightened when discussions were underway to extend the deadline by which the company would meet the requirements of its environmental remediation and management agreement. The company threatened to close its plant if the extension was not granted. This would have meant the loss of thousands of jobs and would negatively impact the local economy. In addition, the company has funded many social and health programs in the city. Those who thought its presence was beneficial viewed organizations studying the company, or those who were critical of its impact, with considerable distrust. When members of the Movement for the Health of La Oroya organized a sit-in, they were attacked.82 There have also been demonstrations by workers in support of the company.

Some people have been forced to ask the Ministry of the Interior for protection, fearing for their personal safety. An important aspect of the right to freedom of expression and opinion is the issue of access to information for citizen participation. Participation requires informed and organized citizens who manage to make their voices heard and who can transform their demands into proposals. Informed citizens can also monitor public management and act as a counterweight to political power. The General Environmental Act says that "every person has the right to participate responsibly in the decision-making process, as well as in the definition and application of policies with respect to the environment and its components adopted at all levels of government."

When Doe Run Peru applied for an extension of the deadline set in its environmental remediation and management agreement, the Ministry of Energy and Mines invited individuals, local people, and local and regional authorities to public hearings and workshops. Approximately 19,700 people participated. However, some civil society participants said the invitations were sent only to people who benefited from the company's social programs. These participants said the meetings had to be held by law and they questioned the wisdom of holding consultations on subjects that the general public did not know enough about because of the lack of information.

CONCLUSIONS AND RECOMMENDATIONS

Doe Run Peru is the main source of employment in the Junín region and has contributed to important social projects, including initiatives to prevent and/or alleviate the effects of contaminants emitted by its smelter complex. It is not, however, implementing appropriate technological responses aimed at reducing levels of contamination in La Oroya. This lack of appropriate remedy undermines the ability of people living in

La Oroya to fully enjoy their human rights. Despite widespread evidence that its smelter complex is the source of virtually all toxic emissions in La Oroya, Doe Run Peru has postponed the construction of a sulphuric acid plant that would significantly reduce sulphur dioxide emissions. The company agreed to take these measures within a 10-year period when it purchased the La Oroya complex in 1997. By not honouring its original agreement, Doe Run has allowed its operations to continue to have a negative impact on the ability of the people of La Oroya to enjoy the human right to health, to adequate housing, and to clean water. These negative impacts are experienced primarily by women.

Agreements signed by Doe Run Peru and the Ministry of Health do not address the key problem of pollution. Instead, they focus on reducing exposure to pollutants, rather than reducing the actual level of pollutants. In terms of work, women face greater risks and have less protection because of the nature of their work, doing laundry and industrial cleaning where their exposure to toxins is high. They are not able to enjoy the human right to favourable conditions of work.

The state has failed to protect the human right to health by not holding the company to the original terms of its contract, which includes the projects set out in the environmental remediation and management program. This is particularly troublesome because pregnant women and children under three years of age are most at risk from the high levels of lead in the area. The Ministry of Health has not implemented an emergency program to protect and restore the health of people in the area despite a ruling by the Court of Constitutional Guarantees directing it to do so within 30 days of that ruling.

The Ministry of Health has also failed to conduct scientific research on the impact of lead pollution, especially with regard to women's reproductive health. The ministry has not established specialized medical services, which should include oncologists and gynecologists able to deal with cases of cervical and breast cancer that may be related to pollution. The state has not addressed the problem of inadequate housing caused by the company activities, particularly in La Oroya Antigua. The inadequacies include poor access to good quality water. Women are particularly affected by this problem, given their family responsibilities. Information on environmental management and on the impact of pollution on human health is difficult and sometimes impossible to get. The safety of groups trying to publicize the problem is threatened. This limits public participation in important decisions concerning the smelter complex thereby impeding the full realization of the human right to freedom of opinion and expression.

Recommendations for the Government

The government should establish a system to monitor progressive realization of human rights in La Oroya, with a specific focus on the human rights of women. The national government has the ultimate responsibility to respect, protect and fulfill human rights. With this in mind, it must ensure that the activities conducted by Doe Run Peru do not undermine the full implementation of human rights in La Oroya.

In the area of health, the government program should include scientific research on the impact that toxic emissions from the smelter complex have on health. Special attention should be paid in this research to the human rights of women and to the protection of women's reproductive health. A strategy should be designed to improve health services in La Oroya, with a view to enhancing their availability, accessibility, acceptability and quality. A gender focus (with a reproductive health approach) should be adopted in the design of this strategy so that women enjoy all dimensions of the right to health as described in this report (presence of specialists, monitoring of health services for pregnant women, implementation of nutritional plan for disadvantaged children, etc.). A statistical health registry should be established to track female patients in La Oroya and determine the true health situation in the area.

On housing, the government should adopt a law to implement the human right to adequate housing. People living in La Oroya Antigua should be resettled in safer housing. This should be done in consultation with the community, ensuring that the people participate in the design of the resettlement program and that they fully agree with its terms and implementation. More research should be conducted on water supplies in La Oroya, with a view to determining the precise effects of Doe Run's activities on water quality, and ultimately to improve both the quality and accessibility of water, especially in La Oroya Antigua. Again, the research should place emphasis on the human rights of women. Regarding conditions of work, an investigation is needed into whether subcontractors are abiding by all the conditions needed to establish favourable conditions, especially for women.

The state should also ensure access to all relevant information about the activities of Doe Run Peru in order that informed citizen participation contributes to decision-making processes. Effective participation will also require measures to protect freedom of expression. The government should provide information and training on the effects of environmental pollution and it should implement programs designed to protect people living in the Mantaro River basin from the harmful effects of pollution.

In applying these measures, the government should ensure efficiency and interdepartmental coordination of activities carried out by the responsible state bodies. Local authorities should establish mechanisms to enhance transparency and meaningful participation by citizens in all administrative initiatives related to this matter.

For the Company

Doe Run Peru must invest responsibly in the modernization of its technology, including the construction of sulphuric acid plant. The company must ensure that the working conditions of all of its employees, including subcontracted labour, meet international labour standards. The company should support inquiries aimed at promoting human rights and not obstruct efforts by its employees or others in local communities to advocate for better respect for human rights. Doe Run Peru should not oppose any effort by the Government of Peru or civil society aimed at promoting and protecting human rights.

8

WOMEN'S AND GIRLS' RIGHT

The idea of reparation can have multiple and sophisticated meanings: legal meanings, social justice meanings, and meanings involving the will to shared historical memories and a common understanding of the contribution that victims and survivors bring to rebuilding trust.

From a women's rights perspective, reparation also corresponds to women and girls' capacity to rebuild their lives by restoring their dignity and their sense of self. To rebuild their lives not as they were prior to war or conflict, but in a way that transforms sociocultural injustices and structural inequalities that predate the conflict. Reparation is about the political meaning of caring.

Many members of the Coalition for Women's Human Rights in Conflict Situations have worked to encourage reparation for sexual military slavery. Many came to the Coalition in the middle of the 90s driven by the need to ensure gender justice at the ICTR. We came together because we needed to "look after", to end impunity for violations of women's integrity.

The shame and secrecy, the concealment, the denials and indeed the continuation of violations must also be kept in mind when addressing the need for reparation for sexual crimes in times of conflict. The pressing need to rebuild one's relationship to oneself, to one's family and to one's community obliges us to demand that the state take an active role in enabling victims to move ahead and become true citizens in their society. Indeed, reparation is also about ensuring that victims can contribute to rebuilding their society.

Caring is an active manifestation of awareness. Politically, this means a will to change, to move ahead. Peace must mean more than the mere absence of war. Caring is about what we make of what was made of us. Women and girls' right to reparation is not only about restitution, compensation, preservation of memory and access to judicial redress, it is about women playing an active role in repairing the social fabric and building afresh a just and equal society.

Women survivors, activists and jurists from Sierra Leone, South Africa, Sudan, Kenya, Rwanda, Burundi and DRC have joined their sisters of Peru, Chile, Guatemala, Colombia, India, France, Great Britain, Belgium, United States and Canada to develop the Nairobi Declaration. They have done so in the hopes that women's NGOs, women's network and human rights NGOs throughout the world will endorse this Declaration, and that committed States will seek to ensure that international, regional and national mechanisms - both judicial and non-judicial - understand the benefit and value of this Declaration and start promoting its principles.

At the International Meeting on Women's and Girls' Right to a Remedy and Reparation, held in Nairobi from 19 to 21 March 2007, women's rights advocates and activists, as well as survivors of sexual violence in situations of conflict, from Africa, Asia, Europe, Central, North and South America, issued the following Declaration:

DEEPLY CONCERNED that gender-based violence, and particularly sexual violence and violations against women and girls, are weapons of war, assuming unacceptably alarming proportions as wars, genocide and communal violence have taken their toll inside and between countries the world over within the last two decades;

BEARING IN MIND the terrible destruction brought by armed conflict, including forced participation in armed conflict, to people's physical integrity, psychological and spiritual well-being, economic security, social status, social fabric, and the gender differentiated impact on the lives and livelihoods of women and girls;

TAKING INTO CONSIDERATION the unimaginable brutality of crimes and violations committed against women and girls in conflict situations, and the disproportionate effects of these crimes and violations on women and girls, their families and their communities;

ACKNOWLEDGING that gender-based violence committed during conflict situations is the result of inequalities between women and men, girls and boys, that predated the conflict, and that this violence continues to aggravate the discrimination of women and girls in post-conflict situations;

TAKING INTO CONSIDERATION the discriminatory interpretations of culture and religion that impact negatively on the economic and political status of women and girls;

TAKING INTO CONSIDERATION that girls specifically suffer both from physical and sexual violence directed at them and from human rights violations against their parents, siblings and caregivers;

BEARING IN MIND that girls respond differently than women to grave rights violations because of less developed physical, mental and emotional responses to these experiences. Noting also that girls are victims of double discrimination based on their gender and age.

TAKING INTO CONSIDERATION the roles and contributions of women and girls in repairing the social fabric of families, communities and societies, and the potential of reparation programs to acknowledge these roles;

BEARING IN MIND advances in international criminal law that confirm gender-based crimes may amount to genocide, crimes against humanity and war crimes;

RECALLING the adoption by the UN General Assembly in October 2005 of the Basic Principles and Guidelines on the Right to a Remedy and Reparation for Victims of Gross Violations of International Human Rights Law and Serious Violations of International Humanitarian Law;

TAKING COGNIZANCE of the existence of international, regional and national judicial and non-judicial mechanisms for individual and collective, symbolic and material reparation, and the enormous challenges of catering for all victims and survivors, individually and/or collectively;

CONCERNED that initiatives and strategies at the local, national, regional and international levels to ensure justice have not been effective from the perspectives of victims and survivors of these crimes and violations in a holistic manner;

Declare as Follows:

1. That women's and girls' rights are human rights.
2. That reparation is an integral part of processes that assist society's recovery from armed conflict and that ensure history will not repeat itself; that comprehensive programmes must be established to achieve truth-telling, other forms of transitional justice, and an end to the culture of impunity.
3. That reparation must drive post-conflict transformation of socio-cultural injustices, and political and structural inequalities that shape the lives of women and girls; that reintegration and restitution by themselves are not sufficient goals of reparation, since the origins of violations of women's and girls' human rights predate the conflict situation.
4. That, in order to accurately reflect and incorporate the perspectives of victims and their advocates, the notion of "victim" must be broadly defined within the context of women's and girls' experiences and their right to reparation.
5. That the fundamental nature of the struggle against impunity demands that all reparation programmes must address the responsibility of all actors, including state actors, foreign governments and inter-governmental bodies, non-governmental actors, such as armed groups, multinational companies and individual prospectors and investors.
6. That national governments bear primary responsibility to provide remedy and reparation within an environment

that guarantees safety and human security, and that the international community shares responsibility in that process.

7. That the particular circumstances in which women and girls are made victims of crimes and human rights violations in situations of conflict require approaches specially adapted to their needs, interests and priorities, as defined by them; and that measures of access to equality (positive discrimination) are required in order to take into account the reasons and consequences of the crimes and violations committed, and in order to ensure that they are not repeated.

FURTHER ADOPT THE FOLLOWING GENERAL PRINCIPLES AND RECOMMEND that appropriate bodies at national, regional and international levels take steps to promote their widespread dissemination, acceptance and implementation.

Basic Principles Relating to Women's and Girls' Right to a Remedy and Reparation

A - Non-discrimination on the basis of sex, gender, ethnicity, race, age, political affiliation, class, marital status, sexual orientation, nationality, religion and disability.

B - All policies and measures relating to reparation must explicitly be based on the principle of non-discrimination on the basis of sex, gender, ethnicity, race, age, political affiliation, class, marital status, sexual orientation, nationality, religion and disability and affirmative measures to redress inequalities.

C - Compliance with international and regional standards on the right to a remedy and reparation, as well as with women's and girls' human rights.

D - Support of women's and girls' empowerment by taking into consideration their autonomy and participation in decision-making. Processes must empower women and girls, or those acting in the best interests of girls, to determine for themselves what forms of reparation are best suited to their situation. Processes must also overcome those aspects of customary and religious laws and practices that prevent women and girls from being in a position to make, and act on, decisions about their own lives.

E - Civil society should drive policies and practices on reparation, with governments striving for genuine partnership with civil society groups. Measures are necessary to guarantee civil society autonomy and space for the representation of women's and girls' voices in all their diversity.

F - Access to Justice. Ending impunity through legal proceedings for crimes against women and girls is a crucial component of reparation policies and a requirement under international law.

ACCESS TO REPARATION

A - In order to achieve reparation measures sensitive to gender, age, cultural diversity and human rights, decision-making about reparation must include victims as full participants, while ensuring just representation of women and girls in all their diversity. Governments and other actors must ensure that women and girls are adequately informed of their rights.

B - Full participation of women and girls victims should be guaranteed in every stage of the reparation process, i.e. design, implementation, evaluation, and decision-making.

C - Structural and administrative obstacles in all forms of justice, which impede or deny women's and girls' access to effective and enforceable remedies, must be addressed to ensure gender-just reparation programmes.

D - Male and female staff who are sensitive to specific issues related to gender, age, cultural diversity and human rights, and who are committed to international and regional human rights standards must be involved at every stage of the reparation process.

E - Practices and procedures for obtaining reparation must be sensitive to gender, age, cultural diversity and human rights, and must take into account women's and girls' specific circumstances, as well as their dignity, privacy and safety.

F - Indicators that are sensitive to gender, age, cultural diversity and human rights must be used to monitor and evaluate the implementation of reparation measures.

KEY ASPECTS OF REPARATION FOR WOMEN AND GIRLS

A - Women and girls have a right to a remedy and reparation under international law. They have a right to benefit from reparation programs designed to directly benefit the victims, by providing restitution, compensation, reintegration, and other key measures and initiatives under transitional justice that, if crafted with gender-aware forethought and care, could have reparative effects, namely reinsertion, satisfaction and the guarantee of non-recurrence.

B - Governments should not undertake development instead of reparation. All post-conflict societies need both reconstruction and development, of which reparation programmes are an integral part. Victims, especially women and girls, face particular obstacles in seizing the opportunities provided by development, thus risking their continued exclusion. In reparation, reconstruction, and development programmes, affirmative action measures are necessary to respond to the needs and experiences of women and girls victims.

C - Truth-telling requires the identification of gross and systematic crimes and human rights violations committed against women and girls. It is critical that such abuses are named and recognized in order to raise awareness about these crimes and violations, to positively influence a more holistic strategy for reparation and measures that support reparation, and to help build a shared memory and history. Currently, there is a significant lack of naming and addressing such abuses in past reparation programs and efforts, much to the detriment of surviving victims.

D - Reconciliation is an important goal of peace and reparation processes, which can only be achieved with women and girls victims' full participation, while respecting their right to dignity, privacy, safety and security.

E - Just, effective and prompt reparation measures should be proportional to the gravity of the crimes, violations and harm suffered. In the case of victims of sexual violence and other gender-based crimes, governments should take into account the multi-dimensional and long-term consequences of these crimes to women and girls, their families and their communities, requiring specialized, integrated, and multidisciplinary approaches.

F - Governments must consider all forms of reparation available at individual and community levels. These include, but are not limited to, restitution, compensation and reintegration. Invariably, a combination of these forms of reparation will be required to adequately address violations of women's and girls' human rights.

G - Reparation processes must allow women and girls to come forward when they are ready. They should not be excluded if they fail to do so within a prescribed time period. Support structures are needed to assist women and girls in the process of speaking out and claiming reparation.

H - Reparation must go above and beyond the immediate reasons and consequences of the crimes and violations; they must aim to address the political and structural inequalities that negatively shape women's and girls' lives.

9

WOMEN RIGHTS IN ASIA PACIFIC

INTRODUCTION

Unless women are involved in the decision and policymaking process at all levels of the state, changes in women's political and to some extent social and economic status will continue to be marginal. Since the early part of 1990s, particularly after the Beijing Conference on Women and Development and the Second United Nations Conference on Human Settlements (Habitat II), women's role in local, provincial and national political processes has been discussed throughout the region. Moreover, the Beijing+5 and Istanbul+5 reviews identified women and politics and women and local government as important crosscutting issues. Local government is the level of government where women can enter political life with relative ease, as the costs of mounting election campaigns are relatively low and issues at the local level tend to motivate women to enter politics. Moreover, local governments are good training grounds for women politicians who want to reach higher levels of elected or appointed office in government.

Moreover, women in politics and in decision-making positions in governments and legislative bodies provide opportunities for "transformative leadership" by redefining political priorities, placing new items on the political agenda that reflect and address women's gender-specific concerns, values and experiences and provide new perspectives on mainstream issues.

While some countries in Asia and the Pacific have taken positive actions to promote the participation of women in local government and decision-making, nowhere in the region are women proportionately represented in local government, political parties or civil society organizations unless these are women oriented in nature. Even in countries where opportunities for women's representation and participation exist, women have not been able to effectively utilize these. The reasons are multiple: patriarchal social systems, social and cultural prejudices, financial dependence of women, lack of media support and exposure to political processes and limited training opportunities for women. Women may also be discouraged from seeking political office by discriminatory attitudes and practices, family and child-care responsibilities, the high cost of seeking and holding office and by the criminalization of politics.

ASIA-PACIFIC SUMMIT OF WOMEN MAYORS AND COUNCILLORS

To promote the participation and representation of women in local government the United Nations Economic and Social Commission for Asia and the Pacific (UN ESCAP) has been implementing the multi-phase Advancement of Women in Urban Local Government project since 1999. The first phase of the project culminated in the first-ever Asia-Pacific Summit of Women Mayors and Councillors, which was held at Phitsanulok, Thailand, from 19 to 22 June 2001. The discussions at the Summit were based on a comparative analysis of the reports on the "State of Women in Local Government" prepared in the 14 participating countries. Each report contained:

- An in depth qualitative analysis of issues in women's participation and representation in government.
- Relevant gender statistics.
- Steps already undertaken by governmental and non-governmental organizations and political parties to increase the roles of women in local government and in gender sensitizing of local governments.

- Further steps needed to promote the role of women in local government.
- Profiles of successful elected and appointed women in local government, emphasizing the factors that contributed to their success, as well as, hindrances and difficulties they faced.

The Summit was attended by over 200 participants from 24 countries in the Asia-Pacific region. More than half of the participants were women elected or appointed to local government. In addition, high-level government officials, NGOs, and academics participated.

The Phitsanulok Summit provided a forum to exchange experience, to review and discuss issues, strategies and approaches in promoting women's participation and representation in local government, as well as, in depth discussions on good governance, gender budgeting, and transformative leadership. The Summit culminated in the adoption of the Phitsanulok Declaration on the Advancement of Women in Local Government, which calls for:

- The preparation and implementation of national action plans on advancement of women in local government
- The convening of national summits of women mayors and councillors
- Establishment of national networks and resource facilities on women in local government, linked to a regional network and resource facility.

Advancement of Women in Urban Local Government: Phase II

In the second phase of the project, UN ESCAP plans to assist selected countries in implementing the country-level actions outlined in the Phitsanulok Declaration. The objectives of Phase II of the project are to:

- Increase the awareness of the transformative role women can play in local government and the issues and constraints they face while working with and leading local governments.

- Assist women's organizations and women in local government to develop sustainable and self-financing National Resource Facilities that would promote and coordinate actions to increase the participation and representation of women in urban local governments.

These objectives are to be realized through the organization and convening of National Summits of Women Mayors and Councillors and the implementation of National Action Plans on the Advancement of Women in Urban Local Government.

The Need for National Summits

The Phitsanulok Summit was a milestone in promoting increased representation and participation of women in local government. Considerable momentum was built at the Summit, which now needs to be converted into actions at the country level. However, although over 200 women mayors and councillors, members of parliament, activists and academics participated at the Summit, by its very nature the Summit was exclusive. Given the total number of women in local government in the Asia-Pacific region, a small number of them participated at the Summit. Moreover the working language of the Phitsanulok Summit was English, which also restricted participation to those who were relatively fluent in English.

While the Phitsanulok Summit generated considerable media attention, this was relatively short-lived. Sustained awareness of the issues of women in local government at the country-level could not be created due to the regional nature of the event.

While considerable cross-fertilization of ideas took place and experiences and strategies were explored and exchanged, due to the regional nature of Summit, detailed attention to country-specific situations, issues and strategies was limited. With twenty-four countries participating, issues and strategies were aggregated to arrive at common positions.

To noticeably improve the situation of women in local government, sustained efforts are needed at the country-level. These include preparation and implementation of national action plans, establishing networks and resource facilities for women in local government, providing regular training for women in local government and identifying resources at the local level that will contribute to addressing the issues of women in local government. To initiate these actions in a participatory manner the Phitsanulok Declaration calls for the organization of national summits, "(i) to develop country-level strategies, (ii) to establish country-level networks of women in local government, (iii) to identify country-level training providers and training needs, (iv) to advocate policy and legislative changes and (v) to mobilize the required human and financial resources." The national summits will also raise awareness of the issues of women in local government at the country-level.

Objectives of the Guidelines

The objective of these guidelines is to assist governmental and non-governmental organizations to plan, organize and convene national summits of women mayors and councillors.

The process outlined in these guidelines emphasizes inclusiveness and broad participation. It consists of a number of phases:

- Establishment of a committee of initiators
- Convening of a preparatory meeting
- Preparation of background documentation and discussion papers for the National Summit
- Convening of the National Summit
- Monitoring of post Summit actions

These guidelines contain both requirements to ensure that the process of organizing the Summits is inclusive and bears results and suggestions that may or may not be followed by the organizers. The suggestions are clearly marked as such.

THE STEERING COMMITTEE

The process of planning, organizing, convening a National Summit and monitoring its follow-up actions needs initiators. While international organizations can initiate this process, country-level initiators need to be identified to ensure ownership of the process and to make it more effective and sustainable, A multi-actor Steering Committee is recommended to ensure that the planning, preparation and organization process is participatory and inclusive and carries the necessary political weight,

Responsibilities of the Steering Committee

The responsibilities of the Steering Committee are to:

- Ensure effective and timely preparations for and organization and convening of the Preparatory Meeting and National Summit
- Monitoring of the follow-up actions of the National Summit, particularly the establishment of the national resource facility and network on women in local government and the implementation of the National Action Plan on the Advancement of Women in Local Government.

Composition of the Steering Committee

The committee of initiators should comprise:

- Senior officials from national government ministries dealing with women in development, local government and urban affairs
- Associations of local governments, women in local government, if such exist
- Key local government/public administration training and research institutes
- Key NGOs dealing with women in development issues
- Selected country-based donor organizations within and outside the United Nations system

Care should be taken to balance the need for participation and inclusiveness with practicality. To make its work effective, the committee of initiators should not exceed ten persons. To make sure that the Steering Committee has political weight, it should be convened and chaired by a senior-level national government official, preferably at the Ministerial level. To ensure continuity one of the member organizations of the Steering Committee should assume the role of secretariat, organizing the meetings of the committee, keeping records and following-up of discussions and decisions.

If local government associations exist and have the required capacity, the planning, preparation and organization process of the National Summit should be anchored in these associations. This will ensure sustained action by the stakeholders themselves and will also lead to gender mainstreaming in local governments.

PREPARATORY MEETING

Unless intensive substantive preparations are undertaken before convening the National Summit, these would end up being one-shot publicity event. To ensure that this does not happen and to ensure that the preparations for the Summit are owned by a majority of the stakeholders, the convening of a Preparatory Meeting is recommended.

Objective and main tasks of the Preparatory Meeting

As the name indicates, the main objective of the Preparatory Meeting is to prepare for the National Summit. While the organization of the Summit remains the responsibility of the Steering Committee, the outcome of the Preparatory Meeting will determine the Summit's substantive content.

The main tasks of the Preparatory Meeting should be:

- Identify issues that need to be addressed and strategies to address the issues based on the presentation of the Report on the State of Women in Urban Local Government
- Further develop issues and strategies for discussion at the Summit
- Draft the National Action Plan on the advancement of women in local government for discussion at the Summit

Tasks before the Preparatory Meeting

The main tasks before the convening of the Preparatory Meeting are:

- To review, update and discuss the country report on women in urban local government prepared by national experts for UN ESCAP.

SUGGESTION

If the information, data and issues listed in the report are not sufficient, the Steering Committee may need to appoint a member or group of members to update or improve the report. The existing reports can be downloaded from <http://www.unescap.org/huset/women/reports/index.htm>. The Guidelines of the preparation of country reports on women in local government can also be downloaded from the same URL. Based on the issues contained in the report prepare issue papers for presentation at the Preparatory Meeting. Organize the Preparatory Meeting, including:

- Deciding the dates and venue
- Engaging professional facilitators to conduct the group sessions of the Preparatory Meeting
- Identifying participants and issuing invitations
- Organizing logistics of the Preparatory Meeting

The first meeting of the Steering Committee should be used to:

- Formalize the composition of the Steering Committee, including appointment of its secretariat
- Clarify the objectives and main tasks of the Steering Committee
- Identify resources to accomplish the tasks
- Decide on a schedule and assign responsibilities for accomplishing the tasks

The Steering Committee should meet for subsequent sessions as when required.

Composition, duration and structure of the Preparatory Meeting

As the Preparatory Meeting will be a working meeting, the number of participants should be kept to between thirty and forty. In addition to the members of the Steering Committee, key women in local government, representative of NGOs and academics should be invited. Care should be taken to ensure that a majority of the participants are either women in local government, represent associations of local government or are from organizations that have worked on women in development issues, particularly on issues of women in politics and decision-making. The duration will depend on several factors, including among others, the availability of resources and the number and complexity of issues under consideration. The duration of the Preparatory Meeting should not exceed 5 days.

Day One: Morning Session

Opening ceremony

The Meeting should be opened by the chairperson/convenor of the Steering Committee. Opening ceremony should be kept as brief as possible. It is recommended that the opening ceremony should not exceed 15 minutes.

Introduction and overview session

The introduction and overview session should be used to "break the ice" among participants and to provide them with the overview of the Preparatory Meeting and the National Summits. There are several means of "breaking the ice." An experienced facilitator should be engaged to conduct this session. The introduction segment of the session should take about 45 minutes. It should be done skilfully as group synergy would be very important for achieving high-quality outputs.

SUGGESTION

One method is to pair participants and allow them five minutes to find out as much about each other as possible and then to introduce each other. A presentation should be made in the overview segment of the session, providing information on the:

- Asia-Pacific Summit of Women Mayors and Councillors and the Phitsanulok Declaration
- Establishment of .Steering Committee and the organization of the National Summit

- The objectives and expected outcomes of the Preparatory Meeting and the programme of the Preparatory Meeting

Care should be taken to allow time for questions and answers at the end of the presentation.

This will ensure that the participants are well aware of the objectives, expected outcomes and programme of the Meeting.

Presentation of the Report on the State of Women in Urban Local Government

Under this segment of the morning session, the updated Report on the State of Women in Urban Local Government should be presented. Care should be taken to address issues and recommendations contained in the report, rather than on statistics and data.

Discussions and Identification of Key Issues from the Report

This segment of the session should be moderated by an experienced facilitator, who should focus the discussions around the identification of issues. Care should be taken to prioritize the issues and come up with a list of around 5 to 7 issues slated for action.

Day One: Afternoon Session

Working Group Discussions

Participants should be divided into groups. Each group should discuss one issue. The number of groups would therefore depend on the number of issues identified. The task for each group is:

- Explore the various aspects and sub-issues of the issue under discussion
- Develop strategies and actions to address the issue into short, medium and long term actions
- Identify resources needed to implement these actions, including identifying organizations responsible for undertaking these actions.

- Determine simple and easily measurable performance indicators to monitor the progress in the implementation of the identified actions and strategies

Each working group should be requested to identify two to three persons who would take extensive notes in the working group as well as in the plenary, when the report of their working group is presented. These persons would also represent their working group in a working group that would compile the national action plan on advancement of women in urban local government, based on the working group reports and discussions of the plenary. To ensure that working group discussions remain focused and working groups complete the tasks assigned to them in the given time, an experienced facilitator should moderate each working group. The facilitators should use techniques that ensure contribution of all participants to the discussions.

Facilitators should draw the attention of participants of each working group to the shopping list of actions and strategies contained in the Phitsanulok Declaration. However, discussions should not be limited to actions and strategies contained in the Phitsanulok Declaration alone and participants should be encouraged to formulate other actions and strategies.

SUGGESTION

The facilitators should not present the outcomes of the discussions in the plenary, and should ensure that participants select someone from the group to do so.

Box 1: Suggested Structure of the National Action Plan

The National Action Plan could be divided into three segments:

1. Preamble and overall vision
2. Specific issues and actions
3. Institutional support mechanisms

Preamble and Overall Vision

This segment should describe the rationale behind the National Action Plan and the Process by which it was formulated and adopted. It should also describe the overall vision or goal (the improved situation that one would like to see in the future).

Specific Issues and Actions

Each identified specific issue, that is relevant to increasing the participation and representation of women in urban local government, and actions needed to deal with it, should be dealt with separately. The structure for this segment could be:

1. Existing situation: This section should describe specific existing situation pertaining to the particular issue
2. Desirable future situation: This section should describe the desired future situation. This section could also be formulated in terms of objectives.
3. Actions needed to achieve the desirable situation: This section should describe the activities needed to reach the desirable future situation or to meet the objectives. Activities should be divided into immediate, mid-term and long-term time frames. Each activity should be accompanied by a specific date by which it should be accomplished. Care should be taken to ensure that the dating is practical and achievable.
4. Resources needed to accomplish the actions: This section should describe the monetary and human resources needed to accomplish each activity. It should also identify the organizations responsible for accomplishing these activities.
5. Indicators to measure Success: Performance indicators should be developed at two levels to measure whether the desirable future situation has been reached and whether individual activities have been successful. Performance indicators should be both quantitative and qualitative and should be easily and cost effectively measurable.

Institutional Support Mechanisms

This segment could be devoted to institutional support required to implement the National Action Plan. For all practical purposes this segment would describe the terms of reference of the National Resource Facility and Network of Women in Urban Local Government.

At least one of the working groups should concentrate on developing the terms of reference for the National Resource Facility and Network of Women in Local Government inclusion in the National Action Plan.

Day Two: Whole day

Working Group Discussions Continue

Day Three: Morning session

Working group discussions continue/preparation of working group reports to the plenary

Box 2: National Resource Facility and Network of Women in Urban Local Government

The National Resource Facility and Network of Women in Urban Local Government should be an organization serving the needs of women in urban local government. Its mission should be to become the definitive organization on issues related to women in urban local government. It should, among others, undertake the following functions:

1. Serve as a repository and clearing house for information on women in urban local government, including:
   a. Studies on issues related to women in urban local government
   b. Training opportunities for women in urban local government, including maintaining a database of training needs and training providers
   c. Statistics on women in urban local government
2. Coordinate, facilitate and monitor the implementation of the National Action Plan on the Advancement of Women in Urban Local Government
3. Advocate the role of women in urban local government through:
   a. Development and dissemination of profiles of successful women in local government

   b. Lobbying federal, provincial and local governments, political parties etc. for changes in legislation to increase the effective participation and representation of women in urban local government

   c. Undertaking periodic media awareness campaigns

4. Promote networking among women in urban local government through:

   a. Maintaining and disseminating a database on women in urban local government

   b. Issuance of a regular newsletter

   c. Organizing periodic seminars and conferences on issues related to women in local government

   d. Initiating mentoring and other programmes that strengthen personal relationships among women in urban local government

   e. Initiating sub national associations of women in urban local government

As access to e-mail and the Internet has become available in almost all cities and towns of Asia and the Pacific and as utilizing this medium considerably reduces the costs of communication, the National Resource Facility should make full use of these electronic mediums and undertake most its functions through it.

Day Three: Afternoon session

Presentation of Working Group Reports

Each working group should be allowed about 20 minutes to present their report. After each presentation, adequate time should be allocated for discussion.

Day Four: Whole day

Meeting of the working group compiling the National Action Plan

The working group should compile the National Action Plan based on the discussions held in the working groups and on the group presentations made and discussions held in the plenary. They should note that their main task is to compile the National Action Plan and not formulate one. Consequently they should closely follow the working group presentations and discussions in the plenary. Their main task would be essentially ensuring that there is no duplication or contradiction in the actions, schedules, responsibilities and resources proposed by the working groups. They would also need to prioritize actions. Criteria for prioritizing should be simple and practical. In other words actions that are relatively easy to undertake and for which resources are already available or can be accessed with relative ease should be prioritized as immediate actions. To keep momentum and to build upon success it is important that actions begin almost immediately after the National Action Plan is approved by the National Summit.

SUGGESTION

As participants will be a mixture of those working on women-in-development issues and women in local governments, the study visits should focus around issues of concern to them. These may include women-livelihood programmes, community-based development programmes, low-income housing, urban environmental management programmes, including solid waste management, water and wastewater management etc. As not all of the participants would wish to go to all of the study visits, study visits should be divided into three to four groups.

Day five: Whole Day

Presentation of and discussion on the compiled National Action Plan on the Advancement of Women in Urban Local Government

The chairperson of the Steering Committee should chair this session. During the presentation and discussion all of the participants of the working group, that compiled the National Action Plan, should sit up front in a panel. This will assure the larger group of transparency in decision-making and compilation process and show that the compilation was undertaken through consensus. One or two of the panelists should make the presentation, while the others should intervene as and when necessary to answer questions, clarify points and enter into discussions. In addition to presenting the compiled National Action Plan those making the presentation should describe the task assigned to the working group and the process that the working group adopted in completing these tasks.

Discussions should focus on the substance of the action plan rather than on editorial issues. Often such plenary meetings end up "dotting the I's and crossing the T's." Care should be taken to avoid this. Participants should be informed that editorial changes would be made after the meeting and that the draft National Action Plan would be sent to them for their comments before it is disseminated to the participants of the National Summit.

CLOSING CEREMONY

SUGGESTION

After the official closing statements, selected participants should be allowed to make brief statements in which they could convey their thanks, their commitment to the National Summit and the cause of advancing the representation and participation of women in urban local government etc.

NATIONAL SUMMIT

The National Summit should not be seen as an end in itself, but rather as an important milestone or starting point for actions to increase the representation and participation of women in local government.

Objectives and main tasks of the National Summit

As stated earlier, the Phitsanulok Declaration calls for the organization of national summits to:

- Develop country-level strategies,
- Establish country-level resource facilities and networks of women in local government,
- Identify country-level training providers and training needs

- Advocate policy and legislative changes
- Mobilize the required human and financial resources.

In addition to the above, another objective of the Summit is to raise awareness of the issues of participation and representation of women in local government and the transformative role that women play when in positions of decision-making.

Preparations for the National Summit

The main task of the Steering Committee after the Preparatory Meeting would be the organization of the National Summit. Specifically it should:

- Prepare and disseminate the draft of the National Action Plan and other relevant documents to all participants of the Preparatory Meeting and set a date by which comments on the draft should be sent back.
- Revise and further update the report on the State of Women in Local Government.
- Identify organizations willing to host the National Resource Facility and Network of Women in Urban Local Government
- Decide on the venue and dates for the National Summit
- Prepare and send invitation to participants of the Summit, including conference information kit or aide-memoire
- Incorporate the comments, as necessary and disseminate the final draft of the National Action Plan and other relevant documents to the confirmed participants of the Summit
- Develop a media strategy for the Summit. The media strategy should be developed in partnership with both tele- and print journalists. In this process journalists from national wire services would be particularly useful as their stories are carried in several newspapers.
- Arrange other logistical details.

SUGGESTION

After the Preparatory Meeting the Steering Committee may wish to increase its membership to include some of the organizations, institutes and individuals that participated in the Preparatory Meeting. It may change its name to National Committee on the Advancement of Women in Local Government

Composition, duration and structure of the National Summit

The number of participants to the Summit should be determined only by availability of resources and logistical arrangements. A successful and relatively inclusive Summit would require about 200 to 250 participants. A majority of the participants should be women in urban local governments (mayors and councillors). This would ensure that the decisions of the Summit reflect their needs and demands as they see them and not as other organizations see them.

As the Summit will involve a considerable number of people, logistics and costs, it is recommended that the duration of the Summit be three days or a maximum of four days.

SUGGESTION

If logistics and costs permit, the Summit should be organized in a city or town headed by a woman mayor of chief executive. This would not only be symbolic, it would also provide interesting opportunities for field visits. While selecting the venue, care should be taken to balance symbolism with logistical ease and costs. Similar to the Preparatory Meeting, while the Steering Committee would determine the final structure, the following structure is recommended:

Day one: Morning Session

Opening Ceremony

The Head of State or Government should open the Summit. This would reaffirm the Government's commitment to seriously addressing the issue of advancement of women in local government. The opening ceremony should not exceed 60 minutes.

Presentation of the revised report on the State of Women in Urban Local Government

Similar to the presentation of the report in the Preparatory Meeting, the presentation at the Summit should focus more on issues rather than on statistics. The presentation should not exceed 20 minutes. At the end of the presentation adequate time should be allocated for participants to air their views.

Presentation of the National Action Plan

The presentation of the National Action Plan should not exceed 30 minutes. Participants should be informed in advance that they will get an opportunity to review and discuss the National Action Plan in working group discussions in the afternoon of day one and on the morning of day two. At the end of the presentation only questions of clarification should be entertained from the participants.

Day one: Afternoon Session

Working Group Discussions

As it would be cumbersome and time consuming review the National Action Plan and propose amendments or additions to it in a plenary session participants should be divided into groups. Each group should discuss one section of the national action plan. To ensure that group discussions remain focused and the task assigned to them is completed on time an experienced facilitator should moderate each working group. The Initiators should ensure that the facilitator and at least one participant of each group is well versed with the National Action Plan so that she/he can inform working group participants whether an activity that they wish to propose is covered under another section of the National Action Plan. A note describing the offers received by the Steering Committee on the hosting of the National Resource Facility and Network of Women in Urban Local Government should be provided to the working group discussing this aspect of the National Action Plan. They should be requested to review the offers and select the host. Each working group should be required to nominate one person to present their work at the plenary.

Day Two: Morning session

Working group discussion continue

Day Two: Afternoon session

Presentation of Working Group Reports

Each working group should be allowed 15 to 20 minutes to present their reports. After each presentation, adequate time should be allocated for discussions.

Day Three: Morning session

Study Visit for Participants

Amendments proposed to the National Action Plan should be incorporated while participants are on study visit.

SUGGESTION

If possible the amended National Action Plan should be reproduced and distributed at the beginning of the Afternoon session. If the Summit is being organized in a city headed by a woman mayor or chief executive, study visits should highlight innovations that she has introduced. Otherwise study visits should follow the same guidelines as outlined earlier for the study visits of the Preparatory Meeting.

Amendments proposed to the National Action Plan should be incorporated while participants are on study visit.

Afternoon session

Adoption of the National Action Plan

The amended National Action Plan should be presented to the Plenary. Final corrections/amendments should be incorporated during the plenary session itself and the National Action Plan should be adopted by the Summit.

Establishment of the National Resource Facility and Network of Women in Local Government

A formal announcement should be made on the selection of the organization or organizations, which would host the National Resource Facility and Network of Women in Local

Government. A letter of agreement on the hosting arrangements should be signed between the host organization/s and other relevant organizations, among or outside the Steering Committee.

FOLLOW-UP ACTIONS OF THE SUMMIT

As stated above the facilitation and monitoring of the National Action Plan would become the task of the National Resource Facility and Network of Women in Local Government. It is recommended that the Members of the National Committee on the Advancement of Women in Local Government become members of a board overseeing the work of the National Resource Facility and Network of Women in Local Government. However, it is most likely that there will be an interim period between the establishment of the National Resource Facility and Network at the Summit and its full operationalization. In this interim period the National Committee should undertake the followi©ng key actions after the Summit:

- Publish the National Action Plan and disseminate it as widely as possible.
- Prepare the report of the National Summit and disseminate it to the participants of the Summit and others concerned.
- Facilitate and monitor the operationalization and functioning of the National Resource Facility and Network. This may require, among other things:
- Following up on promises of resources made at the Summit
- Ensuring that the host organization or organizations meet the commitments and schedules set in the letter of agreement
- Assist the host organization or organizations in overcoming bureaucratic hurdles
- Monitor and report the progress in the implementation of the National Action Plan until such time as the National Resource Facility and Network can assume these functions.

BIBLIOGRAPHY

Bell, L.: *Good Girls/Bad Girls: Feminists and Sex Trade Workers Talk Face to Face*, Toronto: The Women's Press, 1987.

Fozzard, S.: *Surviving Violence: A Recovery Program for Children and Families*, Geneva, International Catholic child Bureau, 1995.

George, K. K.: *Limits to Kerala Model of Development: An Analysis of Fiscal Crisis and Its Implications*, Thiruvananthapuram, Centre for Development Studies. Monograph Series, 1993.

Hiew, C. C.: *Child Prostitution: Social and Psychological Factors*, Sukhothai University, Bangkok, 1992.

Judith, E.: *The Sexual Exploitation of Children*, Cambridge, Polity Press, 1986.

Kevin, Major: *Free the Children: A Young Man's Personal Crusade Against Child Labor*, New York, HarperCollins, 1998.

Miller, Barbara: *The Endangered Sex: Neglect of Female Children in Rural North India*. Ithaca, Cornell University Press, 1981.

Noble, Christina: *Nobody's Child: a Woman's Abusive Past and the Inspiring Dream that led to Rescue the Street Children of Saigon*, New York, Grove Press, c1994.

O'Grady, R.: *The Rape of the Innocent*, Bangkok, ECPAT, 1994.

Rozario, Sr. R. M.: *Trafficking in Women and Children in India*, Uppal Publishing House, New Delhi, 1988.

Sturdevant, S. P. and Stotzfus, B.: *Let the Good Times Roll: Prostitution and the Military in Asia*, CIIR, The New Press, 1993.

INDEX

□□□